W. Hollar delineauit et sculpsit Aqua forti 1674

HM The Queen in Garter Robes on the West Steps, St George's Chapel, Garter Day 2010
© Paul Macneil

The Book of the Poor Knights of Windsor

and

The Military Knights of Windsor

Edited by The Revd Michael Boag, BA, Minor Canon, Succentor and Dean's Vicar
of St George's Chapel, Windsor

consisting of

The History

by

Mr Peter Begent with additions by Major Richard Moore and edited by Mrs Jennifer Moore

The Roll

by

The Revd Edmund H Fellowes, CH, MVO, MA, Mus Doc, Minor Canon of Windsor

with

additions and amendments by Major Richard Moore

Appendices

compiled by Major Richard Moore

The publication of this book has been made possible by
the generosity of
His Grace the Duke of Wellington, KG
The Revd Fr Michael Seed, SA
Mr & Mrs Yoyo Allalouf
Mr & Mrs Rashid A W Galadari
Mr Hassan Jameel
Mr & Mrs Walid Juffali
Prof N. David Khalili KCSS and Mrs Marion Khalili KSS
Mr & Mrs Ilyas Khan
Mr & Mrs Christian St. John Sweeting KCSG
and the Moore family in memory of Charles Edward Moore who died aged 44 in 2010.

ISBN: 978-0-9567699-0-9

This book replaces the Historical Monograph,
'The Military Knights of Windsor 1352-1944'
by Edmund H Fellowes, CH, MVO, MA, Mus Doc, Minor Canon of Windsor
Printed and Published for
The Dean and Canons of St George's Chapel, Windsor Castle.

Published by The Military Knights of Windsor
and produced by
Mr Richard Model of RM Print Consultancy,
Windsor

2011

CONTENTS

Illustrations

Foreword

The Military Knights of Windsor by their presence and their bearing add greatly to the services at St George's Chapel, but few know of their long and distinguished history.

Since their creation in 1348, the Alms (or Poor) Knights have prayed for the Monarch and for the Knights of the Garter. They form an essential part of the College of St George and of Windsor Castle. Indeed, it is said that in the middle of the seventeenth century, during the Interregnum, when the Dean and Canons were ejected from the Castle, the Poor Knights continued the tradition of uninterrupted worship until the restoration of Chapter by King Charles II. Although not all the Poor Knights were soldiers, the majority were. Most regiments have provided at least one Military Knight during their existence.

This book contains a unique and much needed account of the history of the Military Knights. The reader will find countless examples of bravery and chivalry. However, not all of them have been without blemish; the bad apples are also faithfully recorded.

To Major Richard Moore and his wife Jennifer we owe our thanks for the meticulous production of this excellent work.

The Lord Carrington, KG, GCMG, CH, MC, Chancellor of the Order of the Garter

Introduction

This book replaces the historical Monograph, 'The Military Knights of Windsor' by The Reverend Edmund H Fellowes, Minor Canon of Windsor, published in 1944 by the Dean and Canons of St George's Chapel in Windsor Castle. This is primarily a book of reference consisting of the History, the Roll and additional information.

The History was rewritten by Mr Peter Begent and handed over to me when I was acting as Staff Officer in 2000 just before he died. Due to personal circumstances nothing happened until 2004 when it became possible to start work on a new book. The first thing my wife and I did was to number all the Poor and Military Knights in seniority order as detailed in Fellowes' book and produce an index. It became apparent that there were many errors particularly as regards the names of regiments. As we started going through the list making corrections and adding facts from the internet and other modern sources we decided that it would not be too difficult to re-order the list to date of death and produce a Book of Remembrance. The Book of Remembrance was dedicated at the Garter Requiem Eucharist in 2008.

During the year it took for the Book of Remembrance to be handwritten, we went through every entry checking on the facts. Having the facility of the Internet, that had not been available to Edmund Fellowes, it was possible greatly to increase many of the facts concerning individual knights. Lieutenant Colonel Charles Webb (646) very kindly undertook research at the National Army Museum and in the Army List to ensure that the names of regiments were correct. Over the years the army organisation has changed. Here we have tried to show as far as possible the regimental names as they would have been during the Poor or Military Knight's service.

With the new history, rearranged by my wife Jenny, and the enhanced Roll of Poor and Military Knights it was decided to try to put together a book that is historically accurate, interesting to all, informative, colourful and at times amusing. We have added additional information which it is hoped will be found to be of use.

It became apparent, as we were putting it all together, that the story of the Poor Knights and the Military Knights is a history of the British Army. Of the 109 regiments of Line Infantry only 26 did not provide a knight. They have fought in almost every battle, skirmish or incident in which we, as a nation, were involved. They have fought from Agincourt to the Armada, Arras to Alamein, Arnheim to Aden, and that is just the As. They have had outstanding examples of bravery, dedication and chivalry. In June 1947 'Peterborough' in *The Daily Telegraph* reported that four Military Knights had ten DSOs between them and a total of fifteen between the thirteen Military Knights. There have also been some 'bad apples' that add spice.

It is not a book to sit down and read like a novel but one to dip in and out of. We hope some people will find it an inspiration for further research and exploration. Above all we hope it is enjoyed.

Major Richard Moore (637)
Mrs Jennifer Moore

(3)   (7)   (10)   (8)

The Poor Knight of Windsor

His helmet now shall make a hive for bees,

And lover's sonnets turn to holy psalms:

A man-at-arms must now serve on his knees

And feed on prayers which are Age's alms.

But though from Court to cottage he depart,

His Saint is sure in his unspotted heart.

And when he saddest sits in homely cell

He'll teach his swains this carol for a song:

Blest be the hearts that wish my Sovereign well,

Curst be the souls that think her any wrong.

Goddess, allow this aged man his right

To be your bedesman now that was your knight.

★★★★★★★★★★★★★

Taken from George Peele's 'Polyhymnia' this song was introduced at 'the annual exercise in arms', held in the Queen's presence at the Tilt-yard in Westminster, 17 November 1590.

Some of the shields of the early Poor Knights

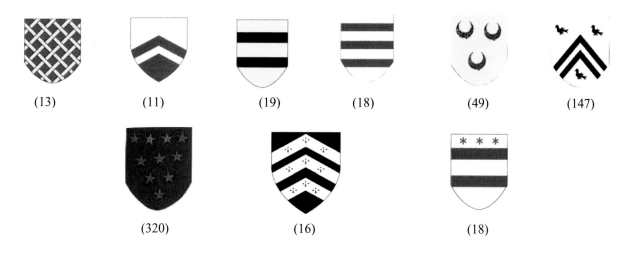

(13)   (11)   (19)   (18)   (49)   (147)

(320)   (16)   (18)

THE MILITARY KNIGHTS' PRAYER

Almighty God,

Thine arm is strong to defend and save;

Hear us as we remember before Thee

Our Royal Founder, King Edward III,

Who, in gratitude for victory won,

And of his charitable purpose,

Caused the Alms Knights to be formed.

Grant that we, the Military Knights of Windsor,

By dutiful obedience to our ancient calling in offering prayer,

Both for the person and the kindred of the Sovereign

And for the Companions of the Most Noble

Order of the Garter, living and departed,

May prove faithful to our solemn trust.

Through Jesus Christ, our Lord.

AMEN.

Two Poor Knights of Windsor
The Garter Procession 1663
By Sir Peter Lely

Two Poor Knights of Windsor
Garter Procession 1663
By Sir Peter Lely

The Poor Knights of Windsor

The Beginning

The theological doctrine of Purgatory, a place of cleansing, of expiation and of waiting, where prayers made for the soul of the deceased might ease and aid his path to heaven, formed the basis of the great Chantry Movement which by the fourteenth century had become one of the dominant features of church life. A chantry was a legal obligation whereby in return for endowments these prayers were to be regularly offered. The size of the endowment naturally determined the arrangements. Perhaps prayers might simply be offered at one of the altars situated within the church or chapel; it may be that a particular altar would be assigned, or indeed an enclosure or a building in which prayers were to be said would be erected – a Chantry Chapel – and even a Chantry priest or priests appointed whose main or even sole duty was to officiate therein. Particularly generous endowments might also allow the appointment of a group of men known as Almsmen or Bedesmen who would be accommodated and maintained from the chantry endowment, in return for which they would daily assist with their prayers the passage of their benefactor's soul through Purgatory.

St George's Chapel has occasionally been described as essentially a chantry. This is perhaps an exaggeration, for the purposes of its establishment, enunciated by various documents associated with its foundation, do not refer exclusively to intercession for the souls of the dead. The Letters Patent of 6th August 1348, which express King Edward's intentions, certainly lean towards such intercessions, for they state that the King wills the canons and ministers 'celebrate divine service there according to an ordinance to be made for him and for his progenitors and successors, in part satisfaction of whom, in the last day of judgement he will have to give account.'

The name by which the bedesmen would come to be known has occasioned some discussion. In the Letters Patent of 1348 they are called Milites Pauperes, in the Papal Bull of 1350 Militis Regni Anglie, whilst the College Statutes also use the term Milites Pauperes. The early Garter Statutes in the Registrum Ordinis refer to Milites Veterani whilst the French version uses Povres Chevaliers. The argument turns then upon the construction of the word milites. In Classical Latin Miles is a soldier; a knight would be Eques which signifies perhaps more than a soldier but less than a knight. Perhaps a satisfactory translation might be 'impoverished warriors'.

Whatever the strength of this argument may be, it must be emphasized that the terms used in the several documents refer not to the name of the body but the qualification for admission. Although not a few of the early bedesmen had been dubbed knights, being described in their Letters Patent of Appointment as 'Chevaler' (sic), knighthood never seems to have been a requirement for admission, nor does the appointment confer knighthood and members are not, simply by virtue of their appointment, styled 'Sir'. Bedesmen were to be appointed as members of the College but there is no direct reference in the College Statutes as to how the veterans were to be appointed although the Garter Statutes provide that 'they shall be nominated in the same manner as the Canons'. How the Canons were chosen in the early days is however by no means clear. At first sight the position seems clear for Article 1 of the College Statutes, repeating the provision of the Bull of 1350, states that the patronage is reserved to the Crown. However the Garter Statutes provide that the Canons shall be presented by the Founders, a term which means the current Knights of the Garter. If any of the Canons so presented shall die, his successor is to be appointed by the Sovereign. A further provision supplements these arrangements by requiring that, should the Sovereign be abroad, the Warden (Dean) is to advise him of any vacancy in order that he may appoint a successor.

King Edward III

King Edward's Letters Patent provide that there should be twenty-four, the same number as the Priests, that is the Canons and the Priest Vicars who formed the ecclesiastical membership. Thus, whilst the prime intent of Edward's Foundation was to celebrate the Opus Dei, the Divine Office of daily public prayer, this was closely allied to, and was almost overshadowed by the duties appertaining to a chantry. The Bull of Clement VI dispatched from Avignon on 30th November 1350, which authorised the establishment of the College of St George, refers to the King's proposal, and states that it is 'for the increase of divine worship to order for his own salvation and that of the souls of the other faithful'. Neither the Statutes of the College nor the early Garter Statutes require the Poor Knights to pray for the Order as a whole. The College Statutes enjoin simply that they shall pray for the good estate and for the souls of King Edward lll and his progenitors, for the Bishop of Winchester and for their successors. They are to attend the chief Mass of the day and that of the Blessed Virgin Mary as well as Evensong and Compline. At each of the services they are to say the Ave Maria one hundred and fifty times and after each ten the Lord's Prayer. A requirement of the whole College imposed by the early Garter Statutes was that Masses were to be offered for all Christian souls.

The Statutes of the College drawn up by William Edyngton in 1352 state that the purpose of the establishment is 'for evermore to pray for the happy estate of our Sovereign Lord the present King for his successors and for our own and for the soul of the said King and our own after the departure from this life'. Also in the Statutes of 1352 the number of both Priests and Bedesmen had risen to twenty-six, reflecting, it is thought, an increase in the establishment of the Knights of the Garter. The records which would allow the numbers and succession of Poor Knights in the fourteenth century to be known with certainty are incomplete, but the surviving Patents of Appointment, together with the Attendance Register and the College Accounts, suggest that it is unlikely that any appointment was made before 1353 and perhaps even later, and that, until the reign of Mary I, there were never more than three Poor Knights in post at the same time. The reason would appear to be financial, for the intention of Edward lll to provide endowments which would finance the College with sufficient income was never fulfilled, although the revenue which it enjoyed was generally adequate, since most of the salaries paid were dependent upon attendance. It may therefore be suggested that the number of Poor Knights appointed was deliberately suppressed to keep the expenditure within the limits of the funds available.

An analysis has shown that between 1352 and 1368 nineteen Canons were appointed seemingly without royal patronage. and it may be that the 1415 Statutes serve to authenticate these appointments and to confirm that the practice is to cease. It seems likely that the early appointments of the Poor Knights followed a similar pattern, for no record of the issue of Letters Patent, which would indicate a royal appointment, is to be found until 1377. A list (which would probably be incomplete) of the names of the early Poor Knights can only be compiled from the Treasurers' Rolls, a number of which have not survived, the Attendence [Attendance] Registers which commence only in 1384, the Injunctions issued to the College following the Visitation of 1378 and in the Patents appointing their successors. At the Garter Feast of 1376 the Poor Knights were supplied with robes by the Wardrobe. From 1377 all the surviving early patents of appointment of bedesmen are by the Great or Privy Seal, a practice which continued until August 1623.

The Chapel Archives contain fascinating records of disciplinary offences. Even those in post had cause for complaint, for the Visitation of 1378 shows that the Warden, William Mudge or Mugge, together with the Chapter, had failed to pay them the forfeitures for non-attendance or a share in gifts made by the Knights of the Garter, and he was ordered to make up the arrears. The Visitor's Injunctions seem to have been obeyed only in part for, although the accounts show sums were paid in respect of forfeitures during the remainder of the year to Michaelmas 1378, no mention of the arrears is to be found. The Visitor also criticized the Poor Knights. Two only were in post, Thomas Tawny (2) and Sir John Breton (3). Both, although married, kept women in adultery, whilst Breton was said to be insolent, seldom came to Chapel and when he did immediately fell asleep. In passing it should be observed that although the Poor Knights were rebuked, the Warden appears to have been blamed for failing to exercise his disciplinary powers. He was also criticised for failing to discipline the Canons, one of whom seldom attended Chapel and instead went hunting or fishing, whilst another was both profligate and a poacher and when he did come to Chapel was irreverent and exchanged jokes with the laity. The Warden was also threatened with instant suspension for failing to pay the salaries of the Priest Vicars.

The Chapter was also neglectful in the payment of other dues. The early Garter Statutes provided that a share of the Installation Fees which are ordered to paid by each Knight Companion should accrue to the Poor Knights; but those of the Earl of Arundel and of Sir Henry Percy, both of whom were installed in 1388 were shared between the Canons and the Priest Vicars, the claim of the Poor Knights being ignored.

Each was to receive twelve pence per day in respect of his attendance, together with forty shillings per annum for his general maintenance, whilst as a member of the College he would be provided with accommodation. Each bedsman was to be given a red cloak bearing an escutcheon of the arms of St George but without any encircling Garter, this latter provision being made in the early Garter Statutes. Should a bedsman fail to attend, his daily payment was to be withheld and distributed among his colleagues. This monetary provision was generous indeed, the daily rate being equal to that paid to a Canon, although of course the latter was entitled to other and additional perquisites. The total salary of £20-4-0d a year plus accommodation and occasional additional fees might be compared to the salary paid a little over a hundred years later to those employed upon the building of the new chapel where the head carver, William Berkeley, and the principal smith, John Tresilian, were paid £24-5-0d per annum whilst the master mason William Vertue who was also a designer received only £12-0-0d. These financial provisions were to be the cause of considerable difficulty. The charitable intention of the Founder was emphasised by the provision that the bedsmen were to be military veterans in needy circumstances, and that should any of them acquire property of the value of £20-0-0d per annum or more he should lose his place.

In addition he was entitled to a share of the Installation Fees payable by a Knight of the Garter as well as sundry occasional fees. His robes were supplied by the College and as a member of that body he would receive free accommodation. An additional perquisite was what came to be called Residence Money. This arose from a medieval custom whereby during the first three weeks of his residence each Canon was to invite three poor persons (including Poor Knights) to supper. Each of the guests was to say the Psalter for the souls of the Knights of the Garter, living and departed following which they were to be served personally by the Canon and each given one penny. This perquisite was, at some unknown date, commuted to a monetary payment which, at the end of the nineteenth century amounted to £19-10s and was divided equally between the Knights.

Administrative necessity must have required the body to be accorded a name. What this may have been in the early days is not known, but by the early years of the fifteenth century the increasing use of English caused the Milites Pauperes to be called 'Poor Knights' and the name stuck, for in a petition presented to Parliament by the College of St George, reference is made to 'a Warden, Chanons, Poure Knights and other Ministres'. The requirement that a Poor Knight must remain unmarried was novel and first appears in the Marian Statutes. In the medieval period this was not a condition of appointment and the Account Rolls of the College show gratuities and other sums being paid to widows of Poor Knights, including several payments to the widow of Sir John Grimsby (10) (died 1413) who was employed as a seamstress. The new provision was at first fairly strictly observed.

No Garter Statutes of the fourteenth century appear to have survived, the earliest copy being that of a compilation of Statutes issued in 1415 which provide that, 'twenty-six veteran Knights who have no means of sustenance shall have there in the honour of God and of the Blessed George a sufficient maintenance that they may continually serve God in prayers'. These Statutes established that appointments of Canons and Poor Knights would be by royal patronage. They were amended in 1421.

The Visitation of 1430 names no offenders but reminds the Knights that they are to obey the Dean. As the financial mismanagement seems hardly to have improved since the previous Visitation, the Canon Treasurer was also castigated, ordered that the fees due to the Poor Knights be paid, and threatened with loss of his own fees if delay in payment should again occur.

Many of the early Poor Knights, if not most, were former soldiers. Those who were knighted and carried shields have them shown around the poem in the preface. Of particular note is Sir John Trebell (16) who fought at Agincourt as a 'Chevalier lance ' in the retinue of Sir Thomas West. He had a garden in the castle for which he paid the Constable of the Castle the rent of one rose on Midsummer day. Sir William Crafford (20) served in Normandy after the siege of Harfleur and was wounded and taken prisoner. Sir Robert Champlain (42) is described as a 'Knight Crosse 'who was commended by Popes Pius II and Paul II for fighting for the Hungarians against the Turks.

The financial responsibilities devolving upon the Chapter which gave rise to the difficulties so apparent in the fourteenth and early fifteenth centuries were removed when in 1483 an Act of Parliament provided for the incorporation of the Dean and Canons and expressly relieved them of the requirement to provide funds for the payment and maintenance of the Poor Knights. The Act says that in respect of payment 'our said Sovereign Lord hath otherwise provided'. Of this 'provision' no tangible evidence has been found. Poor Knights continued however to be appointed and since their names appear in the Treasurer's Rolls it must be assumed that, although legally not bound to do so, the Chapter continued to pay them. Indeed when the provisions of the Act which related to the Poor Knights was challenged in the early years of the reign of Henry VIII the Chapter, in reply to a petition stated that it had paid the Poor Knights from the time of Henry IV to that of Henry VII. Perhaps as an insurance against future claims Chapter had procured an exemplification of the Act of 1483 dated 4th February 1503.

A number of appointments made at this time suggest that some direct or indirect royal augmentation of the payments may have taken place, for the appointees, far from being 'impoverished warriors', were royal servants, and others were almost certainly in receipt of funds from other sources, who probably regarded the position as a sinecure. They included James Fryse (27) who, appointed in 1475, is in 1481 described as one of the King's physicians; John Sigemond (29) 1478 a Groom of the King's Chamber; Thomas Holme (36) 1482 Clarenceux King of Arms; Lewis Caerlyon (47) 1491, King's physician; John Mewtes (52) 1503, the King's French Secretary; the organist of St Alban's Abbey, Robert Fairfax (55) 1509 and a judge, Bartholomew Westby (54) 1514 who apparently continued to sit as a Baron of the Exchequer.

That no legal liability for the payment of the Poor Knights fell upon the Chapter was acknowledged by Henry VIII, who in 1511 asked the Dean and Canons to pay Peter de Narbonne (49), a Poor Knight appointed in 1493, an annuity of 20 Marks (£13-6-8d) per annum. Chapter agreed to do so and received the King's 'hearty thanks' and a promise that they would not be asked to bear the charge of any other Poor Knights until lands had been provided, the revenues of which would be sufficient to pay the salaries and fees. In fact at least two appointments were made in 1514 and possibly one in 1515 but from that date, despite the continuing reference to them in the revisions of the Garter Statutes of 1519 and 1522 (where their numbers were reduced to thirteen), no firm evidence exists to show that any Poor Knights were appointed during the remaining years of Henry's reign. In 1519 the Garter Statutes were revised and in 1522 were reissued. It is these Henrician Statutes, together with additional Statutes and Chapter Decisions, which still govern the Order to the present day.

It was not until the revision of the Garter Statutes by Henry VIII in 1522 that the College as a whole was required to pray for the Sovereign, the Knights of the Order living, the souls of departed Knights and for all Christian souls. In addition the College Statutes require that at all the principal Masses of the day a special Collect is to be said for the King. Of the form of this Collect no evidence has been found. What appears to be a Tudor interpolation in the Black Book, the first surviving register of the Order of the Garter which dates from c.1534 suggests the term Milites Eleemosyne, Alms Knights, but although this name is sometimes used, the term Poor Knights is that by which the body was generally known for the first five hundred years of its existence.

The task of implementing Henry VIII's will fell upon his children and his executors. Although Edward VI excluded any reference to the Poor Knights from his revision of the Garter Statutes of 1553 it may well be that the omission was because of the association of that body with religious observances, particularly that of praying for departed souls, an anathema to the young King and his protestant ministers. Nevertheless an indenture of 4 August 1547, followed by Letters Patent dated 7 October in that year granted lands to the Dean and Canons and specified the purposes to which the profits were to be applied. The total which would accrue annually to the Chapter was estimated to be £600 of which £283.18.4d was to satisfy the charges of the Poor Knights. These lands came to be called the lands of the New Dotation.

Queen Mary I continued to implement the intentions of her father by nominating nine of the thirteen Poor Knights of the new establishment and by providing accommodation for them It is uncertain where the two or three Poor Knights of Edward III's Foundation, who were in post at any one time, lived. The work of providing accommodation for the thirteen who were now to be appointed began in February 1557. Six houses, which had been built in 1359/60 against the south wall of the Lower Ward between its central tower and that at the eastern end, now Henry Ill's Tower, were renovated and each provided with a cellar. To the west of the central tower six new houses were built together with a common hall and a kitchen. The latter utilised the thirteenth century drum tower which protrudes from the wall on the southern (outer) side. Above the door of the hall was painted St George's Cross within the Garter. The western houses together with part of the hall were built of stone from the Lady Chapel of the suppressed Reading Abbey. The central tower, which was at one time a belfry and had been surmounted by a spire, was allocated to the Governor of the Poor Knights and the arms of King Philip of Spain and Queen Mary were placed above the entrance.

Whilst Queen Mary, in furtherance of her father's will, caused draft Statutes for the new establishment of Poor Knights to be prepared, it was in the first year of the reign of Queen Elizabeth I that formal Statutes, albeit based upon the Marian draft, were issued. Articles 1, 2, 3, 20 and 25 of the Statutes are concerned with the qualification for admission. The candidates must be gentlemen brought to necessity after service in the wars, in garrisons or in other service of the Sovereign; must be and remain unmarried, and must not have committed any serious crime. Should they come into an estate worth £20 per annum or more or convicted of a serious offence they are to be dismissed. Henry VIII's will required the wearing of a long white gown with the Arms of St George encircled with a garter upon the breast and a red mantle. The draft Statutes of Philip and Mary and those apparently first adopted by Elizabeth specify a gown of violet and a mantle of murrey, the latter having a Cross of St George without a garter upon the left shoulder. Whether this specification was the result of a scribal error or no, the Statutes dated 30 August 1559 which appear to be those finally implemented, specify a gown of red and a mantle of blue or purple with a badge or escutcheon as before and garments of these colours, save that the mantle is described as violet were being provided by the Dean and Canons in 1559/60. It is not certainly known for how long the College paid for gowns and mantles.

Neither the College nor the early Garter Statutes specifically require the Poor Knights to attend the Garter ceremonies, nor do the later Statutes issued for their governance by Queen Elizabeth in 1559; the latter simply requiring them to stand at their doors at the entrance and departing from the castle of the Sovereign or his Lieutenant and the Knights Companions. The Poor Knights had however, certainly from the reign of Henry VIII if not before, always attended the services at Windsor and the Elizabethan Statutes provided that they should sit together at the Garter Dinner. In early Tudor times the procession from the Upper Ward to St George's Chapel was largely upon horseback and no evidence has been found which shows that the Poor Knights took part in it, their appearance being confined to the processions within the Chapel.

Queen Elizabeth 1

The Elizabethan Statutes maintained the scale of attendance money but abolished the sum payable for general maintenance. They also established a fee for attending the quarterly Obit Service which was to be 20 pence for each Poor Knight with an additional 2 shillings for the Governor. Obits, days upon which benefactors of the College were especially remembered in prayer, usually the dates upon which they had, or were said to have, died and which the Poor Knights were to attend, were numerous and Ashmole prints a list of them as in 1547/8. In 1559 these were gathered together in quarterly Obits when a special prayer was ordered to be said. Probably the earliest version of today's Garter Prayer it reads: 'God save The Queen and all the Companions of this Order.' By the time of James I it had expanded and now read: 'O Lord long preserve James our King and all the Companions of this Most Noble Order of the Garter.' In his letter to Ashmole, Evans says that it now reads: 'God save our gracious Sovereign and all the Companions of the Most Noble Order of the Garter. Amen'.' The use of this wording continued until about 1920.

The Lands of the New Dotation were expected to produce sufficient revenue as well as other payments which were set out in an Indenture of 1559. This indenture, whether or not it was sealed on behalf of the Crown, was never formally executed by the Dean and Canons and was to be the cause of disquiet and dissatisfaction for three centuries. Over the years general inflation and improvement in land values caused the revenue produced by the New Dotation to increase considerably. The Poor Knights and others, including the lay clerks, payments to whom were included in the indenture, continually demanded that their income be enhanced in line with the increase in the revenue received by the Chapter. The Dean and Canons continually refused. From time to time the persons affected submitted petitions and even had recourse to counsel's opinion, but to no avail.

In the reign of Queen Elizabeth I the Poor Knights were required to attend morning and evening prayer daily as well as the quarterly Obits. They were also in their daily prayers to pray for the Sovereign and for the Companions of the Order. The requirement as to attendance was modified over the years. Generally the requirement that the Knights be poor appears to have been followed although notable exceptions occur. One of the most surprising discoveries during current research through the Internet was that Captain Jonas Bodenham (153) had been Lieutenant under Sir Francis Drake in the Revenge at the battle of the Armada.

As the records become more detailed we learn of the indiscipline. In 1596 John Norton (99) was said to have spoken with contempt of the Statutes using foul language (which is noted in detail) but his punishment, if any, is not recorded. Two years later Nicholas Whittacres (104) was accused of living in adultery with Elenora Samson. He was dismissed.

On 5 October 1603 James I having regard to the small salaries received by the Poor Knights, doubled them, ordering a further 12 pence per day to be paid from the Exchequer. In the early seventeenth century there are a number of cases involving rudeness, quarrelling and fighting which were punished by fines and suspensions.

From the reign of James I, the Poor/Military Knights have processed both to and within the Chapel at Garter ceremonies. The responsibility for the Poor Knights' robes was cast upon the College by the Elizabethan Statutes and in September 1609 one Roger Jones of London was appointed to make robes at a cost of £2.13.4d per annum. In January 1613 the Poor Knights were warned to provide fit robes for the Garter Installation of the Elector Palatine, but whether this means that they are to provide their own robes or to turn out in clean and decent order is not clear.

Previous military service was generally observed. Indeed it was reiterated at a Chapter of the Order in 1613 when it was decided to cancel the appointment (in reversion) of one Edward Harris as he was a 'mere mechanic'. There were however some periods, notably in the early years of the reign of George Ill when there was some laxity and it is noticeable that in the seventeenth and eighteenth centuries a number of patents appointing Poor Knights refer to service 'by land and by sea'. In August 1623 it was ordered that the future appointments of Poor Knights should be made under the Great Seal of the Order. In 1623 Miles Hughes (143), who had a patent in reversion was excluded as he was married. He protested that his wife was dead and from the tone of the entry in the Register it seems that the Chapter of the Order hearing the case felt sorry for him. He was later appointed but in 1630, further complaint being made, he admitted that his wife was still alive. Although the Chapter before which he was summoned appears to have been interrupted he seems to have been dismissed. It may be noted that when Hughes' case was being considered in 1623 other married Poor Knights were in post but were 'left to the mercy of the Sovereign', it being considered that the appointments had been made in ignorance of the Statute. By the end of the seventeenth century it became the practice to insert in the patent of appointment a dispensation which allowed a candidate to be a married man or to marry after appointment.

In the seventeenth century the Elizabethan establishment of thirteen Poor Knights was increased by a second foundation. This originated in the Will of Sir Peter le Maire dated 8 January 1631 under which the sum of £1,500 was bequeathed to his brother-in-law Sir Francis Crane to be expended upon such charitable purposes as Crane might see fit. Sir Francis, who was Chancellor of the Order of the Garter from 1628 until his death in 1636, proposed to increase the number of Poor Knights to eighteen and to this end by his Will settled lands to the value of £200 per annum to the intent that each of the five Knights, two to be regarded as of the foundation of Peter le Maire and three of his own, should receive £40 per annum. Further, he provided that monies should be made available for the building of new additional lodgings. Sir Richard Crane, the brother of Sir Francis, was his executor but was negligent in carrying out the testator's wishes, and little had been done to implement the provisions of the bequest when he too died. Although Sir Richard, presumably in furtherance of his brother's bequest, by his Will of September 1645 charged his Manor of Carbrook in Norfolk with the payment of £200 per annum, his executors challenged the provision and a series of legal actions ensued. The matter was not finally settled until 1659 when it was confirmed the Manor should stand charged with £200 per annum as salaries for the Knights and £30 per annum for the maintenance of their lodgings.

The Commonwealth

Following the battle of Edge Hill in October 1642, Colonel Venn was detached from the Parliamentary Army to occupy Windsor Castle. The Dean and Canons were removed from their livings and ejected from their houses. The Poor Knights of Windsor were, however, sympathetically treated by the Roundheads. Their pay was continued out of the confiscated Chapter livings and they were allowed either to 'abide in their houses or else have the allowance of the profit that is made from keeping prisoners in them'. One of the prisoners, a Mr Thomas Knyvett of Ashwell Thorpe, near Norwich, writes to his wife 'From our pallas at Windsor Castle, 22 April 1643. You may now write Lady, for we are all Poor Knights of Windsor. They have lodged us in their houses. Poor men, they have been turned out and us put in, and ere long we shall be as poor as they. We had but two rooms for seven of us the first night and one bed for all. I hope you will now say we lay like Pig-hogs indeed. We are since better accommodated, thanks be to the good women here, who are full of courtesy, yet still seven to our rooms and house of office.'

On 19 May 1643 the King notified Sir Thomas Rowe, Chancellor of the Order of the Garter, that he would not fill the vacant Poor Knights' Places until he had spoken to him. The petition presented to the King, presumably in 1643, was signed by eleven Poor Knights. The Dean and Canons had already left the Castle and no records were kept by them after 1642 until 1660. Possibly no vacancies were filled until Oliver Cromwell made appointments and details of the Protector's appointments are very incomplete. The Poor Knights who signed the

1643 petition were: Samuel Hull (125); Henry Browne (139) Governor; John Daye (140); William Lowe (150); Richard Ousley - signature appended (152); Abel Barnard (154); William King (155); William Meysey (156); Lieutenant Sebastian Westcott (157); Captain Huh Done (158); Thomas Browne (159).

During the Civil War and the following Protectorate, despite the occupancy of the Castle by parliamentary forces and the ejection of the Dean and Canons, the Poor Knights appear to have remained in post, for on 24 June 1643 the (parliamentary) House of Lords recommended that the Poor Knights be paid from the lands sequestrated from the Chapter or else allowed to profit by maintaining prisoners in their houses.

Parliament set a Commission in 1654 to inquire into this particular organisation, with the result that it was satisfied that it was one of the Charities maintained according to the intention of the Founders and that it should continue in being. In the same year Ordinances were issued 'for the Continuance and Maintenance of the Poor Knights', from which the following is quoted: 'We do establish thirteen Poor Knights, one of them to be their Governor, who have served the Commonwealth as Commissioned Officers in the Army and are now out of commission and incapable of doing service either by reason of age or for want of some limb lost in their service… to be placed in the said Alms Houses. '

It may be noted that by an ordinance of 2 September 1654, Cromwell having appointed new governors who were to oversee the affairs of the Poor Knights, ordered them to require the executors and administrators of the le Maire and Crane estates to settle the outstanding matters. Perhaps in consequence of this injunction and before the final settlement, the first five additional Poor Knights of what was to be called Crane's or the Lower Foundation were appointed, as eighteen Poor Knights were present at Cromwell's funeral in November 1658. There is some confusion over the names of those said to have been appointed by Cromwell but it is noticeable that none of these appearing in a certificate of 1660 as being the first Poor Knights of Crane's Foundation appear in the list of those attending the funeral. It would seem therefore that the appointments were short lived. New Statutes were made, probably soon after the appointment of the governors. These, although not as comprehensive as the Elizabethan Statutes, bore a strong resemblance to them.

The Elizabethan Statutes provide that the Knights, 'shall be placed within the Church where the Dean and Canons shall think best to hear the Divine Service together where they shall least trouble the Ministers of the Church.' This seems to have been settled as being in front of the lower or sub-stalls, that is at pavement level, at the eastern end of the Quire. There is some confusion of evidence as to the form of seating. Thirteen chairs lined with scarlet provided for the Poor Knights appeared in the chapel inventory for 1643 and were, according to Ashmole seized by Colonel Venn the Parliamentary Governor of the Castle in May of that year.

As before, there were to be thirteen Poor Knights who had served in the army, but the selection was to be made only from those who fought for Parliament. Of these one was to be the governor to whom the remainder were to be obedient. He was to be elected, the chosen candidate being required to receive a minimum of nine votes. The candidates for admission as Poor Knights must not have been convicted of any serious offence and if convicted after appointment are to be dismissed. The salary is not specifically awarded by the Statute but there is an implication that it is to be to be £40 per annum, for the cost of the cloak to be worn as 'uniform' and which was to be issued every two years is to be deducted from it.

The Poor Knights were to attend a Prayer Meeting in the Common Hall every day by 9 am, when the cloak was to be worn and when attending church they were to be placed in such a position that 'they may hear without disturbing or being disturbed'. Married men were not excluded from appointment but were required to give security to the Corporation of Windsor in respect of any charges which might be incurred by or on

Quire looking East 1660
By Wenceslaus Holler
The Poor Knights' seating was in the front row nearest the altar.

behalf of their wives and children. If they wished to marry after appointment they were to obtain the consent of the Governors or face dismissal. They were not to haunt taverns and were to reside in their lodgings unless permission was obtained from the Governors, or upon a vote, nine were in favour of leave being granted. They were to be present at a formal reading of the Statutes at least once a year. Any who came into possession of land worth £45 a year or more, or of a sum exceeding £500 was to lose his place. In 1654 the matter was addressed by Cromwell's Council which made an ordinance for the 'continuance and maintenance of the Almshouses and Almsmen called Poor Knights' the preamble stating that 'the Lord Protector being zealous to continue ----- all Works and Foundations tending to ----- Charitable and Pious uses ----- had resolved to settle and establish forever ----- the Foundation. The ordinance appointed twenty-six men including the Provost of Eton and the Mayor of Windsor, the latter being ex-officio, as governors of the charity and transferred to them the ownership and management of the lands of the New Dotation. They were to exercise discipline over the Poor Knights 'according to such Statutes as are to be found or by such other Statutes, Rules and Orders as shall at any time be conceived or made by the said Governors'.

The new lodgings ordered by Sir Francis Crane were built in the Lower Ward of Windsor Castle backing on to the western wall where the guardroom now stands. They were also a product of the Protectorate, being constructed in or about 1657 at a cost of £1700. They consisted of a single block of five houses divided by pilasters with a pedimental gable in the middle; each had a garden in front. They were considered to be beyond repair and destroyed in 1847, apartments over Henry VIII Gateway and what is now known as the Salisbury Tower being provided for the then displaced Poor Knights of the Lower Foundation.

King Charles II

Upon the Restoration some of the Cromwellian appointees were retained and some dismissed. The governance of the Elizabethan Statutes was restored. Under both the Edwardian and Elizabethan Foundations the responsibility for the discipline of the Poor Knights was exercised by the Dean and Canons. In early times the Knights were undoubtedly members of the College and swore obedience to the Dean. It has been argued that the Act of 1483 which incorporated the College and, at least technically, relieved it from paying them, severed the Knights from College membership, but whatever construction might be placed upon this statute there seems little doubt that the re-foundation by Elizabeth I created a new body. Nevertheless discipline was still to be maintained by the Chapter although the Poor Knights were also required to be obedient to their Governor. The oath required under the new arrangement however was not of obedience to the Dean or to the Governor but to obey the Statutes. In a similar manner Military Knights today make a solemn declaration that they will observe the regulations made for their governance.

The ordinance of 1654 required that when the additional Poor Knights should be appointed they should be under the same 'Governance and Rule' as those of the older foundation. This provision was confirmed in more detail by Charles II when at a Chapter of the Order held on 14 January 1661 it was ordered that the Knights of the new foundation should be subject to the same rules as those of the Elizabethan Foundation, have the same privileges and wear the same habit. In 1661 Captain Nicholas Burgh in a letter to Ashmole says that he has not received his salary from the Dean and Canons, 'noe, not soe much as for my Roabe and Gowne' which suggests that by that date the Poor Knights were in receipt of an allowance to provide their own robes.

Four drawings by Hollar show the Quire in 1660 and in 1663. The one dated 1660 looking eastward undoubtedly shows the furnishing at or immediately before the Restoration of Charles II. Bench seating without arm rests extends in front of the lower stalls. Two versions of a drawing of the same view dated 1663 show, in the first, the bench seating as before, but in the second printed by Ashmole, the seating occupied by the Poor Knights is provided with arm rests. Yet another view also dated 1663 but looking westward shows no bench seating at the eastern end at all, but individual chairs. From Hollar's drawing it seems possible that individual seating for the Poor Knights was supplied at the Restoration, but if so, for how long it continued is uncertain.

It may be noted that whatever may have been the early feeding arrangements, by the seventeenth century the hall and kitchen were being let as residential accommodation. On 9 April 1668 a Captain Wildbore was authorised by the Dean and Canons to live in the Poor Knights' Hall. On 4 June 1670 however Chapter ordered the Poor Knights to reoccupy the hall from Michaelmas and not to let it again. The accommodation, now known as Garter House, is today occupied by the Superintendent of the Castle.

With the advent of the Book of Common Prayer it may be that one of the prayers for the King in the English Communion Service, or perhaps that appointed for use at Morning or Evening Prayer was used, but certainly by 1669-70 Canon George Evans writing to Ashmole says that the prayer then used was that which is now substantially contained in the suffrages of the Litany and reads: 'Almighty God we beseech thee to keep thy Servant Charles our King and Governor and so to rule his heart in thy faith, fear and love that evermore he may have affiance and trust in thee and ever seek thy honour and glory; through Jesus Christ Our Lord. Amen.' The use of this prayer at Matins and Evensong may have been peculiar to St George's. With small amendments to the wording this same prayer continues to be used daily at the Communion Service, but that used at Morning and Evening prayer varies.

Some of the appointments towards the close of the seventeenth century were given to Naval officers. For instance Captain Richard Loudon (241) had 'served above forty years in the Royal Fleet and above twenty as a Captain in ships of war.' Captain William Rayer (240), also appointed in 1691 had 'served as a Lieutenant at sea.'

By a decision of a Chapter of the Order of the Garter held on 18 June 1701 the salary and the Exchequer Money which would be payable to a Poor/Military Knight, should there be a vacancy, was to be paid to the Governor.

The eighteenth century saw an outbreak of non-residence. Poor Knights were required, unless leave were obtained, to reside in their houses. Any who failed to do so were formally warned upon two occasions and if non-residence continued, were dismissed, and there appears to have been a spate of admonitions and dismissals between 1774 and 1778.

During the reign of George III, the standard of qualification for the appointments was not maintained and few had seen military service. Mark Anthony Porny, (364) a Master at Eton College, who was appointed in 1781, upon his death in 1802, left a large estate including £4,000 to fund a school so the requirement that an estate of not more than £20 per annum was not strictly enforced. Some of the strange appointments included Sir John Dineley Bart (377) who was such an eccentric that he became a tourist attraction in his own right (See Annex for a full text); and Charles Haynes (384), who following his death was hanged in effigy from the Market House for bribery during the Windsor Borough Election of 1802.

By the late eighteenth century a schedule was in place which provided that six Poor Knights would be in residence at any time. The rota, based upon the number allocated to their houses, specified a residence of four months every year, each period lasting one month. Thus for example the occupants of houses 1,4,6,9,11 and 14 were required to be in residence in March, June, September and December. The present bench seating with its splendidly carved arm rests was provided by Henry Emlyn during the refurbishment of 1785-91.

Notable soldiers during the eighteenth century were Captain William Thorne (399) who was present at the capture of Quebec and was wounded at the siege of Yorktown. Major Edward Fuller (402) was present at the Battle of Minden and other actions during the Seven Years War. Many fought in Marlborough's campaign and in the war in America and in India. Charles Wise (310), who had been one of the two Turkish Moslem boys aged seven or eight captured by the Duke of St Albans at the battle of Belgrade in 1688, and brought up in his home, was a Poor Knight from 1742 to 1743.

The abuse of patronage in the appointment of civilians was brought to the King's notice in about 1809 and it was determined that subsequently none should be appointed but 'decayed and disabled Officers of His Majesty's Forces 'In 1817 the Poor Knights and the Minor Canons were warned not to let their houses and in 1828 the

Captain Nicholas Burgh

Chapter concerned itself with the nuisance caused by beating carpets in front of the Poor Knight's lodgings and ordered it to cease. In 1841 George Lawrence (435) was reported for 'peevish and irritating' conduct and' giving utterance to ----- very in-justifiable expressions.' He was admonished and 'desired to regulate his conduct so that no complaints of a similar nature might render interference by the Chapter again necessary'.

On the day following the Feast Day of the Garter Knights, the medieval practice of an annual event was held celebrating the heraldic achievements when swords, helms, crests and banners of the Knights who had died during the previous twelve months were offered at the Altar. The ceremony was last observed in full in 1805. No personal Installations of Knights Companions took place between 1805 and the revival of Installations in 1948 when the then Dean of Windsor, Bishop Hamilton, introduced an informal ceremony in which, during Evensong, the banner was to be brought in procession by the Military Knights and, being received by the Dean was placed upon the Altar. Prayers were then to be said for the Companion and for the Order. These informal arrangements were officially approved by King George VI in January 1952.

The ceremony of the installation of a Poor Knight before the nineteenth century is not known but the description by Lieutenant Fowler (418) of his installation in 1826 is echoed in modern practice. He describes his arrival at the Castle where he reported to the Governor of the Poor Knights, and his reception by the Chapter Clerk who, having received his Patent together with his fees, was responsible for making the necessary arrangements with the Dean or in his absence with the Canon in Residence. The fees, which have remained unchanged were 17/2d or in modern terms 86 pence. Shortly before Matins on the day of his arrival, Fowler attended the Chapter House (now the Vestry) to take the oaths of allegiance and supremacy. He remained in the Chapter House until after the Psalms when, supported by the two junior Poor Knights he was led into the Quire. Upon entry they advanced a few paces and bowed to the Altar, turned and bowed to the Sovereign's Stall, turned again and bowed to the Altar. He was then installed in the fourth stall nearest the Altar on the Sovereign's side. Afterwards he attended at the Vestry and swore to observe the Statutes.

By 1827, if not before, the uniform was certainly being provided by the Knights themselves for Fowler says that 'New Robes cost about £9, but they can be purchased second hand'. From at least the early nineteenth century the accounts confirm that Robe Money continued to be paid in lieu. The robes prescribed by the Elizabethan Statutes continued to be the official dress until the nineteenth century, save for the period under Cromwell when gowns of a 'sad grey colour' displaying the Arms of the Commonwealth were worn.

The Military Knights of Windsor
King William IV

On 17 September 1833 a Garter Statute introduced a number of changes, including the change of name whereby for the future the Poor Knights were to be called Military Knights. This was in part due to the embarrassment caused by the word 'Poor' to the then occupants of the posts, all of whom were military men, and which had been the subject of scurrilous verses in a local newspaper. The change was also in part due to the fact that by this time a further establishment of impoverished naval lieutenants had come in to being. The title by which this new body was incorporated was 'The Poor Knights of Windsor of the Foundation of Samuel Travers' but unofficially the members were referred to as 'Naval Knights'. Partly in response to this and partly because the Poor Knights had become exclusively military, the members assumed an unofficial title; Dean Legge in 1805 described the older foundation, perhaps colloquially, as 'Military Poor Knights'. Two members who died in 1822 are described in the Burial Register as 'Military Knights', whilst two years later the Reading Mercury referred to Captain Edward Skilton as a 'Military Knight, thus anticipating the Garter Statute which was to settle the matter.

For almost two hundred years, although subject to the same conditions, appointments to the two foundations, the Royal or Upper and Crane's or the Lower were, as a general rule, distinct, and only rarely was promotion made from the Lower to the Upper. After 1833 when the 'military' nature of the appointment was well established it became the custom for the senior Military Knight in Crane's Foundation to be promoted to the Royal Foundation when a vacancy occurred.

The Garter Statute also authorised a new military style uniform. It states that the dress shall be that 'which We as Sovereign have been graciously pleased to prescribe and assign to them'. This prescription has not been found and it has often been asserted that the dress was that of unattached officers, that is officers not attached to a particular regiment, and reference is made to the Dress Regulations of 1834 where that uniform is described. Lieutenant George Sicker (438), describes in detail the uniform which he wore at his installation in 1838 including the embroidery on the tail of his coat, so it is probable that what was prescribed was not the uniform of unattached officers but an adaptation of that dress. This view is supported by the fact that a specimen made for the King's approval and presented to Lieutenant Samuel Ragg in September 1833, a few days after the issue of the Statute was worn by him at a Review in the Home Park. The first occasion upon which all the Military Knights appeared in the new uniform was upon Christmas Day 1833.

The uniform consisted of a scarlet tail coat with a blue collar and cuffs, the tail having the Arms of St George embroidered thereon, gold epaulettes with the Cross of St George in silver with the badge of rank above, blue trousers, a crimson sash, a black sword-belt and a sword with simple gilt quillons and grip. The Knights were to wear a black cocked hat with feathers of red and white [a red and white plume]. This uniform continues to be worn, save that although the Dress Regulations for unattached officers of 1834 prescribed blue trousers with a red stripe upon the outer seam, those worn by the Military Knights had no such stripe. A petition from the Knights to Queen Victoria requested that the stripe be added and that the black sword-belt be replaced by a white cross-belt. In August 1897 permission was given to add the stripe but authority to wear the white cross-belt was refused. The white cross-belt together with a plate embossed with the Garter Star and a Crown was however authorised for use at a date between 1904 and 1908.

The undress uniform consisted of a blue frock coat together with a forage cap, although the latter was to be worn only in inclement weather. Wearing of the cap was discontinued in 2009. This uniform is worn between Remembrance Sunday and Easter save for Christmas Day or when a ceremony such as the presentation of a banner or the Installation of a Military Knight takes place. On these occasions full dress is worn.

It would appear that the Robe Money paid by the College in lieu of robes was never increased despite the greatly increased cost of the uniforms which the Military Knights were expected to provide. Fowler states that the cost of new robes was about £9. He makes a careful note of the sums which Military Knights were now required to expend.

Full Dress

Scarlet Dress Coat	5/15/ 6
Pair of Gold Epaulettes	4/ 0/ 0
White Waistcoat	1/ 1/ 0
Blue Pantaloons	2/ 4/ 0
Sword-belt complete	1/ 1/ 0
Sword	2/ 2/ 0
Regulation	1/16/ 0
Cocked Hat trimmed	3/10/ 0
	£21/ 9/ 6d

Extras
Epaulette Box	3/ 6d
Hat Case	2/ 0d
	5/ 6d

Undress
Cap complete	1/ 6/ 0
Blue Frock Coat	4/12/ 0
Blue Pantaloons	2/ 3/ 0
White waistcoat	1/ 1/ 0
	£9/2/0

For how long the responsibility for the provision for uniform lay with the Military Knights is uncertain but by the reign of Edward VII and probably for some time before, the full dress was supplied the Crown. As late as 1963 the undress uniform was required to be provided at the charge of the individual Knight but today if items of full or undress cannot be supplied from stock they are issued at the Crown's expense.

Eventually in Victorian times, after the matter had been raised in Parliament, the dispute over who should pay the Military Knights reached the Court of Chancery where the Attorney General brought an action against the Dean and Canons. The Court found for the Chapter and the Attorney appealed to the House of Lords. One of the points raised was that since the Chapter had not formally assented to the indenture it was not bound by its terms. Thus presumably it was not required to pay the Military Knights at all. The Lords would have none of this. The Dean and Canons had accepted the lands well knowing the purpose for which they were provided and in equity they were bound to observe the conditions which were intended to be attached to the gift. Nevertheless, although the arguments on both sides were rehearsed in great detail and carefully considered the Lords, with considerable regret, held that despite the fact that the balance from the New Dotation after paying the salaries was more than £14,000, the clear intention of the Crown as donor was that the Poor/Military Knights should receive a fixed salary. Thus, since it was further held that the gift of lands was to a charitable body (subject to certain disbursements being made), the Dean and Canons were entitled to the surplus. At considerable cost to the Chapter the matter was finally settled.

The lodgings of the Military Knights have been much altered over the years. In the early nineteenth century Wyatville, in his general restoration and rebuilding, completely rebuilt the drum tower and replaced the picturesque brick chimneys and garden walls with stone, whilst in about 1840 Blore pierced the walls with additional windows on the suggestions of Prince Albert. The doorways to the lodgings are Victorian in origin.

During the nineteenth century several Acts of Parliament had reduced the number of Canons in collegiate bodies by formally suspending the numbers authorised by their Statutes of Foundation and transferring the monies which would have been paid to them to a central fund controlled by the Ecclesiastical Commissioners. As a result the establishment at Windsor was reduced from a Dean and twelve Canons to a Dean and four Canons. In 1861 a further Act provided that the endowments of one of the suspended canonries of Windsor should be transferred to the Military Knights, £20 being awarded to the Governor, the remainder being divided between all thirteen Knights.

By his will dated 10th September 1869 General Sir George Bowles bequeathed the sum of £2038-6-8d. which was invested to provide an additional income for the Military Knights of Crane's Foundation. This together with the monies arising from the original endowment was transferred to the Royal Foundation upon the absorption of the Lower Foundation under the Act of 1919. As the absorption of the Lower Foundation proceeded, the houses which the members had occupied since the destruction of their lodgings were let and the rents initially utilised to supplement the income of the Military Knights in general.

In the middle years of the nineteenth century regular attendance at the daily services was small and in December 1870 a royal warrant dispensed with compulsory attendance at chapel, providing that the Military Knights might attend or not as they should think proper. This warrant was varied by Edward VII who issued orders providing, inter-alia, that the Military Knights should all attend Sunday morning service unless special leave was obtained. These provisions are repeated in the current Regulations with the requirement of the Elizabethan Statutes that the Sovereign and the Knights Companion are to be remembered in the daily prayers of the Military Knights.

For many years the process of appointment required fees to be paid to the several persons involved, principally to the Home Office, which then provided the documentation to the Chancellor whose Secretary applied not the signet but the Great Seal of the Order and to the College. The Home Secretary's fees were waived in 1865 and in 1875 it was decided to dispense with Letters Patent and issue a Warrant under the Royal Sign Manual, countersigned by the Chancellor to which the Signet not the Great Seal would be applied. In 1885 the reduced fees payable to the Chancellor upon the issue of a Warrant rather than Letters Patent were waived leaving only those to the College.

Outstanding and especially interesting officers in the nineteenth century include Captain John Duncan King (459) who was an excellent artist with paintings exhibited in the Royal Academy and eight in the Royal Library in Windsor. Colonel Sir John Milley Doyle KCB (463) had a very colourful career commanding Portuguese Forces. Colonel Francis Cornwallis Maude VC CB (540) has 76 Battery Royal Artillery named after him 'Maude's Battery'. Captain John Purcell (534) was shipwrecked with a party of the 50th (Queen's Own Regiment) in November 1844 on the Andaman Islands where they remained in great privations for fifty five days. Lieutenant Colonel Bryan Turner Tom Lawrence VC (591) won his award serving as a Sergeant in the 17th Lancers in South Africa. Nineteen Military Knights had fought in the battle of Waterloo.

A great deal of difficulty arose during the closing years of the nineteenth century much of it being connected with the remuneration paid to the Military Knights who at one time, ignoring the Dean and Canons, petitioned the Commander in Chief to be allowed to set up in trade or business. The Dean was incensed and persuaded the War Office to ignore any communications received from the Military Knights. Hardly had the dust settled when an acrimonious dispute arose principally concerning the difference in pay between the Knights of the Crane Foundation and those of the Royal Foundation. This had to a certain extent been mitigated in 1833 by a policy of promoting Knights from Crane's to the Royal Foundation as vacancies occurred.

The protagonist in this affair was Colonel Francis Maude VC, CB (540) who, whilst having only a small income, had been refused promotion because he was bankrupt. Not only did he and others write to the War Office and The Queen, but in the course of the campaign published articles in the press attacking both the financial arrangements and their operation by the Chapter, one of the more colourful phrases being that it was easier to take butter from a dog's mouth than to obtain money from the Dean and Canons! Although it took some time it is probable that this agitation was one of the factors which eventually led to the amalgamation of both bodies.

Additional fees, not all of which continue to be paid, included Obit Money, a sum of 20 pence being payable to each Knight for his attendance at the quarterly obit with an additional 2 shillings for the Governor. Installation Fees payable by each new Knight of the Garter were ordered to be shared with the Poor Knights. This fee is the only Installation Fee now payable, the remainder having been abolished by a Garter Statute dated 12th April 1904. £1.05 is paid by the Dean and Canons to each Military Knight present at the Installation and is funded by a sum of £150 payable from the Exchequer to cover this and as a contribution to the maintenance of the Chapel. Another fee payable to each Military Knight by the Dean and Canons is the sum of £2.10 for the attendance at Royal Funerals.

Early in the twentieth century, during thc hearing of an action in the Chancery Division, Mr Justice Byrne severely criticised the conduct of one of the parties, a Military Knight, Major Charles Strutt (553). (See annex for full text) The criticism was considered so serious that Counsel's opinion was sought as to whether Strutt could be dismissed. The advice was that nothing could be done since despite the judge's strictures upon Strutt's conduct he had not offended against the Elizabethan Statutes. This result led to the issue in 1905 of Letters Patent declaring that Military Knights hold office and may be dismissed at the Sovereign's pleasure. At the same time the responsibility for the discipline of the Military Knights was transferred to the Governor and Constable of Windsor Castle. The Dean continues however to be responsible for the general welfare of the Knights.

In 1905 a discussion took place upon a proposal to evict the Military Knights and to use the houses as accommodation for members of the Lord Chamberlain's Department. Viscount Esher, writing to Archbishop Davidson on 23 February says that he has been appointed chairman of a committee to make recommendations as to how the residential privileges of the Military Knights may be abolished. Davidson, previously Register (as Dean of Windsor) and Prelate (as Bishop of Winchester) of the Order, returned the next day a scathing three-page reply in which he says that the proposal was being made by people who are totally unaware of the facts, that it would be an act of vandalism and would rightly be attacked by responsible and historically-minded people throughout the country. Nothing more was heard of this proposal. The houses, suitably refurbished from time to time, continue to be occupied by the Military Knights.

In 1919 the Military Knights of Windsor Act provided that the Lower Foundation should be absorbed into the Upper Foundation and from the time these provisions were fully implemented the establishment of the Military Knights has consisted of thirteen, one of whom is the Governor. Since 1906 the latter has always been a retired Lieutenant General or a Major General. Seniority within the Military Knights is determined by the date of installation, not the military rank.

In about 1920 the Garter Prayer assumed the form used today: 'God save our Gracious Sovereign and all the Companions, living and departed, of the Most Honourable and Noble Order of the Garter. Amen.'

Until 1922, if not later, the practice of a dispensation which allowed the candidate to be a married man or to marry after appointment continued, but in modern times the Statute has been ignored and the conditions of entry, far from permitting the Military Knights to marry or to be married, now requires them to be married on appointment. Although not a Garter celebration the Military Knights attend the quarterly Obits in uniform but do not formally attend the Requiem which, while not initially described as such, was revived in 1966, and is held on the day following Garter Day. A Garter ceremony in which the Military Knights take part is the Presentation of the Banner following the death of a Knight Companion. If the funeral of a KG takes place at St George's, the Banner is often presented at that time, but usually the ceremony takes place during special Evensong held sometime later. This ceremony is redolent of medieval practices when on the day following the Feast Day the heraldic achievements (swords, helms, crests and banners) of the Knights who had died during the previous twelve months were offered at the Altar, and was last observed in full in 1805.

Queen Victoria's first Mattins in St George's Chapel 1837
Two Naval Knights and four Military Knights are in the stalls.
The Military Knights' uniforms are incorrect.

Ceremony of Installation of Garter Knights 1840
The occupants of the stalls below the Garter Stalls are
thought to be Canons and the Military and Naval Knights

Until 1975 when the finances were reorganised rent was paid to the Military Knights. Although they no longer receive Obit Money and the rents formally received in respect of the accommodation of the Superintendent of the Castle and of Crane's Lodgings have been commuted to a subvention from the Privy Purse, they continue to receive their ancient stipends together with sums in lieu of robes and residence money. They also receive their share of monies from the suspended canonry, the Exchequer Money of James I and those arising from the Crane and Bowles Trusts. Installation Fees and Royal Funeral Fees continue to be paid.

The present bench seating with its splendidly carved arm rests which was provided by Henry Emlyn during the refurbishment of 1785-91 and which was still in the early nineteenth century referred to as 'chairs', was occupied by the Knights until Sunday 29 November 1942 when they moved to their present position in the lower or sub-stalls.

The practice of the Military Knights entering and leaving the Quire in marching order dates from 17 April 1927. At the Sunday morning services it was the custom for the Military Knights to enter in procession via the north east entrance to the Choir and to move straight into their seats omitting the old-time obeisance to the Altar. There was a good deal of dissatisfaction about this as lacking in suitable dignity and it was also felt that as the representatives of the Knights of the Garter, the Military Knights ought to sit in the Garter Stalls and not in the front row alongside the choir boys. Incidentally these front seats are very uncomfortable and are not made for full grown men, so a round robin was sent to the Governor signed by all the Knights asking for a meeting to be called to discuss these and other points. The meeting was held and it was decided to make it the first of regular quarterly meetings to be held after the Obit services. It was agreed to enter the choir on Sundays via the West entrance from the nave and two by two to bow to the altar before moving into their seats. It was also decided that the Governor should make application for places to be allotted to the Military Knights in the Garter Stalls. The application was warmly approved by Lord Wigram and the Dean undertook to see the King about it and ask for his sanction. On Sunday 13 September 1942 the new form of entry commenced with the obeisance to the altar which was met with general approval.

On 13 November the Governor received a letter from the Privy Purse saying that the King had approved and ordered that the Knights should occupy seats in the middle row of stalls, immediately in front of the Garter stalls, and that these should be their permanent seats which they would not be displaced from when the Garter Knights occupied their stalls. Brigadier Pelly (598) writes in his diary, 'This is, I think, a most satisfactory arrangement which commences happily on Sunday 15 November, the day the church bells were rung to celebrate the victory of the 8th Army over Rommel in Egypt, the first time they have been rung for 2½ years, since the fall of France.'

On 8 May 1945 a service to celebrate VE Day was held in St George's Chapel. The Military Knights paraded in Full Dress (scarlet) for the first time since the beginning of the war with the exception of the Dean's Installation. From then on it has been worn for parades throughout the summer months.

During the two world wars in the twentieth century there were so many outstanding officers it would be difficult to single any out. However two officers merit special mention. Brigadier General Raymond Pelly CB, CMG, DSO, (598) who was an accomplished musician, a friend of The Reverend Edmund Fellowes and maintained a diary from 1942 to 1952 when he died. The other is Major Gordon Mitchell MBE, BEM (631) who was given a special award by President Mitterand of France for his work with the SAS in Normandy before D Day.

At the end of June 1947 Peterborough, in *The Daily Telegraph*, wrote of two naval officers who had eight DSO between them. Brigadier Pelly wrote and gave him a list of DSOs among the Military Knights. Peterborough commented on 7 July 1947 as follows: 'collectively the 13 Knights have a remarkable collection of decorations. Four have 10 DSOs between them. Lt Col Plunkett (583) has three DSOs, an MC and DCM; Lt Col J A Fraser (597) has three DSOs and a DCM; Lt Col R Pennell (587) and Brig Gen Pelly (598) each have a DSO and bar. Five others have a mere single DSO, making 15 in all. Between them the 13 Knights have 15 other decorations.'

Outstanding among the post World War II officers is Major General Sir Peter Downward, KCVO, CB, DSO, DFC (633) who was seconded to the Glider Pilot Regiment from the Parachute Regiment and flew as a second pilot in an Avro York (related to the Lancaster Bomber) in the Berlin Air Lift. Unusually for a soldier at that time he was awarded the Distinguished Flying Cross in the Korean war. Today's Military Knights have served in Malaya, Borneo, Kenya, Cyprus with the United Nations, Aden, with Ghanaian Forces in the Congo, the Multi-National Force Sinai and of course Northern Ireland.

Appointments continue to be made by the Sovereign. Applicants apply for registration to the Military Secretary at the Ministry of Defence. They must not be more than 65 years of age when the appointment is made and be medically fit to undertake the duties. The candidate would normally have a long and distinguished military career and, apart from pensions, was, until recently required to have a private income below limits which were set from time to time by the Keeper of the Privy Purse. Today a strict rule is no longer observed but regard is still paid to the candidate's financial situation. This Military Knight (637) was required to furnish the interview board with a certified true copy of the previous year's income tax return, presumably to show that he was, and still is, 'a gentleman brought to necessity'. He attends an interview board and if found to be acceptable is placed upon a waiting list.

When a vacancy occurs a selection is made from the list by the Governor of the Military Knights, further enquiries are made as to his health, and he is interviewed, together with his wife, by the Constable and Governor of Windsor Castle, the Governor of the Military Knights, the Dean of Windsor and others. If the candidate is successful the Keeper of the Privy Purse is notified and the Sovereign asked to approve the appointment. A Warrant of Appointment is drawn by the Ministry of Defence and forwarded to the Keeper of the Privy Purse who submits it to The Sovereign for signature, following which it is sent to the Chancellor of the Order of the Garter who, having arranged for the Signet to be applied by the Secretary of the Order, countersigns the document.

Today the oaths are no longer taken but before Evensong the new Military Knight attends in the Vestry before the Dean and makes a solemn declaration to observe the Regulations for the Governance of the Military Knights of Windsor. At the end of the Psalms, escorted by two supporters and followed by the Governor he enters the Quire. As the party advances through the Quire it halts and bows to the Altar, moves forward, turns about and bows to the Sovereign's Stall. During the further advance these obeisances are twice repeated. The Knight then enters his stall which today is always the second lower stall from the gangway on the north or Prince's side. The Dean then says: 'The Lord preserve you in your going out and your coming in from this time forth for evermore. Amen.' There then follows the Lord's Prayer, special prayers and Evensong continues.

The houses, suitably refurbished from time to time continue to be occupied by the now Military Knights. They have been brought up to modern standards with central heating. The responsibility for furnishing and minor running costs rests with the occupant. They pay Council Tax through their stipends and water and sewerage rates at local council level direct to Buckingham Palace.

Uniform is worn at the morning service on Sundays, Garter Day, at Obit Services, at the presentation of a banner and upon other occasions as may be approved. It may not be worn outside Windsor Castle without special permission. Troops stationed at the Castle pay compliments to the Military Knights.

The Military Knights are listed in the 'Active Army List ' and regard themselves as the oldest formation in the British Army. Whilst unlikely to be called for active service, one was recalled to fight in the Peninsula during the Napoleonic War and during World War II some helped to man the Berkshire Home Guard. At the start of the Falklands conflict in 1982 a Military Knight who was visiting his daughter in Buenos Aires was in danger of being taken as a prisoner of war. The 85 year old former Quarter Master of the Scots Guards was whisked home via South Africa.

Most have duties within the organisation such as Staff Officer, Funerals Liaison, Uniforms, Flat allocation and Liaison with the Household Property Section. Two work for the College of St George, one as Clerk to the 'Companions and Friends of St George's' and one as Concert Manager. One wife is in charge of the flowers in St George's and most help on special occasions such as Christmas and Easter. Being able to take VIP visitors on guided tours of the State Apartments is one of the requirements. Guided tours of the chapel are also undertaken.

Peter J Begent

Peter Begent lived from 30 May 1930 - 7 July 2001. On leaving school he entered health service administration and rose through the ranks, to become an Associate of the Chartered Institute of Secretaries and Administrators along the way. His monument in this regard is probably Wexham Park Hospital, where he actually died, which he guided from before the first sod was turned until after completion when it was at its peak as a centre of healing. After this period he started his own accountancy practice in Burnham, which was later joined to a larger practice.

An erudite and rigorous self-taught scholar of history he became a considerable expert on heraldry. He is the co-author (with Humphrey Chesshyre, sometime Clarenceux King of Arms and Garter secretary [2006]) of 'The Order of the Garter'. He wrote and edited several monographs on the architecture and heraldry in St George's Chapel, Windsor and was the accepted authority on the stained glass of the Chapel.

He had a grant of arms from the College of Heralds which incorporated his interest in archery and the City of London.

After the devastating fire of 1992 at Windsor Castle, Peter was called in as an heraldic authority on the restoration project for the several hundred shields and banners in St George's Hall and was personally complimented by both HM The Queen and HRH The Duke of Edinburgh.

An enthusiast for Belgian beer, engendered on numerous trips to Knokke to shoot popinjay (Belgian-style archery), he enjoyed good food and wine. He was Master of the Bowyers Company 1996-1998, during which period Past Master Sir Roger Cork, his close friend, was Lord Mayor.

Bibliography

G.H. Cook, Medieval Chantries and Chantry Chapels (1968)

A. Kreider, English Chantries the road to Dissolution.

C.Danielle, Death andBurial in Medieval England (1997)

F.H. Stratman, A Middle English Dictionary (1891. Reprint 1967).

St George's MS Papal Bulls 3

A.K. Roberts, St George's Chapel, Windsor Castle 1348-1416 (1947

W. St John Hope, Windsor Castle, An Architectural History (1913)

Peter J. Begent and Hubert Chesshyre, The Most Noble Order of the Garter 650 Years (1999)

E.H. Fellowes, The Military Knights of Windsor 1352-1944 (1944)

E. Ashmole, The Institution, Laws and Ceremonies of the Most Noble Order of the Garter (1672)

The Black Book (1724)

E.H. Fellowes and E.Poyser The Baptism, Marriage and Burial Registers of St George's Chapel Windsor (1957)

S. Bond The Monuments of St George's Chapel Windsor(1958)

Dean Legge's Book St George's M.S. X 23

The Prayer Book of 1552.

P. J. Begent, 'The Feast of St George as Observed on 23rd April 1805 ' Friends Report (1992/3)

Bodl. MS Ashmole 1125

Lambeth Palace Library, Randall Davidson Papers III

P .Clissold, 'Samuel Travers and the Naval Knights of Windsor' Friends Report (1976/7) p346.

King's Regulations for the Army (1908).

Peter J. Begent, 'The Appointment and Installation of a Poor Knight in 1826' Friends Report (1993/4) pp 194-7.

M.F. Bond, The Inventories of St George 's Chapel, Windsor Castle 1384-1667 (1947)

Tighe and Davis II p 181 quoting Lords Journals IV

Acts and Ordinances of the Interregnum 1642-1660 (Reprint 1982)

S. Bond, The Chapter Acts of the Dean and Canons of Windsor (1966)

Statutes for the Poor Knights of Windsor

Queen Elizabeth 1

Henry the Eighth projected the restoration of the thirteen original knights; and Queen Elizabeth devised for the government of the charity, the following rules. '

1. That there be thirteen poor knights, all gentlemen, one whereof to be governor, that have spent their time in the wars, or other service of the realm, having little or nothing to live upon to be elected by the sovereign and successors.
2. The governor and knights must be unmarried, yet that the crown may dispense withal; and upon their marrying are to lose their place.
3. None deformed, and convicted of heresy, felony, or any notable crime, is to be admitted of the thirteen, and after admittance, so convicted, to be expelled.
4. Each knight to have yearly, for their liveries, a red gown of four yards, and a mantle of blue or purple of five yards, at 6s. 8d. Per yard. [Approx £0.33p]
5. An escutcheon of St George embroidered without the garter, to be upon the left shoulder of the mantle.
6. The charges of the cloth, making, lining and embroidering to be paid by the dean and chapter, out of the revenue of the foundation.
7. That the knights attend morning and afternoon divine service, within the college in their ordinary apparel, without a reasonable let to be allowed by the governor.
8. That they keep their lodgings appointed, and table in a common hall appointed, and to have their provisions by a common purse, except for a reasonable cause, may be licensed to the contrary by the dean, and that license not to endure for above twenty days in a year, excepting only for sickness.
9. They are not to haunt the town, nor public houses, nor call any woman into their lodgings, without reasonable cause and license of the dean.
10. Twelve of them to be obedient to him appointed to be governor, and all thirteen to the dean and chapter, in the observance of these statutes.
11. The thirteen knights to have places in the church, where the dean and canons shall think best to hear the divine service together.
12. To be present at the quarterly service, for the memory of the patrons and founder of the college, and especially of King Henry VIII and Queen Elizabeth, and have each of them, at that time, twenty pence, and the governor, two shillings. The said service to be the Sundays next, before the quarter days, the Annunciation, Saint John Baptist, Michaelmas, and Christmas.
13. Any of the twelve knights disobeying the governor, in any of these statutes, to incur the forfeiture the dean and chapter shall put on him, the governor to report the offence, which if more heinous, the dean and chapter are to give a warning, and register the same, and after a second warning, expulsion is to follow; the like punishment to the governor, disobeying the dean and chapter in the observance of these statutes.
14. The penalties of the punished to be employed by the dean and chapter at their discretion, upon any of the ministers or choristers of the church.

15. Upon the king or queen's coming to or going from Windsor, the thirteen knights are to stand before their doors in their apparel, and do obedience.
16. At the keeping of the feast of St George, they are to stand likewise in their apparel before their doors, at the coming and going out of the lieutenant, and of the other knights'-companions.
17. At every feast of St George they shall sit in their apparel at one table, and have allowance of meat and drink at the royal charges.
18. They are daily in their prayers to pray for the sovereign, and the knights'-companions.
19. They are always to lie in their lodging, and upon lying out of them and the college, without license from the dean, to forfeit twelve pence.
20. If lands or revenues of £20 per annum fall to any of the poor knights, he is to be removed, and another put into his place.
21. They are every day (excepting cause of sickness) to be present at divine service in the college, as aforesaid, and receive a daily distribution of twelve pence per day, to be paid them monthly, if it may be, or at least in such sort as the other ministers of the chapel be paid; and he that shall absent himself one day, without leave from the dean, shall lose his distribution of twelve pence.
22. The governor is to keep a book, and register the absentees, and other defaulters of the statutes, whereof he shall deliver one to the dean, and another to the steward, or him that payeth the poor knights, who, by order of the dean, is to make proper defalcations at the time of paying them.
23. The dean once a year is to appoint a day and hour, at which the poor knights are warned to be present, to hear these statutes read, and any knight absenting himself after that warning, and without license, is to forfeit six shillings and eight pence.
24. Any elected poor knight before he takes any commodity of his room, shall take a corporal oath before the dean, to be faithful and true to the crown, and that for the time of their tarrying there, to truly observe the statutes and ordinances upon the penalties contained in the said statutes. '

The twenty-fifth article is a dispensation for those poor knights chosen before those statutes, who were not certainly known gentlemen, yet men well reported for honesty, and meet to be relieved; but with an intent that none hereafter be admitted, unless a gentlemen born, agreeable to the first order. The annual allowance of each, upon this new establishment, is eighteen pounds five shillings, to be paid by the Dean of Windsor, (but their governor has three pounds six shillings and eight pence more,) besides their gown and mantle mentioned in their statutes. King James I doubled this pension, and made it payable out of the exchequer quarterly.

The Roll

of

The Poor Knights of Windsor

and

The Military Knights of Windsor

by

The Revd Edmund H Fellowes, CH, MVO, Mus Doc, Minor Canon of Windsor

with

additions and amendments

by

Major Richard Moore (637)

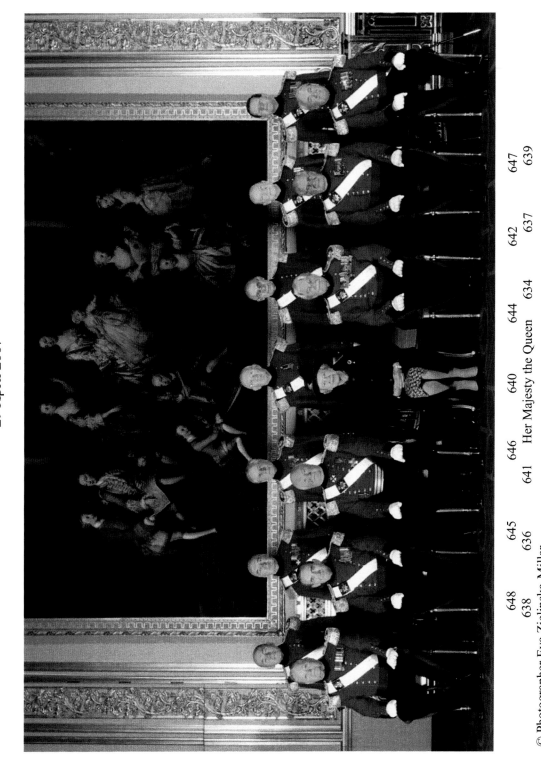

The Military Knights of Windsor
29 April 2007

648   645   646   640   644   642   647
638   636   641   Her Majesty the Queen   634   637   639

© Photographer Eva Zielinska-Millar

26

1.   Robert Beverle (Beverley)   **1368**
Shown in the Treasurer's Roll for 1368 to have received payment as a Poor Knight from May that year until 7 July. Died 7 July 1368 (?)

2.   Thomas Taune (Tawney)   **1376–79**
Appointed before 1376. He received payment as a Poor Knight from 1376 to 1378. He was reprimanded by an Injunction of Richard II in 1378 for unseemly behaviour. He was succeeded by Robert Bitterle (6). Died before June 1379.

3.   Sir John Breton.   **1376**
Appointed before 1376. Described in his Patent as a knight. Received payment as a Poor Knight from 1376 to 1378. He was reprimanded together with Tawney (2) for unseemly behaviour by the injunction of Richard II in 1378. Died before 1384

4.   Richard Stanle (Stanley)   **c.1377–?**
The only record of this Poor Knight is in the Patent of John Brancaster (5) where he is named as his predecessor

5.   John Brancaster   **1377–85**
Patent dated 10 August 1377. The Patent records his good service to the King's father ,The Black Prince, and recommends him on account of his poverty and old age. His name appears in the Attendance Register which begins in October 1384, and his death is recorded there on 9 June 1385

6.   Robert Biterle (Bitterley)   **1379–97**
Patent dated 3 June 1379. Succeeded (2)
After the death of Brancaster (5) he is shown to have been the only Poor Knight throughout the rest of the Attendance Register. It seems he was the sole occupant for about twelve years. He was Succeeded by Sir Nicholas Say (8). Died in 1397

7.   Sir Henry Sturmy   **c.1386**
Held two Patents dated 13 June 1384 showing him as successor to John Breton (3), if the place had not been granted to another by the King and 11 June 1385 nominated him as successor to John Brancaster (5). He is described as a knight in the Patent. Possibly never took up his appointment

8.   Sir Nicholas Say   **1398–1408**
Patent dated 18 September 1398. He succeeded Robert Bitterley (6). Described in the Patent as a knight. Died 19 July 1408

9.   George Muschet   **1402–1411**
Patent dated 27 April 1402. Succeeded John Brancaster (5) whose place seems to have been kept vacant for seventeen years. He is recommended for his great labours and loss in the wars of the King's progenitors. Ralph Whithors (11) nominated to succeed him. Died in 1411

10.   Sir John Grymesby (Grimsby)   **1404–1413**
In his Patent dated 18 December 1403 he is described as 'chivaler' and no doubt held the rank of knighthood. No predecessor is named in the Patent, and for the first time there were as many as three Poor Knights together. Succeeded by Adam Koker (12) in 1413

11.   Sir Ralph Whithors (Whitehorse?)   **1411**
In his Patent dated 15 November 1411 he is described as 'chivaler'. The Patent states that he had laboured long in the wars of Richard II and Henry IV, and had not sufficient means to maintain himself in the knightly order. He may be identical with Ralph, son of Whithors, the King's Esquire, who had a wardship granted him by a

Patent dated 20 December 1376. Ralph had lately been taken prisoner, and this grant was to aid payment of his ransom. There is no evidence to furnish the date of his death

12. Sir Adam Koker   1413–1415
Patent dated 13 May 1413. He is styled 'chivaler'. He was nominated in consideration of his poverty and great age. He was succeeded by Sir William Lyle (13) in 1415

13. Sir William Lyle (Lisle)   1415–1428
His Patent dated 14 February 1415 shows that he succeeded Sir Adam Koker (12). He is described as a 'chivaler ' and was recommended because of his poverty and great age. He was mentioned in a letter of the Dean and Canons, undated but early in the reign of Henry VIII, protesting against the claim of the 'pretend knights' Onerey and Kendall. He was succeeded in 1428 by John Kiderowe (15)

14. Sir Walter Clyston   1423–before 1428.
Patent dated 15 July 1423. He is described as a knight in the Patent. His predecessors and successors names are not recorded. It is presumed that he died before 1428.

No names of Poor Knights are recorded in the Treasurer's Rolls after 1419-20 until 1428-29, when Kiderowe (15) was the sole Poor Knight

15. John Kiderowe (Kithrowe/ Clytherowe/Clitheroe)   1428–1442
In his Patent dated 16 June 1428 he was nominated to succeed Sir William Lyle (13). His appointment was recommended in consideration of his great poverty in old age. He was the only Poor Knight in the years 1429 to 31. His name appeared continuously in the Treasurers Rolls until 1441-42.

16. Sir John Trebell   1431–1438
Patent Dated 23 May 1430. He must have been admitted after 1431 because Kiderowe was the only Poor Knight to receive payment from the Treasurer in the year 1430-31. He served in the retinue of Sir Thomas West at the battle of Agincourt. (From the Roll of the Battle of Agincourt published by the Society of Archers where he is shown as a Chevalier, Lance). He had a garden in the Castle for which he paid a rent of one rose on Midsummer Day to the Constable of the Castle. He died before 11 June 1438 when a grant was made by Letters Patent to John Deepdene (Canon 1430-1460 and Register of the Order of the Garter).
He was succeeded by Richard Lowyk (18)

17. John Salusbury (or Salisbury)   1437/38–1442
His Patent is not to be found in the printed Calendar of Patent Rolls. His name is first appears in the Treasurers' Rolls for 1437-38. He last appears in the Rolls for 1441-42.

18. Sir Richard Lowyk (?Lowick)   1438–1441
Succeeded John Trebell. His Patent, in which he is described as a knight, is dated 13 June 1438 stated that he was to have the house which Kiderowe used to occupy. Kiderowe must have moved as he was still living until 1441/42. Succeeded by Sigismund Ottelinger (19) in 1441.

19. Sir Sigismund Ottelinger   1441–1462
Patent dated 4 May 1441. Described as a knight in his Patent. He was born in Germany, and Letters Patent of the same date granted him Denization. He was appointed a Poor Knight by the advice and assent of the Knights of the Garter in consideration of his poverty and age. He had long service to Henry V and Henry VI in the French wars. He suffered a loss of goods in France in the Rebellion of Paris when he transferred his allegiance to the King of England. He is presumed to have died on 21 October 1462, the last day on which payment was made to him by the Treasurer

20.   Sir William Crafford (Cranford)   **1442–1463**

Patent dated 14 May 1442 in which he is described as a knight. He had served in France and in the Duchy of Normandy after the siege of Harfleur. He was often taken prisoner and wounded grievously in the head. 'That which Henry V gave him wherewithal to live is in the hands of the King's enemies in France, so he is impoverished'. He is presumed to have died 24 June 1463

21.   Robert James   **1451–after 1455**

In his Patent dated 12 August 1451 he is described as 'Late Lieutenant of Bayeux'. He served in the wars of Henry V in France and Normandy over thirty years and was taken prisoner four times. Losing all that he had in the Treaty of Bayeux, he retreated to England in great poverty. There is no evidence to indicate when he died

22.   Sir Walter Cottisford   **c. 1461–1462**

 Patent for Cottisford is to be found in the printed Calendar of the Patent Rolls, but his name appears in the Treasurer's Roll for the years 1461-62, when he received payment for about four months. He may have succeeded Robert James. He was styled 'Sir Wat Cotesford' in the letter of the Dean and Canons in reply to the claim by the 'Pretend Knights'. It is likely that he is to be identified with 'Walter Cotford Kt', who having suffered losses serving in the wars in France and Normandy, was given a grant by letters Patent dated 4 May 1451

23.   William Danyell (Daniel)   **1465–1475**

Patent dated 17 June 1465. His name appears in the Register of daily Attendances at the Chapel Services which begins in June 1468. Died on 17 March 1475 when he was succeeded by James Frus (27).

24.   John Pesmerch (Peasmarsh)   **1465–1480**

Patent dated 14 November 1465. He is described in the Patent as 'the King's Esquire'. His name is mentioned in the Treasurer's Rolls until 1479/80.

25.   Thomas Gray   **1467–1468**

Patent dated 22 October 1467. He died 8 September 1468 and was succeeded by Hugh Jones, or Johns (26)

26.   Hugh Johns (Jonys or Jones)   **1468–c. 1480**

Patent dated 15 December 1468. His attendance was maintained regularly until July 1479 when the Register ends.

27.   James Frus (Fryse)   **1475–after 1481**

No Patent has been found for his appointment, but he was admitted 20 March 1475. He is described in the Register as *medicinae doctor*. He had been granted certain tenements in Westminister by Letters Patent dated 29 January 1481, in which he was described as one of the King's physicians

28.   William Saunderson   **1480–before 1485**

Patent dated 8 May 1460. He was nominated in consideration of laudable and faithful service to the Crown. There is no positive evidence that he was ever admitted

29.   John Sigemond   **1480–1482**

His name is found only in the Patent of Thomas Holme, who was nominated to succeeded him. In that Patent Sigemond is described as 'late one of the Poor Knights'. Holme was to have his house and Garden. In a grant dated 20 June 1478 Sigemond was described as 'one of the grooms of the King's chamber'. The John Sigemond (53) appointed a Poor Knight in 1510 may have been his son

30.   Sir Christopher Furneys (Furness)   **c. 1481**

His Patent is dated 28 August 1481, but there is no evidence that he was ever admitted

31.   Walter Harneys   c. 1481
Patent dated 21 November 1481. No evidence of admission

32.   David Thomas   1482–before 1485
Patent dated 25 January 1482. It is stated in the Patent that he was one of the Esquires of the Household.

33.   Thomas Grenfeld (Grenfell?   c. 1482
Patent dated 14 March 1482. There is no evidence to show whether he was admitted. Recommended for good service to the King and to the King's brother, Richard, Duke of Gloucester.

34.   Laurence Faireclow   c. 1482
Patent dated 16 March 1482. There was no evidence to show whether he was admitted. He is described as one of the King's servant and one of the Marshals of the King's Household. He is recommended for his good service to the King in all his victorious conflicts and necessities

35.   Laurence Leventhorp   c. 1482
Patent dated 18 March 1482. There was no evidence of admission

36.   Thomas Holme   1482–1485
His Patent is dated 29 March 1482. It is stated that he was to have the same rights 'as David Thomas hath' (32), and the house and Garden of John Sigemond (29) 'late one of the Poor Knights'. Was Clarenceux King-of Arms. He was still living in 1484, but is not among the Poor Knights named in the Treasurer's Roll for 1485

37.   Richard Assheton   c. 1482
Patent dated 4 June 1482. No evidence of admission

38.   Thomas Crabbe, Esquire   1482–1485
One of the Marshals of the Hall of the household of the King's first son, Edward, the Prince of Wales. 'For his good service to the King in his conflicts and necessities and to the King's said son.' His name appears in the Treasurer's Roll for 1485

39.   Henry Sewall   1484
Patent dated 23 February 1484. No evidence that he was admitted.

40.   William Ballard alias Marche?   1484
In the Patent of Thomas Gibbes the promise of the first vacancy was stated to have been given to 'William Ballard alias Marche', and Gibbes was to have the second vacancy. If he was admitted in 1484 he was no longer a Poor Knight in 1485

41.   Thomas Gibbes   1485
His Patent is dated 18 January 1485, giving the details stated above under Ballard's name. He seems to have been succeeded in the end of the same year by Sir Robert Champlain (42).

42.   Sir Robert Champlain   1485–before 1489
Patent dated 8 December 1485 in which he is described as a 'Knight Croyse'. It seems he had taken part in the Civil Wars with Henry VI against King Edward IV, shortly after whose coming to the Crown betook himself to Hungary to fight the Turks, and bore himself as a Christian Knight. He took with him an Equipage of three servants and four horses. Commended by the Popes Pius II and Paul II, the Emperor and Matthias, King of

Hungary. He was dangerously wounded and taken prisoner several times. His ransom was 1500 ducats, and having lost his fortune, he was without means to live. There is no date or record of his death

His name does not appear in the Treasurer's Roll for the year 1485 but there is a gap in the series after this until 1489-90. If he was admitted he must have died before that year.

43.   Roger Tonge   1485–1502
Patent dated 24 November 1485. He was recommended as a Poor Knight because of his great losses and 'maims' in the service of Henry VI. He died at the end of 1502, for the Patent of John Meautis (52), names him as his predecessor.

44.   Richard Thame   1486–?
Patent dated 3 June 1486. He must have held the position for a very short time if he was ever admitted.

45.   William Stoughton (Stockton)   1486–1491/92
His Patent is dated 4 October 1486, and a mandate to admit him is dated 14 November 1486. He had spent his whole of his youth in the service of Henry VI , and had suffered great persecution and losses. He was succeeded by Lewis Caerleon (47)

46.   John Charleton   c.1486–1493
Patent dated 15 November 1485. He first appears in the Treasurer's Roll in 1489-90, and for the last time in 1492-93 when he was paid till 16 January 1493. He was succeeded by Peter de Narbonne (49).

47.   Lewis Caerleon (Carlyon or Carly)   1491–after 1493/94
Patent Dated 14 September 1491.He is described in the Patent as a doctor of medicine. He was one of the King's physicians. He had previously received from the Crown of 40 marks for life; and another grant of 20 marks was dated 27 November 1486

48.   John Lewis   1492–after 1499
No Patent for his appointment has been found. His name appears in the Treasurers' Rolls regularly from 1491-92 until 1499 after which date no names of Poor Knights are given in the Treasurers' Roll.

49.   Peter De Narbonne (Nerbon)   1493–after 1512
His Patent, dated 23 January 1493, states that he was to succeed John Charlton (46). He was a native of Brittany and was granted letters of Denization 2 April 1490. He served as a Poor Knight for many years in the reign of Henry VIII under special conditions. In compliance with the King's wishes the Dean and Canons contributed 20 marks per annum to his support. They received thanks from the King who admitted that the Chapter were under no obligation to do this. He was still living in 1512. He was Barber to Henry VII and granted coat of arms 23 June 1502

50.   Henry Spencer   after 1493
Patent dated 29 October 1493. He was one of the Yeoman of the Crown and was recommended for good service in his youth to Henry V, and having suffered tribulations and loss under Henry VI. Probably not admitted

51.   Charles de Bresy   after 1493
His Patent is dated 24 November 1493, nominating him to be one of the Alms Knights, 'the first and second vacancies excepted'. Almost certainly not admitted

52.   John Meautis (Mewtes)   1503–after 1518
His Patent is dated 8 January 1503, nominating him as successor to Roger Tonge. He held the important post as 'Secretary of the French tongue to the King'. He Nearly lost his life in the riots of 'Evil May Day '1517.

Note. On 1 May 1517 rioters attacked foreign workers and residencies in Stepney. 137 Flemish people were killed. The riot was suppressed by Cardinal Wolsey. 60 rioters were hanged.

53.   John Sigemond   1510–?

Patent dated 2 June 1510. In it he is described as 'Sewer of the King's Hall, now in his old age. Possibly the son of John Sigemond (29)

54.   Bartholomew Westby   1514–?

Patent dated 5 May 1514. He formerly served as Baron of the Exchequer, appointed by Letters Patent dated 2 June 1509

55.   Robert Fayrfax (Fairfax)   1514–24 October 1521

Patent dated 10 September 1514. He is described as one of the Gentleman of the Chapel, i.e. the Chapel Royal. He was a famous musician, and his work as a composer is well known today. He was Organist of St Alban's Abbey. He took the degree of Doctor of Music at Cambridge in 1501. He was head of the singingmen at the funeral of King Henry VII and at the coronation of Henry VIII. In 1520 he headed the Gentlemen of the Chapel Royal to the great Anglo-French summit at the Field of the Cloth of Gold. Henry VIII made Fayrfax a Poor Knight to supplement his existing income. He was accounted the prime musician of his day.
He died 24 October 1521 and was buried at St Alban's Abbey.

56.   Robert Harrison   1515–?

Captain Coley-Bromfield gives the name of Robert Harrison on the authority of a Dr Evans as having been appointed a Poor Knight in 1515. No evidence has been found among the memoranda of Evans or elsewhere but there must be some evidence for discovering the full name and date of appointment

No Letters Patent after that of Robert Fayrfax (55) are known to exist. It is improbable that any further appointments were made until 1558 when Queen Mary nominated nine Poor Knights under the new establishment in 1558. There is also a large gap in the series of annual Rolls kept by the treasurers of the College during these same years.

57.   James Crane   1558–1559

First Governor of the Poor Knights

Nominated by Queen Mary. He died shortly afterwards and was succeeded as Governor by John Acton (69).

58.   Michael Whiting   1558–1568/69

Governor of the Poor Knights 1567–68

Nominated by Queen Mary. He succeeded John Acton(69) as Governor of the Poor Knights in 1567-68, and was succeeded by Francis Ingloss(79).

59.   Silvester Glossop (or Clessop)   1558–1571

Nominated by Queen Mary

60.   Hugh Johns (Jones)   1558–1560

Nominated by Queen Mary. He died 26 September 1560. He was succeeded by John More(72)

61.   Robert Case   1558–1561

Nominated by Queen Mary. He died 18 January 1561. He was succeeded by Thomas Walkley(73)

62.   John Brigsby   1558–1560/61

Nominated by Queen Mary

63.   George Fothergill   1558–1560/61

Nominated by Queen Mary

64.   George Thackwell   1558–1563/64

Nominated by Queen Mary.

65.   William Berd   **1558–1559/60**
Nominated by Queen Mary.

66.   Thomas Kemp   **1558–1574/75**
Nominated by Queen Elizabeth 'by byll assigned', dated 16 December 1558. He was a merchant of Bristol and
owned a ship called the Trinity. Associated with the Mary Rose which foundered in the Solent with great loss of
life in 1545. First occupant of No 8 Lower Ward. His shield is carved on the left of the fireplace in No 8 Lower
Ward.

The names of Poor Knights were no longer entered into the Stewards' Accounts after 1574-75

67.   William Barrett   **1559–1560/61**
Nominated by Queen Elizabeth

68.   William Cowper (Cooper)   **1559–1574/75**
Nominated by Queen Elizabeth

69.   John Acton   **1559–1567**
Governor of the Poor Knights 1559–67
Nominated by Queen Elizabeth. He succeeded James Crane (57) as Governor of the Poor Knights in 1559-60.
He died 16 June 1567 when he was succeeded by Michael Whiting (58)

70.   John Pasfeld   **1559–1574/75**
Admitted in 1559, apparently in succession to James Crane (57)

71.   Henry Mounteney   **1559–1561**
Admitted in 1559, apparently in succession to William Berd (65). He died 8 July 1561. He was succeeded by
Thomas Bainbrigg, or Bainbridge (74)

72.   John More   **1560–after 1563/64**
Admitted in 1560 in succession to Hugh Jones (60)

73.   Thomas Walkley   **1561–1571**
Admitted 1561 in succession to Robert Case (61). His name appears for the last time in the Stewards' Roll for
March 1571

74.   Thomas Bainbrigg (Bainbridge)   **1561 after 1575**
He was admitted in 1561 in succession to Henry Mounteney

75.   John Brooke (Broke)   **c. 1563–?**
His name only appears in the steward's Account for 1563-64. He may have succeeded George Fothergill (63)

76.   Robert Jerningham   **1563/64–after March 1571**
Admitted in 1563-64. His name appears for the last time in March 1571. He may have succeeded John Brigsby
(62)

77.   Robert Corbett   **1563/64–after March 1571**
Admitted in 1563-64. His name appears for the last time in March 1571. He may have succeeded William
Barrett (67)

78.   William Turner   **1566/67–after 1575**
Admitted in 1566-67. His name appears regularly in the Steward's Rolls until 1574-75.

79. Francis Ingloss (Inglois/Engloss)   **1566/67–after March 1571**
Governor of the Poor Knights 1568–1571
Admitted in 1566-67. His name appears for the last time in March 1571, when he was Governor of the Poor Knights, having succeeded Michael Whiting (58) in that office after the year 1568-69. He was succeeded as Governor by William Palmer (81) before 1574-75.

80. Thomas Palmer   **1566/67–after March 1571**
Admitted in 1566-67. His name appears in the Steward's Roll for the last time in March 1571

81. William Palmer   **1567–1587**
Governor of the Poor Knights 1575–1587
Admitted in 1567-68. His name appears for the last time in the Steward's Accounts for 1574-75, in which year he was Governor of the Poor Knights in succession to Francis Ingloss (79). He was appointed as Governor on the nomination of Lord Leicester. He was succeeded as Governor by David Price (91). He died in May 1587.

82. Roger Wentworth   **1570/71–after 1574/75**
Admitted in 1570-71 in succession to Michael Whiting (58). Patent dated 9 June 1567. His name appears in the Steward's Roll of 1574-75. Served under Sir Edward Gray at Leith as a demilance, and at Newhaven under Captain Twilie (?). He also served under Lord Williams of Thame

83. Eustatius Abyngton   **c.1574–1575**
Admitted in 1574.

There are no Steward's Rolls between 1571 and 1574-75. After that date no names of Poor Knights are given in these Rolls

84. John Molesworth   **c. 1574–1575**
Admitted c. 1574

85. Nicholas Waferer   **c. 1574–1575**
Admitted c. 1574

86. George Calwartley   **c. 1574–1575**
Admitted c. 1574.

87. Adam Finmore   **1574–1575**
Admitted 1574. Patent dated 24 December 1574

88. Robert Tyndesley   **c. 1574–1575**
Admitted c. 1574

89. Nicholas Smyth   **1575–?**
Admitted in 1575 and was paid for a short period, as recorded on the Steward's Roll at the end of the year 1574-75. Presumably he was appointed late in that financial Year

90. Raynold Worseley   **1578–?**
Patent dated 7 December 1578. He served in King Edward's time and Queen Mary's with two hundred men. Served as a page in the Court. 'He hath a mayden wyfe'. 'He hath no lands'. *[These details , as mentioned in the Patent, refer to the statutes under which the Poor Knight had to be unmarried and without substantial means.]*

91.   David Price   c. 1580–?
Governor of the Poor Knights–1589–1597
His name comes between those of Worseley (90) and Morgan (92) in a list of six Poor Knights. The space in the
list has been left vacant. He served in the wars in Scotland and at Boulogne, Montreuil and Landrecies. He
succeeded William Palmer (81) as Governor of the Poor Knights on 18 October 1589. He was succeeded as
Governor by Thomas Conway (100) in 1597

92.   John Morgan   1584
Patent dated 18 May 1584.   'He served in the wars in King Henry's time and in Queen Mary's and King
Edward's in Calais, Guienne and Boulogne, at Landrecies under Sir John Wallop; at Musselburgh under Lord
Gray, and in Ireland, `often hurte and maymed '

93.   Percy Conway   1585
Patent dated 24 March 1585.   'He served in the wars in King Edward's time and in Queen Mary's in Scotland
under Mc Hanmer at the burning of Kelso; and at Boulogne under Sir John Gates; in Ireland hurt in service and
hath divers wounds he served the late Earl of Sussex.

94.   ——Dollwin   after 1585–?
His name appears alone in this incomplete manner, as if intended to follow the previous six names on the page.
Evidently the writer was interrupted and the list left incomplete.

95.   George Martin   1590
Patent dated 11 September 1590. There is no actual record of his appointment but it may be presumed. There
are no other known documents supplying information for this period until 1596

96.   Andrew Thistlethwaite   1590
Patent dated 19 September 1590. There is no actual record of his appointment, but it may be presumed, as in
the case of Martin (95)

97.   Stephen Metcalf   1590
Patent dated 19 September 1590. Described as a Serjeant Trumpeter. His appointment may be presumed as in
the previous two cases.

98.   J. Jobson   1594–1600
A letter dated 13 October 1600 was addressed by him to the Dean and Canons as 'having been late a Poor
Knight ' and giving a release of all demands on the Dean and Canons as a Poor Knight.

99.   John Norton   c.1596–1617
First mentioned in 1596 in the Chapter Acts as being admonished for speaking contemptuously about the
statutes for the government of the Poor Knights. In August 1602 he was charged with 'divers contempts and
misdemeanors', including striking Mr Hook (107) and was suspended from attending chapel.   He
'contumaciously ' attended both Morning and Evening prayer and was subsequently excommunicated and had
his stipend and pay stopped. In September he expressed sorrow and after making a public confession during
Sunday service received absolution. In June 1606 John Norton, being the senior Poor Knight was required to
attend with one other to bring John Massingberd (109) to the Governor's place. He refused declaring
Massingberd to be a 'Pycard, no gentleman and no soldyer'. Norton's wages were stopped again until such time
as he acknowledged his offences. In September 1606, he and John Salisbury (112) were fined Five pounds and
four shillings for continued tumultuous and disobedient behaviour. In October they both acknowledged
themselves to be 'sorye'. On 4 April 1617 he was succeeded by Read Wildgos (138). *See Appendix for the full text*

100.   Captain Thomas Conway   **1597–1606**
Governor of the Poor Knights–1597–1606
He was already a Poor Knight when he was appointed to succeed David Price (91) as Governor of the Poor Knights on 30 September 1597.   He was succeeded by Captain Thomas Muse(120) and by Richard Massingberd(109) as Governor.

101.   George Sheffield   **1597–?**
Admitted 10 July 1597. Patent dated 8 July 1597. He was recommended for good dervice in the wars and was promised the first vacancy that should occur.

102.   Thomas Tucker   **1597–?**
Admitted 10 July 1597. Patent dated 8 July 1597. He was recommended in consideration of his service in the wars, and also because both hands were maimed by an explosion of gunpowder whilst training soldiers in the county of Bucks

103.   Robert Sampson   **1597**
Admitted 23 July 1597. Patent dated 23 July 1597

104.   Nicholas Whittacres (Whittakers)   **1597–1598**
Admitted 25 July 1597. Patent dated 8 July 1597. He was recommended in consideration of his service in the wars. Guilty of adultery with Elenora Sampson and was expelled for misconduct 30 September 1598

105.   Arthur Hygham (Hyam)   **1597–1601**
Admitted 22 December 1597. Patent dated 9 December 1597. Died 1601. Succeeded by Anthony Parkhurst (110)

106.   Robert Teshe   **1599–1610**
Admitted 15 April 1599. Patent dated 13 April 1599. Died 1610 and was succeeded by Robert Stafferton (123)

107.   Thomas Hooke   **1599–1619**
Admitted 4 August 1599. Patent dated 1 August 1599. Died 1619. Succeeded by John Daye (140).

108.   Edward Aymes (Amyas)   **1599– 1625**
Admitted 23 September 1599. Patent dated 20 September 1599. On 11 January 1606 he was charged by the Dean and Chapter for fighting with Parkhurst (110?) at their doors after ten of the 'Clocke in the night to the great troble and Disquietinge of their bretheren'.   He was fined six weeks pay and Parkhurst a fortinghtes. Buried in St George's Chapel 20 October 1625. He was succeeded by Morgan Coleman (144)

109.   Richard Massingberd   **1599–1623**
Governor of the Poor Knights–1606–1623
Admitted 12 December 1599. Patent dated 1 December 1599. Appointed Governor of the Poor Knights 25 June 1606 by the King's order in succession to Thomas Conway (100). His appointment was opposed by 'divers of the Poor Knights ' under the leadership of John Norton (99), 'being the ancientist of them', who objected to Massingberd as being 'no gentleman and no soldier'. The Poor Knights were summoned by the Dean and Chapter 'to hear his Majesty's pleasure touching their Governor'. He died in 1623 and was succeeded as a Poor Knight by Miles Hughes (143) and by Read Wildgos (138) as Governor

110.   Anthony Parkhurst   **1601–?**
Admitted 25 December 1601 in succession to Arthur Hygham (105)

111. Richard Parker   1603–1609

Admitted 9 February 1603. Recommended for good service to Queen Elizabeth in the wars. Died 1609.
Succeeded by William Phillips (121)

112. John Salisbury   1603–1637

Admitted 24 June 1603. Patent dated 13 June 1603. Recommended for good service to Queen Elizabeth in the wars. He was suspended from receiving any wages by the Dean and Chapter on 7 August 1606 together with John Norton (99) for complaining about the appointment of Richard Massingberd (109) as Governor. He was again deprived of his pay on 22 November 1608 for a number of misdemeanours which included saying to the Dean openly in the Chapter that for five years he had continually oppressed him and that his oppression would be the cause of Mr Norton's (99) death, as it had been the cause of Mr Godballes death, one of the clerkes. He submitted his apology on 3 December 1608 before the Dean and Chapter saying that he was 'hertelie sorie'. Died 29 April 1637 and was buried the same day in St George's Chapel. Succeeded by William Meysey (156).

113. Francis Pesemede (Peasmead)   1604–1618

Admitted 11 February 1604. Patent dated 27 June 1603. Recommended 'for divers good considerations'. Died 1618. succeeded by Henry Browne (139)

114. John Muffett   1603

Patent granted dated 12 October 1603 but no evidence that he was ever admitted

115. Ellis Bingham   1604

Patent granted dated 23 October 1604 but no evidence that he was ever admitted

116. Richard Cunliffe   1604

Patent granted dated 3 November 1604 but no evidence that he was ever admitted

117. Laurence Hussey   c. 1604–1609

The date of his admission is not known, nor has his patent been found. It is certain that he was admitted, for John Pierson (122) was appointed in his place in 1609

118. John Hutton   1605–1612

The exact date of his admission is not recorded, but his Patent is dated 22 May 1605. He died in 1612 and was succeeded by Samuel Hull (125)

119. Nicholas Tompson   1605–1629

The exact date of his admission in 1605 is not recorded.. His Patent is dated 25 May 1605. He was recommended for his good service in the wars. On being admitted a Poor Knight he had to renounce a pension of 16d a day, granted to him by Letters Patent dated 30 October 1586. Buried at St George's Chapel 25 September 1629. Succeeded by Henry Sanders (145)

120. Captain Thomas Muse   1607–1629

Admitted 6 December 1606. Patent dated 18 October 1603, granted in consideration of good service done in the wars. He was granted leave of absence on 12 April 1609 'to Travel to the Low Countries where he hath business '. He died 20 November 1629, having been 'found dead in his Chamber with a great part of his body consumed with fire ' [St George's Chapel Burial Register]. He was buried in St George's Chapel 21 November 1629. Succeeded Thomas Conway (100) and was succeeded by Anthony Huggins (146).

121. William Phillips   1609–1610

Admitted 12 April 1609. Patent dated 14 January 1604, granted in consideration of good and faithful service to Queen Elizabeth as one of the pages of her Chamber. Died 1610. Succeeded Richard Parker (111) and was succeeded by Thomas Gardiner (124).

122. John Pierson   **1609–1619**

Admitted 17 December 1609. Patent dated 29 April 1604, granted for good service done to King James. Died in 1619. Succeeded Laurence Hussey (117) and was succeeded by Richard Morris (141)

123. Robert Stafferton (Staverton)   **1610–1613**

Admitted 18 April 1610. Patent dated 4 May 1604. Died 1613. Succeeded Robert Teshe (106) and was succeeded by Jonas Bradbury (130)

124. Thomas Gardiner   **1610–1612**

Admitted 5 September 1610. Patent dated 3 July 1604, granted in consideration of good service done to Queen Elizabeth in the wars. Died 1612. Succeeded William Phillips (121) and was succeeded by William Russell (126)

125. Samuel Hull   **1612–after 1643**

Admitted 22 February 1612. Patent dated 27 March 1607. He was 'sequestrated from his place by occasion of the death of Andrew Lingan'. On being acquitted on the charge of guilt in this affair, he was restored to his place 27 June 1618 plus a restoration of all fees and commodities due to him. He was one of eleven Poor Knights who presented a petition to Sir Thomas Rowe, Chancellor of the Order, dated 21 March 1638, concerning their income; and also a petition addressed to Charles I c. 1643 about arrears of pay. Samuel Hull (200), who was appointed a Poor Knight c. 1660 and died in 1685, was perhaps his son. Succeeded John Hutton (118).

126. William Russell   **1613–5 October 1634**

Admitted 11 January 1613. Patent dated 26 January 1611. Died 5 October 1634 and was buried the next day in St George's Chapel. He succeeded Thomas Gardiner (124) and was succeeded by Jonas Bodenham (153).

127. Daniel Ballard   **1613**

His Patent is dated 23 May 1607. He surrendered his claim to succeed Thomas Gardiner (124) and was not appointed

128. Thomas Gibbs   **1613–1641**

The date of his admission is not known. His Patent is dated 14 November 1610, and admissions at this period follow the date of the Patents after an interval of about three years. He was one of the signatories to the petition of 21 March 1638 (see under Hull 125). He died 7 November 1641 and was buried on 9 November in St George's Chapel. He was succeeded by Thomas Brown (159)

129. William Carus   **c.1613–1620**

The date of his admission is not known. That he was admitted as a Poor Knight is certain as Thomas Domville (142) was nominated to succeed him.

130. Jonas Bradbury   **1613–?**

Admitted 20 May 1613. Patent dated 4 April 1611, and granted for good and faithful service done by sea and land in the time of Queen Elizabeth and also of James I. The date of his death has not been found. Succeeded Robert Stafferton (123)

There is a gap in the records between 1613 and 1617 and there is no evidence to show whether any of these were admitted Poor Knights. It is possible that some were

131. John Derwyn–Water (Derwentwater or Drawater)★   **1611–?**

132. Richard Hales★   **1612–?**

133. Edward Harris★   **1613–?**

134.	William Farmer★	1614–?

135. John Palmer★   1615—?

136. Thomas Bradshaw★   1615–

137. Richard Langley★   1616–?

138. Read Wildgos   1617–1634
Governor of the Poor Knights 1623–1634
Admitted 5 August 1617. Patent dated 4 April 1612. In 1623 he was appointed Governor of the Poor Knights in succession to Richard Massingberd (109). Died 12 December 1634. Buried 14 December in St George's Chapel. Succeeded John Norton (99) and was succeeded by Richard Ousley (152)

139. Henry Browne   1618–after 1643
Governor of the Poor Knights–1634–after 1643
Admitted 26 June 1618. Patent dated 17 May 1612. Succeeded Francis Pesemede (113). In 1634 he was appointed Governor of the Poor Knights in succession to Read Wildgos (138). He was one of the signatories at the head of the list to the Petitions of 1638 and c. 1643 (see Samuel Hull (125). The date of his death is not known.

140. John Daye (Day)   1619–1660
Governor of the Poor Knights after 1643
Admitted 3 November 1619. Patent dated 29 April 1612. . He succeeded Thomas Hooke (107)
On 10 March 1630 he was granted permission by King Charles to travel to Guyana with his wife and family 'for the setling of a Plantacion ' for a period of four years. During this time he was given leave to hire a deputy to attend any feast of St George and Installation. His 'Atturny was to collect all wages, fees, liveries and profits due to him.   In 1634 he was given leave to stay in Guyana for a further four years with the same arrangement for a deputy to stand in for him and an 'Attorney ' to collect his dues including his yearly pension paid from the Exchequer. He was back to sign the petition to King Charles in 1643. He succeeded Henry Brown (139) as Governor of the Poor Knights. Attended Cromwell's funeral in 1658. He died 28 October 1660 and was buried in St George's Chapel two days later

141. Richard Morris   1619–1637
Admitted 3 November 1619. Patent dated 29 April 1613. Died 5 February 1637 and was buried the next day in St George's Chapel. Succeeded John Pierson (122). Succeeded by William King (155)

142. Thomas Domville   1620–1631
Admitted 8 November 1620. Patent dated 15 June 1613. He brought a warrant from six Knights of the Garter for his admission. This was the first warrant from Knights of the Order. He died 17 March 1631 and was buried the next day in St George's Chapel. He succeeded William Carus (129) and was succeeded by Ambrose Jermyn (148)

143. Miles Hughes   1623–1630
Admitted 7 October 1623. Patent dated 16 October 1613. He succeeded Richard Massingberd (109). He was dismissed in 1630 and was succeeded by Sir Francis Tanfield (147)

144. Morgan Colman   1625–1633
Admitted 12 January 1625. Patent dated 6 January 1625. He died 22 February 1633 and was buried in St George's Chapel on 25 February. He succeeded Edward Amyes (108) and was succeeded by John Bray (151)

145.   Henry Sanders   1629–1632

Admitted 1 December 1629. Patent dated 29 September 1629 (?). Died 1632. He succeeded Nicholas Tompson (119) and was succeeded by William Lowe (150)

146.   Captain Anthony Huggen (Huggins)   1629–1631

Admitted 30 December 1629. Died 22 May 1631 and was buried in St George's Chapel but the exact date is not recorded in the Register where he is called Thomas. Succeeded Thomas Muse (120) and was succeeded by Henry Gratwick (149).

147.   Sir Francis Tanfield   1630–1639

Admitted 4 March 1630. Patent dated 21 February 1630. Born in Gayton, Northamptonshire in 1565. He was second cousin to Elizabeth, daughter of Sir Lawrence Tanfield, a subscriber to the Newfoundland company of 1610, and wife of Henry Cary, Lord Falkland. He was knighted in 1603 on the occasion of the Coronation of King James 1. In September 1603 he accompanied the ambassador, Lord Spencer, to the court of the Duke of Wurtemberg. He was Proprietary Governor of the South Falkland colony (in modern Newfoundland). He established the colony at Renews in 1623. The settlers were harassed by migratory fishermen who used the harbour. The settlers returned to England in 1626. He was due to embark on a mission to Ireland in 1630 for King Charles 1. It would seem that he became a Poor Knight instead. He signed the petition of 21 March 1638 (see Hull 125).   Died 9 January 1639 and was buried 11 January in St George's Chapel. Succeeded Miles Hughes (143) and was succeeded by Captain Hugh Done (158).

148.   Ambrose Jermyn   1631–1642

Admitted 4 June 1631. Patent dated 24 May 1631. He signed the petition of 21 March 1638 (see Hull 125), but not that of c.1643 showing that as he died in 1642 this second petition is to be dated at least as late 1643. Died 22 November 1642 and was buried in St George's Chapel 24 November. Succeeded Thomas Domville (142).

149.   Henry Gratwick   1631–1637

The date of his admission is not known but his Patent is dated 16 October 1631. Died 3 November 1637 and was buried the next day in St George's Chapel. Succeeded Anthony Huggen (146) and was succeeded by Sebastian Westcote (157).

150.   Wlliam Lowe   1632–after 1643

Admitted 4 May 1632. Patent dated 23 April 1632. He signed the petitions of 1638 and c. 1643 (see Hull 125). The date of his death is not known. Succeeded Henry Sanders (145).

151.   John Bray   1633–1643

Admitted 7 May 1633 and granted leave of absence for two months. Patent is dated 3 October 1633. He was one of the signatories of the petition of 21 March 1638 (see Hull 125). Died 15 March 1643 and buried 17 March at St George's Chapel. Succeeded Morgan Coleman (144).

152.   Richard Ousley   1634–after 1643

The date of his admission is not known but his Patent is dated 19 February 1634. His name is not among the signatories of the petition of 21 March 1638 but is appended to that of c. 1643 (see Hull 125). The date of his death is not known. Succeeded William Russell (126).

153.   Captain Jonas Bodenam   1634–1637

The date of his admission is not known but his Patent is dated 19 February 1634. He was a Lieutenant in HMS Revenge, Captained by Sir Francis Drake, during the battle of the Armada in 1588. Described as Sir Francis Drake's right hand man he was present at Drake's death, 28 January 1596, and was made an executor of his Will. Died 29 March 1637 and was buried the next day in St George's Chapel. He succeeded William Russell (126).

154.   Abel Barnard   1637–after 1643

Admitted 14 January 1637. Patent dated 10 January 1637. His name appears among the signatories to the petitions of 1638 and c. 1643 (se Hull 125). The date of his death is not known.

155.   William King   1637–after 1643

Admitted 4 march 1637. Patent dated 24 January 1637. Succeeded Richard Morris (141). His name appears among the signatories to the petitions of 1638 and c. 1643 (see Hull 125). The date of his death is not known

156.   William Meysey   1637–after1643

Admitted 7 May 1637. Succeeded John Salisbury (112). His name appears among the signatories to the petitions of 1638 and c. 1643 (see Hull 125). His name also appears, together with those of two others who did not become Poor Knights, in Ashmole MSS, 1115, fo.81, with statements as to their 'Services and testimonies as suitors for the place of a Poor Knight. Meysey could claim long service by land and sea. The date of his death is not known.

157.   Lieutenant Sebastian Westcote   1637–after 1643

The date of his admission is not known but his Patent is dated 21 May 1637. Succeeded Henry Gratwick. His name is among the signatories to the Petition of c. 1643 (see Hull 125). He was possibly the grandson of Sebastian Westcote, Organist of St Paul's Cathedral, 1551-82. The date of his death is not known.

158.   Captain Hugh Done   1639–after1643

The date of his admission is not known but it must have been after his predecessor, Sir Francis Tanfield, died in January 1639. His name is among the signatories to the petition of c. 1643 (see Hull 125). The date of his death is not known.

159.   Thomas Browne   c. 1642–?

The date of his admission is not known but it must have been before the petition c. 1643 was presented because his name is among the signatories (see Hull 125). He succeeded Thomas Gibbs (128). His Patent is dated 18 April 1642. The date of his death is not known.

160.   Thomas Carr   pre 1658–1660

Attended Cromwell's funeral in 1658. He is not listed in the Diary of Thomas Burton Esq volume 2 as being among the Poor Knights in the funeral procession. Died 4 November 1660 and buried the next day in St George's Chapel. Succeeded by John Gill (193)

161.   Richard Pratt   pre 1658–1660

Attended Cromwell's funeral in 1658. He was dispossessed 14 July 1660 with a note added that he was at that date 'in being and put thereunto by Oliver Cromwell and his adherents'. Succeeded by Robert Cave (185)

162.   Captain Fanshaw   pre 1658–?

Attended Cromwell's funeral in 1558

163.   Captain Beale   pre 1658–?

Commanded a company of eighty men in Bristol to which twenty were added and brought onto the Army establishment in 1649. Attended Cromwell's funeral in 1658.

164.   Lieutenant Christopher Parker   pre 1658–1660

Attended Cromwell's funeral in 1658. Succeeded by Samuel Trumball (191).

165.   Cornet Stephens   pre 1658–1660

Attended Cromwell's funeral in 1658. Died before 5 July 1660. Succeeded by Thomas Norwood (184)

166.   Cornet Olner   pre 1658–?

His name is spelt Olmer in British History On Line. Attended Cromwell's funeral in 1658

167.   Lieutenant Mayes   pre 1658–?

Attended Cromwell's funeral in 1658. Succeeded by William Tyrwhitt (186)

168.   Major James Wallinger   pre 1658–?

Attended Cromwell's funeral in 1658. In July 1660 he appealed to the King 'for confirmation of his place which he has enjoyed for some years or he must perish when others are made happy by the blessed Restoration.

169.   Lieutenant Ralph Bankes   pre 1658–died 1660

Attended Cromwell's funeral in 1658. He died in 1660. Succeeded by Samuel Nest (182)

170.   John Grosvenor   pre 1658–1660

Attended Cromwell's funeral in 1658

One of five appointed by Cromwell to Crane's new Foundation. He was dispossessed in 1660 when the Monarchy was restored

171.   Captain Roe   pre 1658–?

Commanding the ship 'Requitall ' of Plymouth he captured the ships 'Mary of St Giles' and 'The Nicholas' that had been trading with ports in France and carrying 'Cloathes provided for His Majesty's Army'. He would seem to have been a 'Privateer' (pirate) holding a Commission from the Earl of Warwick while he was Lord High Admiral. *From the House of Lords Journal volume 7. 26 August 1645.* Attended Cromwell's funeral in 1658

172.   Colonel Herbert   pre 1658–1661

Attended Cromwell's funeral in 1658. Dispossessed in 1661 and succeeded by Captain Thomas Freebody (181)

173.   John Day   pre 1658–25 October 1660

Governor of the Poor Knights–after 1643–1660

It is obvious that Fellows is wrong in asserting that this John Day is different to John Daye (140). Fellows has them both attending Oliver Cromwell's funeral whereas both the British Museum list and British History On line list only show one John Day. Fellows also has them both buried in St George's Chapel on the same day, 30 October 1660 when there was only one funeral. They must therefore be one and the same. He succeeded Henry Brown as Governor of the Poor Knights. He attended Cromwell's funeral in 1658 as Governor. He died 25 October 1660 and was buried in St George's Chapel on 30 October. On 29 October 1660 the Dean and Canons voted £10 for his widow

174.   Captain Cooper   pre 1658–?

Attended Cromwell's funeral in 1658

175.   Major Leventhorp   pre 1658–?

Attended Cromwell's funeral in 1658. He is perhaps identified with Edward Leventhorp who served in the Parliamentary Army

176.   Sir David Hatfield   pre 1658–?

Attended Cromwell's funeral in 1658. There is no record of his name in Shaw's 'Knights of England', but he is styled Sir David in the list of those who attended Cromwell's funeral

177.   Captain Benjamin Burgess   pre 1658–after 1661

Appointed by Oliver Cromwell as one of five on Crane's Foundation. attended Cromwell's funeral in 1658. He was dispossessed by Charles II but recovered his place as a Poor Knight in March 1661 after a tedious Chancery law-suit. Succeeded by Benjamin Lambe (183).

178. Ensign William Carey   pre 1658–after 1660

Appointed by Oliver Cromwell as one of five on Crane's Foundation. He had served in Captain West's company in Colonel Lenthall's Regiment. He was dispossessed on 16 July 1660 by Charles II. He petitioned to have his place continued 8 August 1660 and was readmitted. Succeeded in the first instance by Captain Richard White (196) and ultimately by Captain William Rowlandson (189).

179. John Mountford   pre 1660–?

Appointed by Oliver Cromwell as one of five on Crane's Foundation

180. Ralph Mabb   pre 1660–?

Appointed by Oliver Cromwell as one of five on Crane's Foundation. He took a leading part in various law-suits to establish the claims of the Poor Knights under Crane's new Foundation. He died before 1660

181. Captain Thomas Freebody   1660–1691

Patent dated 26 March 1661, but seems to have been appointed on the Lower Foundation earlier than this, as shown by the bill for his costs in the Crane suit. A Warrant for a vacancy was dated 6 March 1660. It was stated that he had given good demonstration of his loyalty, and by reason of his sufferings was reduced to a necessitous condition. He had been 'seven times imprisoned, four times banished and three times forced to give £1000 security for good behaviour under the late usurpation'. He was to succeeded Herbert(172), 'who was put in by the tyrant Oliver'. He asked in March 1661 for 'conformation of his place, another having been chosen in his place'. This petition was granted. This must refer to second or re-appointment.Buried at St George's Chapel 30 April 1691. Succeeded Colonel Herbert(172) and was succeeded by Gilbert Wye(239).

182. Captain Samuel Nest   1660–1678

Governor of the Poor Knights 1 November 1660–1678

He was admitted as Governor in succession to John Day(173) being 'one of the said Knights (poor) and next in seniority'. He had previously been admitted a Poor Knight 21 June 1660 in succession to Ralph Bankes(169) dec. He was described as 'an ancient soldier, aged and unmarried'. He was engaged in a law-suit with Captain Rowlandson(189) 27 January 1672. His name appears at the head of a list of thirteen Poor Knights who signed a petition dated 27 November 1667 which was presented to the House of Commons concerning arrears of payment due from a Mr Ford MP who was then in possession of the Manor of Carbrooke. Buried at St George's Chapel 24 December 1678

183. Captain Benjamin Lambe   1660–1694

He had served King Charles I faithfully until the end of the war. He was appointed in the place of Benjamin Burgess(177), 'who hath no right to the same'. He signed the petition in 1667 [see under Samuel Nest(182)]. His son was appointed a chorister 24 December 1674. Buried at St George's Chapel 30 September 1694. Succeeded by John Baynes(244).

184. Major Thomas Norwood   1660–1675

Patent dated 5 July 1660. He signed the petition in 1667 (see Samuel Nest). Died 6 August 1675 and buried the next day at St George's Chapel. Succeeded Cornet Stephens(165)

185. Captain Robert Cave   1660–1662

Patent dated 14 July 1660 He was recommended as having lost an arm, being old, and often wounded and imprisoned for his loyalty. He was admonished by the Dean and Chapter on the 15th April 1662 for 'many misdemeanours, as absenting himself above thirty days with out leave, for gameinge, quarrelling and for entertaining Inmates in his lodgings'. He was commanded to dismiss his Inmates and pull down 'the rayles which he hath set up before his house or else be deprived of all emoluments of his place payable by the Chapter until he shall obey these commands'. He was expelled 15 October for his misdemeanours and for refusing to submit himself to the Dean and Chapter. He was succeeded by Captain Edward Palmer(202).

Two Poor Knights of Windsor
The Garter Procession 1663
By Sir Peter Lely

Two Poor Knights of Windsor © Trustees, British Museum
The Garter Procession 1663
By Sir Peter Lely

186.   Capt. William Tyrwhitt   1660–1661

Succeeded Lieutenant Mayes (167). Patent dated 16 July 1660. Admitted 10 November 1660. Died 16 March 1661 and buried in St George's Chapel 20th March.

187.   Thomas Peters   1660–1664

Patent dated 28 July 1660. It was granted in consideration of his having suffered much in the Irish Rebellion. Died 26 November 1664 and buried in St George's Chapel on 2nd December. Succeeded by Francis Harris (204).

188.   Colonel Walter Hastings   1660–1671

Patent dated 1 September 1660. He was notified by the Dean and Canons on 2 October 1665 that his dogs were a nuisance. He signed the petition of 1667 (see 182).

Information was given by two Messengers that were sent to apprehend Mr. Hen. Hastings, that Walter Hastings gave Fire to his Pistol against Mr. Chambers, One of the Messengers employed by both Houses, when he was executing the Warrants of both Houses.

Resolved, That Mr. Walter Hastings shall be forthwith sent for as a Delinquent, by the Serjeant at Arms attending on this House.

From: 'House of Commons Journal Volume 2: 13 July 1642', Journal of the House of Commons: volume 2: 1640-1643 (1802), pp. 669-71.

He was granted leave of absence for a year 17 January 1670, in consideration of his loyalty and many good services. Buried in St George's Chapel 20 October 1671. Succeeded by Thomas Beck (210).

189.   Captain William Rowlandson   after 1660–1677

Succeeded William Carey (178). Patent dated 24 September 1660. It was granted in consideration that he had suffered wounds and imprisonment during seventeen or eighteen years of loyal service. With Pochin (194) and Freebody (181) he signed a demand, addressed to William Crane, but undated, for payment of arrears due to the Poor Knights on Crane's Foundation. He was appointed 'a Commissioner for His Majesty in affairs of weighty concern ' on 25 April 1662 and was granted leave of absence for six weeks. On 13th October 1669 he was granted leave of absence for a year. He was buried in St George's Chapel on 18th May 1677. Succeeded by James Mauleverer (221).

190.   George Barber   1660–1661

Patent dated 11 October 1660. It was granted in consideration of good and faithful service. With Thomas Freebody (181) and William Croome (201) he presented a petition in March 1661 to be allowed to keep his place as a Poor Knight when threatened with dismissal by the Dean on the grounds that he was married. His dismissal was upheld.

191.   Samuel Trumball   1660–1661

Patent dated 5 November 1660. He succeeded Christopher Parker (164). Special permission was granted to allow 'his wife Elizabeth to live in his house being both ancient persons'. He was later dismissed because he was married and £3 was voted to by the Chapter in compensation.

192.   Captain Walter Price   1661–1670

Patent Dated 20 January 1661. He was 'an ancient soldier who had served long in the wars', and was aged and unmarried. He was to come into his place as a Poor Knight on Midsummer Day. He signed the petition in 1667. Buried in St George's Chapel 23 August 1670.

193.   Captain John Gill   1661–1663

Patent dated 20 January 1661. Succeeded Thomas Carr (160). Buried in St George's Chapel 5 July 1663. Succeeded by Richard Vaughan (203).

194.   Captain Robert Pochin   **1661–1668**

Patent dated 20 January 1661. He was stated to be 'aged and unmarried and not so provided with sufficient means of sustentation'. His name also appears in the MSS. as Punchion and Poachin, but it is given correctly in the letter which he signed with Rowlandson (189) and Freebody (181), demanding arrears of pay from William Crane. He was a member of Leicestershire family of Pochin of Barkby. Buried in St George's Chapel 5 August 1668. Succeeded by Edmund Barber (206)

195.   Captain John Beedon   **1661–1673**

Patent dated 20 January 1661. He signed the petition of 1667. Died 25 November 1673 and was buried in St George's Chapel on 27th November.

196.   Captain Richard White   **1661–1672**

Patent dated 20 January 1661. He signed the petition of 1667. He succeeded William Carey (178) when he was dispossessed as having been appointed by Cromwell and his adherents. *Chapter Acts 19 July 1671* ' Captaine White was admonished for his frequent absence from prayers without leave as also for goeing severall tymes out of Towne without leave as also for his inditect dealing with the Governor in receiving summs of money without leave which belong to the Governor to receive and disposing the said summs as he thought good, as also for his contumacious carriag in the Chapter And he was ordered to bring in the £6-13-08 he received of the Green Cloth into the Chapter house and to receive none of his pay 'untill he bring in the said summe'. He was finally deprived of his place as a Poor Knight 24 October 1672. Succeeded by George Huthwaite (211)

197.   Lieutenant–Colonel Anthony Willoughby (Willoby)   **1661–1684**

Patent dated 20 January 1661. He signed the petition of 1667. In 1642 as a Captain he was Governor of the Fort of Galway. Buried in St George's Chapel 14 March 1684.

198.   Captain Nicholas Burgh   **1661–1670**

Patent dated 19 February 1661 in which he is wrongly called Birch. He was a man of exceptional culture and a notable personality. He was an intimate friend of Alias Ashmole, author of *The Order of the Garter*. There are many references to him among the Ashmole MSS. On 28 June 1661 he wrote to Ashmole about the payment of moneys witholden from the Poor Knights; and on 18 December 1661 complaining of his and his 'brother Odensell's (199) ' hard treatment about the suit for Crane's Charity. He was something of a poet and had a fancy to sign his name to his verses in the form of a cypher. He wrote an account of Ludgate Prison, where he was at one time confined, entitled *A Carracter of Ludgate. King Ludd's gate is a place of great receipte.* He excelled as a draftsman; some of his work is now in the Ashmole collection at Oxford. He possibly trained as a goldsmith and was a virtuoso carver. He gave samples cherry stone carvings of St George to the Tradescants for their museum. There is also a draft of St George cut upon a tablet of ivory by him. With a 'Mr Addington ' he measured the West end of St George's Chapel. His portrait in the dress of a Poor Knight is in the Ashmolean Museum though a copy hangs in No 4 Lower Ward. He died 23 June 1670 and was buried the next day in St George's Chapel. He was succeeded by George Bagge (209)

199.   Lieutenant–Colonel Edward Odingsell   **1661–1666**

Patent dated 19 February 1661. Called also Odensells and Odingsells. He was aged and unmarried. Served in Sir William Fairfax's Regiment in Parliamentary Army (*Army List of Roundheads and Cavaliers, by Edward Peacock*). He died late in 1666. he was succeeded by Francis Ranger (205).

200.   Captain Samuel Hull   **1661–1685**

Governor of the Poor Knights 4 January 1679–1685

Patent dated 19 February 1661. He signed the petition of 1667. He was chosen on 19 July 1671 to be co-adjutor (possibly Adjutant/Staff Officer?) to Samuel Nest (182) as Governor of the Poor Knights, pending further arrangements the nature of which is not stated in the Chapter Acts Book. He was appointed Governor of the Poor Knights 4 January 1679 on the death of NeSt Buried in St George's Chapel 7 October 1685. succeeded by Robert Levingston (231) and by James Mauleverer (221) as Governor.

201.   Captain William Croome   1661–1683

Patent dated 1 April 1661. In march 1661 he expressed his thanks for having been granted a place on Crane's Foundation. He was admitted not with standing his being a married man. Elizabeth Croome, his wife, died 4 September 1673 and was buried in St George's Chapel. He signed the petition of 1667. Buried in St George's Chapel 12 May 1683. Succeeded by Nathaniel Rashleigh (229).

202.   Captain Edward Palmer   1662–1676

Admitted 15 October 1662. He succeeded Robert Cave (185). He was brother of the Attorney General and was recommended for faithful service in the wars. He signed the petition of 1667. Died 10 January 1676 and was buried in St George's Chapel on the 13 January. Succeeded by Thomas Trappes (219).

203.   Captain Richard Vaughan   1663–1700

Patent dated 15 July 1663 and admitted on the 28. His admission was granted in consideration of 'great sufferings in his means and hurts in his body'. He behaved himself with great courage in the service of King Charles 1 and lost his sight. He signed the petition of 1667. He was given leave of absence for a year 5 September 1667. He was of the family of Vaughan of Pantglas, Caernavon. He had built and endowed an almshouse for six poor persons in 1700 with the proceeds of £200. He died 5 June 1700 and was buried on 8 June in St George's Chapel. There is an inscribed tablet on the south side wall at the west entrance to the north quire aisle

204.   Francis Harris   1664–1673

Patent Dated 29 November 1664 and admitted the same day. Succeeded Thomas Peters (187). Recommended by the King for the next vacancy in a letter dated 28 September 1663, signed by Sir Henry de Vic (Chancellor of the Order), in consideration of 'his sufferings and losses upon our account during the late troubles in this Kingdom'. He was born in Oxford where his father was a Bailiff on the City Council and held the licence for the Swindlestock Tavern at Carfax. When he died Francis took over the Tavern. He was granted a Bailiff's place on the council and in 1628 was appointed Money Master. In 1633 he was precipitated into the position of Mayor until 1634. Harris was chosen as one of six citizens to attend the Mayor at the Coronation of King Charles II in London on 23 April 1661. On 7 October 1664 he took the oath of obedience and supremacy. On 2 January 1665 the Mayor brought to the council meeting the resignation of Alderman Francis Harris as alderman and coroner. As a token of their love for him the Council gave him £15 out of the city treasure. During his life he fathered at least 15 children all of whom were baptised in St Martin's Church at Carfax. He died 2 July 1673 and was buried in the 5th at St George's chapel. Succeeded by Robert Draper (214).

205.   Major Francis Ranger   1667–1681

Patent dated 31 December 1666. Succeeded Edward Odingsell (199). The date of his admission is not recorded in the Chapter Acts. He had performed sundry useful and faithful service in the late wars to Charles I and Charles II. He was recommended by the King for the next vacancy in letters 14 December 1664 and 22 May 1665. He was buried in St George's Chapel 8 December 1681. Succeeded by David Ogilvy (227).

206.   Captain Edmund Barber   1668–1679

Patent dated 22 May 1665. Admitted 17 October 1668. Succeeded Robert Pochin (194). Recommended by Sir Henry de Vic, Chancellor of the Order of the Garter. Buried at St George's Chapel 6 July 1679. Succeeded by Robert Mainwaring (224).

207.   Thomas Newans   1668

A warrant was issued 19 June 1668 for his admission to the next vacancy as a Poor Knight, with recommendation for faithful services performed to Charles I. It seems that he was actually admitted a Poor Knight, but disqualified soon after admission because he was married

208. Captain William Gardiner (Gardner)   1668–1673

A warrant was issued 19 June 1668 for his admission to the fourth vacancy as a Poor Knight. The actual date of his admission is not recorded. Captains Hull and Barber were requested by the Chapter to enquire into the grounds of Captain Gardiners going out of Town without leave for more than a fortnight. They were unsatisfied with the grounds for his absence. Mr Palmer (202) complained that Gardiner had called him Sirrah (*replaces Sir in imperious or contemptuous use*) and threatened to run him through with his Rapier. Several of the Poor Knights complained of him as being a scandal to the church for his frequent drunkenness. He affronted the ladies 'of honour ' (?) that lodged at his house which came to the knowledge of the King and Queen to their high displeasure. It was decreed to admonish him, register it and to give away 20s of his next months pay to the Quire. Captain Gardiner interrupted the Canon several times and abused Mr Palmer before all the company saying he was fit to go and keep sheep as he formerly did. He was buried at St George's Chapel 16 February 1673.

209. Captain George Bagge   1670–1672

Patent dated 27 June 1670. The date of his admission is not recorded. He succeeded Nicholas Burgh (198). He had served Charles I and Charles II in the late wars. He had 'sustained for his loyalty, great losses and damages which hath reduced him to such exigencies ' that he had no means of livelihood. On 16 November 1652 he was declared in a bill of the House of Commons 'to be a delinquent'. He was appointed to Crane's Foundation. Served both King Charles I and Charles II

210. Captain Thomas Beck   1671–1675

A warrant dated 24 October 1671 nominated him for the vacancy caused by the death of Colonel Hastings (188) who he succeeded. It stated that he had served Charles I faithfully and ' suffered much thereby in his limbs and fortune'. The date of his admission id not recorded. Died 12 January 1675 and buried 14 January. Succeeded by Ferdinando Ivy (220).

211. George Huthwaite   1672–1691

The date of his admission is not recorded, but it was in succession to Richard White (196) who was deprived of his place in October 1672. Buried at St George's Chapel 8 May 1691. He was succeeded by William Rayer (240)

212. Benjamin Poole   1672–1686

The date of his admission is not recorded, but it was in succession the George Bagge (209) who died in January 1672. He was buried at St George's Chapel 2 December 1686.

213. Major Nathaniel Hill   1673

Admitted 19 February 1673. Succeeded William Gardiner (208). Disqualified after his admission because he was married. Succeeded by Thomas Gawdy (215)

214. Captain Robert Draper   1673–1681

The date of his admission is not recorded, but it was almost certainly in 1673 on the death of Francis Harris (204) who he succeeded. In a warrant dated 22 April 1671 he was nominated for the next vacancy, having faithfully served Charles I in all wars since the expedition to the Isle of Rea, 'and now a soldier in our Horse Guards'. Dispossessed 17 November 1675 for misconduct. Re-admitted 18 July 1676. Buried at St George's Chapel 28 April 1681. He was succeeded firstly by Thomas Wright (218) on his dismissal. He succeeded Ferdinando Ivy (220) on his reinstatement. He was succeeded secondly by Edward Montgomery (226).

215. Captain Thomas Gawdy   1673–1680

Admitted 15 November 1673 in succession to Nathaniel Hill (213) on his disqualification. Letters of administration granted by John Durell (Dean) 13 November 1680. Succeeded by Charles Glapthorne (225)

216. Captain Thomas Draper   **1673–1686**

Admitted 22 December 1673. Succeeded John Beedon (195) Buried at St George's Chapel 9 January 1686. Succeeded by Tobias Ewbank (232)

217. Christophilus Wood   **c.1674–1677**

Date of admission unknown. but that he was admitted is shown in the Burial Register of the Chapel, where he is described as one of the Poor Knights. He is also named as the predecessor of Ferdinando Ivy (220) on the latter's readmission in 1677.   Some re-adjustments of his pay was ordered to be made in 1676. Buried at St George's Chapel 7 April 1677.

218. Captain Thomas Wright   **1675–1698**

Admitted 2 December 1675 in the place of Captain Robert Draper (214) who had been dismissed for misconduct in 1675. When Draper was restored to his place 18 July 1676, Wright claimed that he should not be dispossessed, but that Ferdinando Ivy (220), the most recently appointed Poor Knight, should be displaced to make room for Draper. His claim was supported and a fresh patent, dated 5 September 1676, was issued confirming Wright in his place. Died 9 May 1698, aged 84. Buried at St George's Chapel 13 May. Mon. Insc.[Pote, p. 400] Succeeded by Philip Jones (231).

219. Thomas Trappes   **1676–1679**

Admitted 29 January 1676. He succeeded Edward Palmer (202). On Draper's return Trappes, like Wright, claimed that Ivy should be displaced rather than himself. His claim was upheld and a fresh patent issued confirming his place dated 5 September 1676. Buried at St George's Chapel 7 March 1679. Succeeded by George Sayer (223).

220. Ferdinando Ivy   **1676–1695**

Admitted 1 February 1676 in succession to Thomas Beck (210). Patent dated 20 January 1676. On 18 July 1676 Robert Draper (214) having established his claim to recover the place from which he had been dismissed, necessitated the temporary dismissal of one of the three Poor Knights appointed since 17 November 1675. Wright (218) and Trappes (219) successfully established their claims to be retained. Ivy was accordingly dispossessed on 1 December 1676 and promised the next vacancy. This, fortunately for him, occurred very soon through the death of Christophilus Wood (217), and Ivy was re-admitted 11 April 1677. Died 26 November 1695 aged 75 and was buried 28 November in St George's Chapel in the south Choir Aisle, Mon. Insc. [Pote P 377]. Succeeded by John Ormsby (248).

221. James Mauleverer   **1677–1703**

Governor of the Poor Knights 16 November 1685–1703

Admitted 26 May 1677. Succeeded William Rowlandson (189). He was of the family of Mauleverer of Arncliffe, co. York. His family had fought on both sides of the Civil War with Sir Thomas raising a regiment of foot and horse for Parliament and being one of the signatories on King Charles's death warrant and whose son, Sir Richard, fought for the King. He was appointed Governor of the Poor Knights in succession to Samuel Hull (125) 16 November 1685. His Patent is dated 16 November 1685. He died 17 April 1703, aged 75. Buried 20 April at St George's Chapel, Mon. Insc. [Pote, p. 399], in the Dean's Cloister North side wall. Succeeded, when promoted Governor, by Robert Levingstone (231). Succeeded by Thomas Baskerville (257), and by Edmund Hook (250) as Governor.

222. Captain Edward Bromfield   **1678–1682**

Admitted 3 December 1678 in succession to 'Captain Christopher Carey, Deceased'. The name of Christopher Carey is not found in any of the records of the College, either as a Poor Knight or otherwise. Buried at St George's Chapel 3 August 1682. Succeeded by Valentine Crane (228).

223.   Captain George Sayer   1679–1686

His admission is not recorded in the Chapter Acts Book. He succeeded Thomas Trappes (219). Buried at St George's Chapel 5 October 1686 and was succeeded by Daniel Donne (235).

224.   Major Robert Mainwaring   1679–1698

Admitted 28 July 1679. He succeeded Edmund Barber (206). He was one of five Poor Knights on Crane's Foundation who petitioned Parliament 31 December 1692 for arrears of payment on the Carbrook Estate, withheld from them by Sir Robert Clayton, then in possession of that estate. Buried at St George's Chapel 13 November 1698. Succeeded by Alexander Storey (252).

225.   Charles Glapthorne   1680–1693

Admitted 30 October 1680 in succession to Thomas Gawdy (215). Buried at St George's Chapel 1 November 1693. Succeeded by Richard Dobbins (243).

226.   Edward Montgomery   1681–1687

Admitted 27 April 1681 in succession to Robert Draper (214). Died 1687. Succeeded by Alexander James (236).

227.   Captain David Ogilvy   1682–1687

Admitted 30 March 1682 in succession to Francis Ranger (205). He was the second son of Sir David Ogilvy of Innercarity, 2nd Bart. Died 1687 aged 63. Buried at St George's Chapel but the burial is not recorded in the Register. Succeeded by Edward Errington (237).

228.   Valentine Crane   1682–1695

Admitted 28 August 1682 in succession to Edward Bromfield (222). Related to Sir Francis Crane who founded the Lower Foundation. Buried at St George's Chapel 21 April 1695. Succeeded by John Mackenzie (245).

229.   Nathaniel Rashleigh   1683–1686

Admitted 23 May 1683 in succession to William Croome (201). Buried at St George's Chapel 29 January 1686. Succeeded by Sir James Harman (233).

230.   Cornet Edward Barrett   1684–1695

Admitted 31 March 1684 in succession to Anthony Willoughby (197). The House of Commons papers for 2 November 1652 show one Edward Barrett , junior, and a Sir Edward Barrett of Droitwich having their land and estates forfeited for treason. Buried St George's Chapel 25 November 1695. Succeeded by Richard Leader (246).

231.   Captain Robert Levingston   1685–1695

Admitted 17 December 1685 in succession to James Mauleverer (221) when the latter became Governor of the Poor Knights. He served Charles I and Charles II in several expeditions. He was one of the five petitioners on Crane's Foundation in 1692. Buried at St George's Chapel 9 December 1695 (his name is spelt Levelstone in the Burial Register). Succeeded by Thomas Barry (247)

232.   Captain Tobias Ewbank   1686–1689

Admitted 25 January 1686 in succession to Thomas Draper (216). He had served during the wars 'as Captain of Foot and Cornet of Horse under the Duke of Newcastle, and under command of Major Lyttelton in the late rebellion in the West'. Buried at St George's Chapel 22 April 1689. Succeeded by Dodmen Pope (238).

233.   Sir James Harman, Bart.,   1686–1693

The date of his admission is not recorded in the Chapter Act Book but his Patent is dated 5 February 1686. He had faithfully served Charles I in several capacities in the late wars and had suffered great misery and calamity. Buried at St George's Chapel 15 July 1693. He succeeded Benjamin Poole (212) and was succeeded by Richard Loudon (241).

234.   Captain Henry Hastings   1686–1691

Admitted 5 October 1686 in succession to Benjamin Poole (212). Patent dated 18 September 1686. He had 'faithfully served through the whole course of the Great Rebellion, having his share of miseries, and wasted his small fortune'. He was described as 'the great-grandson of George, late Earl of Huntingdon'. Buried   St George's Chapel 16 May 1691. Succeeded by Richard Loudon (241)

235.   Captain Daniel Donne   1686–1697

Admitted 10 November 1686 in succession to George Sayer (223). Patent dated 3 November 1686. He served Charles I during the Rebellion in England and Wales. He was 'most barbarously used after the fight at Worcester.....to the utter ruin of himself and family'. He was one of the five Poor Knights on Crane's Foundation who signed the petition of 1692. Died 8 April 1697, aged 75. Buried 11 April at St George's Chapel [Mon. Insc. Pote, p.401]. Succeeded by Edmund Hooke (250).

236.   Lieutenant Alexander James   1687–1706

Admitted 21 May 1687 in succession to Edward Montgomery (226). Patent dated 20 May 1687; it was granted in consideration of his faithful service and sufferings. He was of the family of James of Grade, near Helstone, Cornwall. He had served Charles II and his royal father 'both in his royall troop of guards in the Earl of Oxford's regiment, and in the islands of Gersey under Sir Thomas Morgan'. Died 29 March 1706 and was buried at St George's Chapel on 4 April. [Mon. Insc. Pote p. 400 Dean' Cloister s North side wall]. Succeeded by Henry Phillips (259).

237.   Edward Errington   1687–1728

Admitted 21 May 1687 in succession to David Ogilvy (227). Patent dated 12 March 1687. He served Charles II faithfully 'in his Royal Troop of Guards under the command of Lord Churchill until disabled by the loss of one of his eyes and almost the sight of the other'. He was one of the five Poor Knights on Crane's Foundation who signed the petition of 1692. Buried at St George's Chapel 23 February 1728. succeeded by Gabriel Mozen (285).

238.   Dodmen Pope   1689–1699

Admitted 13 May 1689 in succession to Tobias Ewbank (232). He had served 'as a soldier under the command of Sir Francis Compton, and in the Royall Regiment of Horse commanded by the Rt. Hon. Aubrey, Earl of Oxford, twenty years last past'. Buried at St George's Chapel 27 March 1699. Succeeded by Robert Thompson (253).

239.   Gilbert Wye   1691–1716

Admitted 5 June 1591 in succession to Thomas Freebody (181). Patent dated 28 May 1691. He had become a great sufferer by losses, wounds and imprisonments for his loyalty and had become aged and infirm. He was one of the Poor Knights of Crane's Foundation to sign the petition of 1692. He died in 1716. Succeeded by Thomas Hawker (271)

240.   Captain William Rayer   1691–1709

Admitted 16 June 1691 in succession to George Huthwaite (211). Recommended for his fidelity and loyalty to Charles I in the wars. He had served Charles II as a lieutenant at sea and in other capacities, and was now aged and infirm. Buried at St George's Chapel 30 August 1709. Succeeded by Thomas Timpson (262)

241.   Captain Richard Loudon, R.N.   1691–1696

The date of his admission is not recorded in the Chapter Acts Book but his Patent is dated 13 November 1691. He succeeded Captain Henry Hastings (234). He had 'served above forty years in the Royal Fleet and above twenty years a Captain in ships of warr'. He had given signal instances of loyalty, courage and zeal in our Service and is now aged and infirm'. He died in 1696 and was succeeded by John Conway (249).

242. Major Roger Thornton 1693–1700
Admitted 12 August 1693 in succession to Sir James Harman, Bart. (233). Patent dated 10 August 1693. He had 'served in the wars all the time of the unhappy Rebellion to the ruin of a very considerable fortune to which he was born, and is now aged and infirm'. Buried at St George's Chapel 28 March 1700. Succeeded by Walter Williams (255).

243. Richard Dobbins (Dobyns) 1694–1699
Admitted 3 April 1694 in succession to Charles Glapthorne (225). Patent dated 30 March 1694. He was 'nobly descended of an ancient family in Worcestershire that was in a flourishing condition before the war. He did in person serve Charles II at Worcester fight, and was forced to go after him beyond sea to the utter ruin of his family'. Died 1699. Succeeded by Hugh Travanion (254).

244. Captain John Baynes 1695–1711
Admitted 13 February 1695 in succession to Benjamin Lambe (183). He had been 'a great sufferer both by losses and imprisonments during the late wars during the unhappy rebellion', and was now aged and infirm. On his tombstone [Pote, p. 401] it is recorded that he was aged 112 at his death. There seems to have been some error as it is extremely unlikely that he was appointed a Poor Knight at the age of 96. His age is not recorded in the Burial Register. Died 3 September 1711 and was buried the next day at St George's Chapel. Succeeded by Benjamin Tattersall (266).

245. Lieutenant John Mackenzie 1695–1720
Admitted 20 June 1695 in succession to Valentine Crane (228). Patent dated 13 May 1695. He had 'for many years served in our Armies and hath signalized himself very eminently and in our sight. He hath received many wounds by one of which he lost an arm….. Though he is younger than the ordinary age of Poor Knights and is a married man, yet we do dispense with the rules'. Buried St George's Chapel 20 May 1720. Succeeded by Richard Williams (275).

246. Lieutenant Richard Leader 1695–1706
Admitted 17 December 1695 in succession to Edward Barrett (230). Patent dated 13 December 1695. he had 'served thirty years in our Guards and is now a lieutenant but disabled from serving us any longer…… We dispense with the Statute' as to his being a married man. Died 17 April 1706 aged 61 and was buried in St George's Chapel 21 April [Mon. Incs. Pote, p. 399]. Succeeded by Anthony Wharton (260).

247. Lieutenant Thomas Barry 1696–1723
Admitted 30 March 1696. Patent dated 23 March 1696 in succession to Robert Levingstone (231). He had 'served in our Army fifteen years and was disabled in our service. Though he is younger than the ordinary age of Poor Knights and is a Married man, yet we dispense with the Statute……' Succeeded by John Folliott (280)..

248. Ensign John Ormsby 1696–1732
Admitted 21 May 1696 in succession to Ferdinando Ivy (220). Patent dated 2 April 1696. Described as 'a gentleman and well descended who hath several years served in our Armies and in the late siege of Namur lost his leg. Though he is younger than the ordinary age of a Poor Knight…. ' His admission was by proxy, a deed for which was executed 16 May 1696 appointing Richard Leader (246) to represent him at the ceremony. This was necessitated by an accident. Owing to his lameness he had to be 'slung out of the vessel' which brought him on his way to Windsor from Holland, by means of a crane. The pulleys either broke or slipped, and his consequent fall disabled him from travelling to take possession of his place as a Poor Knight. Buried at St George's Chapel 2 February 1732. Succeeded by Sir James Holburne (294).

249. Ensign John Conway 1697–1705
Admitted 1 March 1697 in succession to Richard Loudon (241). Patent dated 23 February 1697. He had 'served as an Ensign in our army some years, and by reason of his service had lost his eyes'. Though married, the Statutes were waived. Buried at St George's Chapel 20 November 1705. Succeeded by John Whalley (258)

250. Captain Edmund Hooke   1698–1707

Governor of the Poor Knights 29 May 1703–1707

Admitted 21 January 1698 in succession to Daniel Donne (235). Patent dated 14 January 1698. 'He hath served for several years in our Army with good approbation and is now very old and incapable of further service'. He is described as Gent of Bramshott, Hants. Died 11 June 1707, aged 85. Buried 18 June at St George's Chapel [Mon. Insc. Pote, p. 400]. Succeeded by William Williams (261).

251. Philip Jones   1698–1712

Admitted 1 June 1698 in succession to Thomas Wright (218). Patent dated 4 May 1698. 'he hath served in our first troop of Guards above twenty years with courage and fidelity'. Buried at St George's Chapel 25 September 1712. Succeeded by Edward Butler (268).

252. Lieutenant Alexander Storey   1699–1709

Admitted 24 January 1699 in succession to Robert Mainwaring (224). Patent dated 19 January 1699. He had served above fifty years in the Army and 'hath distinguished himself in many battles where he hath been often wounded'. Died 15 February 1709 and was buried at St George's Chapel 19 February [Mon. Insc. Pote, p. 400]. It is stated that he died at the age of 92 which means he had been appointed a Poor Knight at the age of 82. Succeeded by Alexander White (263).

253. Robert Thompson   1699–1719

Admitted 6 April 1699 in succession to Dodmen Pope (238). He 'served many years in our first troop of Guards in which he hath for divers years carried our Royal Standard, and signalized himself in our late wars in which he received many wounds'. Died 29 December 1719, aged 91 and buried 4 January 1720 at St George's Chapel [Mon. Insc. Pote, p. 401]. His name is wrongly given as Edward in the Burial Register. Succeeded by William Courtney (273).

254. Hugh Trevanion, Esquire   1700–1728

Governor of the Poor Knights 12 July 1707–1728

Admitted 17 May 1700 in succession to Richard Dobbins (243). Patent dated 14 May 1700. He appears to have had no military experience and is styled 'Esquire' in the patent and is described as 'a gentleman very nobly descended, but fallen under great decays of fortune and health'. His patent as Governor is dated 26 June 1707. Buried at St George's Chapel 8 June 1728. Succeeded by Daniel Herbst (286).

255. Walter Williams   1700–1720

Admitted 22 May 1700 in succession to Roger Thornton (242). Patent dated 14 may 1700. he had 'served in the wars for about 50 Years in our Guards and elsewhere'. Died 17 March 1720, aged 72. Buried 25 March at St George's Chapel [Mon. Insc. Pote, p. 399]. Succeeded by John Short. (274).

256. Robert Bouchier   1700–1715

Admitted 11 July 1700 in succession to Richard Vaughan (203). Patent dated 14 June 1700. He had 'served in our Guards these many years. Is a gentleman by descent and now aged and unable to serve'. He is described as of Enstone in Oxon. Died 5 July 1715, aged 81. Buried 9 July at St George's Chapel [Mon. Insc. Pote, p. 399]. Succeeded by Martin Llewellyn (296).

257. Captain Thomas Baskerville   1703–1712

Admitted 18 August 1703 in succession to Edmund Hook (250) on his appointment to Governor. Patent dated 19 July 1703. He was 'plundered for his loyalty and is reduced to a low condition by reason of his great age and infirmity'. He must have lived to a great age, because 70 Years had elapsed since 'in support of Charles I he maintained a Troop of Horse at his own charges'. Died 7 March 1712 and buried at St George's Chapel 12 March. He was said to be 106 at his death. This would mean that incredibly he was 97 when appointed a Poor Knight. His age is not recorded in the Burial Register but is shown on his memorial [Pote, p. 400]. Succeeded by Michael Frances (267)

258. Lieutenant John Whalley   1705–1719

Admitted 1 December 1705 in succession to John Conway (249). Patent dated 27 November 1705. He 'served in our Regiment of Foot commanded by the Hon. Colonel William Tatton, and is aged and infirm by reason of wounds received at the battle of Schellenberg'. (Marlborough's crossing of the Danube in 1704). Buried at St George's Chapel 12 September 1719. Succeeded by Edward Benskin (272).

259. Lieutenant Henry Phillips   1706–1715

Admitted 10 June 1706 in succession to Alexander James (236). Patent dated 20 may 1706. He 'served in our Regiment of Foot commanded by Sir Richard Temple. He served near 40 years with fidelity and is now aged and infirm'. Died 1715. Succeeded by Cyrus Rivers (270).

260. Anthony Wharton   1707–1724

Admitted 30 August 1707 in succession to Richard Leader (246). Patent dated 15 August 1707. His father, Sir Anthony and his five brothers served in the armies of Charles I. He and his family were 'reduced to a low condition by reason of services and sufferings'. Died 1724. Succeeded by Thomas Jordan (281)

261. Lieutenant William Williams   1707–1710

Admitted 26 December 1707 in succession to Edmund Hook (250). Patent dated 20 December 1707. 'In our Regiment of Fusiliers he hath served the Crown above 30 years'. Buried at St George's Chapel 4 March 1710. Succeeded by Alexander White (263).

262. Lieutenant Thomas Timson   1719–1726

Admitted 3 March 1710 in succession to William Rayer (240). Patent dated 8 February 1710. He 'served as lieutenant in our Regiment under the command of Major General Meredith above 20 years'. Meredith's Regiment, later became the 37th Regiment of Foot (The Royal Hampshire Regiment). Died 1726. Succeeded by Richard Bull (284)

263. Lieutenant Alexander White   1710–1741

Admitted 21 October 1710 in succession to Alexander Storey (252) on Crane's Foundation; and on the 15 May 1711 he succeeded William Williams (261) on the Royal Foundation. Patent dated 8 February 1710. He 'served as lieutenant in our Royal Regiment of Foot under the command of the Earl of Orkney 18 Years'. He lost a leg at the battle of Schellenberg. Died 1741. He was succeeded by Robert Lightfoot (264) on the Lower Foundation; and at his death by John Newton (306)

264. Robert Lightfoot   1711–1712

Admitted 15 May 1711 in succession to Alexander White (263). Patent dated 19 March 1711. He 'hath served in our Armies above 20 years in which he hath suffered great losses'. Died February 1712. Succeeded by William Nicholson (265).

265. William Nicholson   1712–1720

Admitted 8 March 1712 in succession to Robert Lightfoot (264). Patent dated 3 March 1712. He had lost both his legs 'in the service of our Regiment of Carbineers under the command of Hon. Colonel Wyndham (Colonel Wyndham was Governor of Bridgewater Castle which he held for the King. His wife, Lady Crystabella Wyndham took a shot at Oliver Cromwell from the castle wall, missed by six feet and felled his aide de camp). Died 1720. Succeeded by John Prince (276)

266. Lieutenant Benjamin Tattersall   1712–1722

Admitted 18 March 1712 in succession to John Baynes (244). Patent dated 3 March 1712. He 'served for 36 years in our Armies, having in our service in Spain almost lost the use of his limbs and hearing. He was born at Haverbit, Suffolk. Died 2 December 1722 aged 77. Buried at St George's Chapel 2 December [Mon. Insc. Pote, p. 402]. Succeeded by William Harland (279).

267.   Michael Francis   **1712–1721**

Admitted 19 April 1712 in succession to Thomas Baskerville (257). Patent dated 5 April 1712. Described as the 'eldest gentleman of our first troop of Guards'. He served in the Army nearly twenty-six years, in which time he was present at the battle of the Boyne. He also saw service in Flanders. He was shot through the arm at the battle of Steinkirk; and at the battle of Landen he received many wounds and was take prisoner. Died 1721 and was succeeded by Henry Peart (277).

268.   Edward Butler   **1714–1739**

Admitted 15 November 1714 in succession to Philip Jones (251). Patent dated 10 November 1714. 'He hath served in our Guards 25 Years and hath behaved himself well in the said service'. Died 19 May 1739, aged 80. Buried 20 May at St George's [Mon. Insc. Pote, P. 402]. Succeeded by Paul le Grandmaison (303).

269.   Martin Llewellyn   **1715–1729**

Admitted 25 August 1715 in succession to Robert Bouchier (256). Patent dated 18 August 1715. He served as a Lieutenant in an independent troop commanded by Captain Thomas Fairfax. He subsequently served as Commissary General of Provisions to Queen Anne's Forces in Portugal. Died 1729 and was succeeded by Jasper Oliver (287)

270.   Cyrus Rivers   **1716–1743**

Admitted 7 September 1716 in succession to Henry Phillips (259). patent dated 18 August 1716. He had served the Crown faithfully for 28 years in three campaigns in Ireland in reduction of that kingdom to their Majestys' obedience. Served in five campaigns in Flanders against the French in the 3rd Troop of Horse Guards commanded by Richard, 4th Earl Rivers. Buried St George's Chapel 20 June 1743. Succeeded by John Rush (312).

271.   Thomas Hawker   **1716–1722**

Admitted 28 December 1716 in succession to Gilbert Wye (239). Patent dated 22 December 1716. 'He is a decayed Gentleman and past employment. Brother-in-law to General Earle, and father to Lieutenant Colonel Hawker, and has likewise grandsons in the service'. Buried at St George's Chapel 12 April 1722. Succeeded by William Tuer (278).

272.   Edward Benskin   **1719–1731**

Governor of the Poor Knights 20 July 1728–1731
Admitted 7 October 1719 in succession to John Whalley (258). Patent dated 2 October 1719. He served several years in the 1st Troop of Horse Guards under command of the Duke of Monmouth. His father and uncle were great suffers in the service of Charles I. Succeeded by Jonathan Bower (292), and by Henry Rogers (288) as Governor.

273.   William Courtney   **1720–1725**

Admitted 27 January 1720 in succession to Robert Thompson (253). Patent dated 27 January 1720. He served the Crown in several employments to the satisfaction of his superior officers. 'Is now reduced and superannuated'. Died 1725. succeeded by John Thompson (283).

274.   John Short   **1720–1731**

Admitted 26 April 1720 in succession to Walter Williams (255). Patent dated 11 April 1720. He had 'served the Crown upwards of 40 Years and is now superannuated'. Buried at St George's Chapel 20 July 1731. Succeeded by Richard Webster (291).

275.   Rice Williams   **1720–1741**

Admitted 11 July 1720 in succession to John Mackenzie (245). Patent dated 25 June 1720. He had served William III at the battle of Beachy Head and siege of Cork, where he received so great a wound in his thigh the surgeons were obliged to cut it off near his body to save his life. The wound being yet uncured he has been at continual expense for surgeons….. and is reduced to the last extremity'. Died 1741. Succeeded by Paul le Grand (305).

276. John Prince 1720–1734

Admitted 4 August 1720 in succession to William Nicholson (265). Patent dated 9 July 1720. He was 'sufficiently recommended by several persons of quality as duly qualified for the place'. Died 1734. Succeeded by Lawrence Ainsworth (296).

277. Henry Peart 1722–1742

Admitted 3 February 1722 in succession to Michael Francis (267). Patent dated 4 January 1722. 'After more than 20 years service to the Crown at sea and on land, and after being in several engagements………he entirely lost one eye and had but very little sight left in the other'. Died 1742.. Succeeded by Joseph Walton (309). Served at Sea and on Land

278. William Tuer 1722–1724

Admitted 2 may 1722 in succession to Thomas Hawker (271). Patent dated 18 April 1722. 'He was a servant to the late Queen Mary at the time of her death, and is now by great losses reduced to a very indigent condition'. Buried at St George's Chapel 23 August 1724. Succeeded by Alexander Fraser (282)

279. William Harland 1722–1730

Admitted 12 December 1722 in succession to Benjamine Tattersall (266). Patent dated 8 December 1722. He served King William III. His father was a Cornet of Horse in Prince Rupert's own Regiment, and he had two uncles that were Captains. He is now very aged'. Buried at St George's Chapel 28 July 1730. Succeeded by Matthew Chauvin (289).

280. John Folliott 1723–1734

Admitted 29 June 1723 in succession to Thomas Barry (247). Patent dated 15 June 1723. 'He served diligently as Coast Officer in the Customs, and was by reasons of ill health obliged to quit the service'. Died 1734. Succeeded by Richard Tildesly (295)

281. Thomas Jordan 1724–1731

Admitted 29 February 1724 in succession to Anthony Wharton (260). Patent dated 24 February 1724. He had 'served well for several years in the 2nd Troop of Horse Guards, being broke by age and sickness'. Died 1731. Succeeded by William Pritchard (293).

282. Alexander Fraser 1724–1736

Admitted 19 October 1724 in succession to William Tuer (278). Patent dated 14 October 1724. He 'served for many years in our Land Service being now superannuated'. Died 1736. Succeeded by Alexander Givans (297)

283. John Thompson 1725–1729

Admitted 12 June 1725 in succession to William Courtney (273). Patent dated 31 May 1725. He had 'served several years in a Regiment of Horse some time commanded by Lord Windsor, and is now superannuated'. Buried at St George's Chapel 12 October 1729. Succeeded by Henry Rogers (288).

284. Richard Bull 1726–1739

Admitted 7 april 1726 in succession to Thomas Timson (262). Patent dated 7 April 1726. He served in Philip's Regiment (later the 40th Regiment of Foot) and had sustained great losses. Died 1739. Succeeded by Richard Kemys (301).

285. Gabriel Mozen 1728–1730

Admitted 31 May 1728 in succession to Edward Errington (237). Buried at St George's Chapel 27 October 1730. Succeeded by Isaac Burrows (290).

286. Daniel Herbst   **1728–1739**

Admitted 28 June 1728 in succession to Hugh Trevanion (254). Patent dated 17 June 1728. Died 6 March 1739 aged 76. Buried 11 March at St George's Chapel 11 March, Mon. Insc.[Pote, p. 366] in South Choir Aisle pavement. Succeeded by Vincent Chateauvert (300)

287. Jasper Olivier   **1729–1750**

Governor of the Poor Knights 5 May 1744–1750

Admitted 29 May 1729 in succession to Martin Llewellyn (269). Patent dated 27 May 1729. Appointed Governor of the Poor Knights 5 May 1744 in succession to Henry Rogers (288). Died 15 May 1750. Buried at St George's Chapel 19 May. Mon. Insc. Deanery Cloisters, West side wall. Succeeded by Nicholas Budiani (326) as Poor Knight and Governor

288. Henry Rogers   **1729–1744**

Governor of the Poor Knights 6 September 1731–1744

Admitted 26 October 1729 in succession to John Thompson (283). Patent dated 23 October 1729. Appointed Governor of the Poor Knights 20 September 1731 in succession to Edward Benskin (272). Patent dated 6 September 1731.

289. Matthew Chauvin   **1730–1741**

Admitted 8 August 1730 in succession to William Harland (279). Patent dated 31 July 1730. Buried at St George's Chapel 3 November 1741. Succeeded by William Ainsworth (308)

290. Isaac Burrows1730–1736 Admitted 5 November 1730 in succession to Gabriel Mozen (285). Patent dated 31 October 1730. Buried at St George's Chapel 30 October 1736. Mon., Insc, [Pote p 400]. Succeeded by Francis Forester (298).

291. Richard Webster   **1731–1750**

Admitted 13 August 1731 in succession to John Short (274). Patent dated 6 August 1731. Buried at St George's Chapel 2 May 1750. Succeeded by John Bill (323)

292. Jonathan Bower   **1731–1741**

Admitted 24 September 1731 in succession to Edward Benskin (272). Died 1741. Succeeded by Samuel Chiswell (304).

293. William Pritchard, (Pridger in Burial Register)   **1731–1739**

Admitted 11 November 1731 in succession to Thomas Jordan (281). Patent dated 4 November 1731. Buried at St George's Chapel 20 September 1739. His name is spelt Pridger in the Burial Register. Succeeded by Samuel prince (302).

294. James Holburne   **1733–1737**

Admitted 17 March 1733 in succession to John Ormsby (248). Patent dated 7 February 1733. Born about 1706 he would seem to have been a Grandson of Major General James Holborne of Menstrie, and born in the county of Clackmannan, by his father's first wife Janet, the daughter of John Inglis of Cramond, and was made a Baronet in 1706, on the 21st of June, he succeeded to his fathers title upon his fathers death in 1736/7. Died 1737. Succeeded by Sir Bartholomew Heyman Bart (299).

295. Richard Tildesly   **1734–1741**

Admitted 19 January 1734 in succession to John Folliott (280). Patent dated 16 January 1734. Died 1741. succeeded by Nathan Carrington (307)

296. Lawrence Ainsworth 1734–1761

Admitted 25 November 1734 in succession to John Prince (276). Paten dated 22 November 1734. Died 1761. Succeeded by Francis Howe (336).

297. Lieutenant Alexander Givans 1736–1748

Admitted 31 January 1736 in succession to Alexander Fraser (282). Patent dated 7 January 1736. He served as a lieutenant to his father, Captain Givans in defence of Londonderry during the siege. Also in the wars in Flanders in General Ross's Regiment (?). Also in Germany at the battle of Blenheim; he was wounded and disabled from service at the battle of Ramillies. Died 1748. Succeeded by John Palairet (319).

298. Francis Forester 1736–1751

Admitted 19 November 1736 in succession to Isaac Burrows (290). Patent dated 11 November 1736. Died 1751. Succeeded by John Gracieux (325).

299. Sir Bartholomew Heyman, Bart. 1737–1742

Admitted 31 January 1737 in succession to Sir James Holburne (294). Patent dated 28 January 1737. He succeeded his father as third baronet in 1723. His eyesight became impaired in his youth and rendered him unfit for military service. The baronetcy became extint on the death of his son. Died 9 June 1742 aged 52. Buried at St George's Chapel. Mon. Insc, [Pote p. 401]. Succeeded by Charles Wise (310).

300. Vincent Chateauvert 1739–1767

Admitted 15 march 1739 in succession to Daniel Herbst (286). Patent dated 13 March 1739. He was temporarily suspended in 1742. Buried at St George's Chapel 22 May 1767. Succeeded by John Morrison (342).

301. Richard Kemys 1739–1750

Admitted 9 May 1739 in succession to Richard Bull (284). Patent dated 3 May 1739. He ' had for many years been in our military service'. Buried at St George's Chapel 22 June 1750. Succeeded by Strickland Lodge (324).

302. Samuel Prince 1739–1746

Admitted 20 November 1739 in succession to William Pritchard (293). Patent dated 26 October 1739. Buried at St George's Chapel 5 August 1746. Succeeded by John Fielding (316).

303. Paul le Grandmaison 1740–1753

Admitted 1 January 1740 in succession to Edward Butler (268). Patent dated 25 October 1739. Died 1753. Succeeded by Edward Smart (317)

304. Samuel Chiswell 1741–1761

Admitted 3 February 1741 in succession to Jonathan Bower (292). Patent dated 31 January 1741. Buried at St George's Chapel 26 February 1761. Succeeded by Thomas Coke (334).

305. Paul le Grand 1741–1745

Admitted 5 February 1741 in succession to Rice Williams (275). Patent dated 31 January 1741. Died 1745. succeeded by John Bowie (315).

306. John Newton 1741–1750

Admitted 10 February 1741 in succession to Alexander White (263). Patent dated 7 February 1741. Died 1750. Succeeded by Sir Evered Alston (320).

307.   Nathan Carrington   **1741–1778**
Governor of the Poor Knights 16 April 1761–1778
Admitted 11 February 1741 in succession to Richard Tildesly (295). Patent dated 7 February 1741. In 1730, one Nathan Carrington, one of the King's Messengers, was held up by a Highwayman near Hounslow Heath whilst carrying letters from Windsor to London. Appointed Governor 16 April 1761 in succession to Nicholas Budiani (326). Patent dated 30 March 1761. Died 1778. Succeeded by David MacCulloch (359) and by Wuilliam Dick (339) as Governor.

308.   William Ainsworth   **741–1748**
Admitted 30 December 1741 in succession to Matthew Chauvin (289). Patent dated 29 December 1741. Died 1748. Succeeded by Henry Taylor (318).

309.   **Joseph Walton**   **1742–1761**
Admitted 7 April 1742 in succession to Henry Peart (277). Patent dated 3 April 1742. Buried at St George's Chapel 23 November 1761. Succeeded by Peter Papon (337).

310.   Charles Wise (Mustapha)   **1742–1743**
Admitted 15 June 1742 in succession to Sir Bartholomew Heyman, Bart. (299). Patent dated 12 June 1742.
Two little Turkish boys about 7 or 8 years old were captured by the first Duke of St Albans, then about 18 years old, at the Battle of Belgrade in 1668. It is likely that they had become homeless orphans as a result of the battle and were rescued by the Duke as an act of kindness. He brought them to England and they lived at his home, Burford House. When they were about 23 they were baptized at Windsor Parish Church and given the Christian names of George and Charles with their surname, Mustapha. They were given the choice of ether returning to their own country or remaining in the Duke's service. George chose to return and Charles to remain. It may be assumed that Charles remained in the service of the Duchess after the Duke's death in 1726. The Duchess died in 1741. The second Duke of St Albans was Governor of Windsor Castle at the time and in favour with George II. He would have had no difficulty in persuading the King to nominate Charles Wise as a Poor Knight at the next vacancy. Buried at St George's Chapel 16 January 1743. He is called William in the Burial Register. Succeeded by Pedro Pineda (311)

311.   Pedro Pineda   **1743–1760**
Admitted 24 January 1743 in succession to Charles Wise (310), Patent dated 22 January 1743. Died 1760. Succeeded by Sir William Wittewronge (332)

312.   John Rush   **1743–1744**
Admitted 25 July 1743 in succession to Cyrus Rivers (270). Patent dated 2 July 1743. Buried at St George's Chapel 30 October 1744. Succeeded by Robert Dixon (314).

313.   Simon Boswell   **1744–1749**
Admitted 5 May 1744 in succession to Henry Rogers (288). Patent dated 2 May 1744. Died 1749. Succeeded by Peter Palairet (321).

314.   Robert Dixon   **1744–1754**
Admitted 10 December 1744 in succession to John Rush (312). Patent 30 November 1744. Describer as 'Robert Dixon the elder'. Buried at St George's Chapel 9 November 1754. Succeeded by Andrew Glass (328).

315.   John Bowie   **1745–1755**
Admitted 22 February 1745 in succession to Paul le Grand (305) Patent dated 19 February 1745. Buried at St George's Chapel 21 March 1755. Succeeded by Thomas Reeve (330).

316.   Sir John Fielding   **1746–1781**
Admitted 25 August 1746 in succession to Samuel Prince (302). Patent dated 15 August 1746

Died 1781. Succeeded by Francis Delavaux (365).

317.   Edward Smart   1747–1753
Admitted 12 December 1747 in succession to Paul le Grandmaison (303). Patent dated 8 December 1747.
Buried at St George's Chapel 2 May 1753. Succeeded by John James (327)

318.   Henry Taylor   1748–1758
Admitted 7 March 1748 in succession to William Ainsworth (308). Patent dated 19 January 1748. Died 1758
Succeeded by George Hay (331).

319.   John Palairet   1748–1775
Admitted 25 April 1748 in succession to Alexander Givans (297). Patent dated 16 April 1748. Was probably the
first occupant of No 58 Greek Street , from 1733 to 1737. He was agent of the States General in London and
French teacher to three of George II's children, and who in 1736 published an Abrégé sur les Sciences et sur les
Arts. Died 1775. He was succeeded by Thomas Gibbons (354).

320.   Sir Evered Alston, Bart.   1749–1750
Admitted 3 October 1749 in succession to John Newton (306). Patent dated 18 September 1749. He succeeded
his brother as 5th baronet. Having wasted his estate, he was compelled to sell the property at Long Ditton,
Surrey, inherited from his mother's family of Evelyn. He died at his house in Reigate, and was buried there 15
April 1750. His son, the 6th Baronet, also became a Poor Knight. Succeeded by Wolf Hoffmaster (322).

321.   Peter Palairet   1749–1776
Admitted 1 December 1749 in succession to Simon Boswell (313). Patent dated 24 November 1749. Died
1776. Succeeded by Bernard Brooshooft (356)

322.   Wolf Hoffmaster   1750–1771
Admitted 6 June 1750 in succession to Sir Evered Alston (320). Patent dated 23 May 1750. Buried at St
George's Chapel 7 May 1771. Succeeded by Stephen Monnet (347).

323.   John Bill   1750–1770
Admitted 10 September 1750 in succession to Richard Webster (291). Patent Dated 18 August 1750. Buried at
St George's Chapel 4 January 1770. Succeeded by George Steidel (346)

324.   Strickland Lodge   1751–1764
Admitted 7 June 1751 in succession to Richard Kemys (301). Patent dated 10 August 1750. In 1725 he and his
wife Susannah became owners of the 'Barton Fair' in Gloucester. It was a major Fair that they retained until his
death. (Barton Fair is described as a great cheese fair attracting livestock, peddlers, gypsies and showmen). Died
1764. Succeeded by William Dick (339)

325.   John Gracieux   1751–1777
Admitted 7 June 1751 in succession to Francis Forester (298). Patent dated 3 June 1751. Died 1777. Succeeded
by David Lauzun (357).

326.   Captain Nicholas Budiani   1751–1760
Governor of the Poor Knights 12 September 1751–1760
Admitted 12 September 1751 in succession to Jasper Oliver (287). Patent dated 9 August 1751. Served as a
Colonel Farrington's 29th Regiment of Foot (Worcestershire). Appointed Governor of the Poor Knights in
succession to Jasper Oliver 12 September 1751. Patent dated 10 August 1751. Buried at St George's Chapel 2
August 1760. Succeeded by Jonathan Maxted (335) and by Nathan Carrington (307) as Governor.

The Lower Ward from the base of the Round Tower c. 1760 by Thomas and Paul Sandy
To the left are the houses of the Upper Foundation and across the centre the houses of the Lower/Crane's Foundation.
Between the two rows of trees there seem to be graves in the grass. There are three Military Knights buried here.

© The Royal Collection

Mary Tudor Tower, c 1760 by Thomas and Paul Sandby

Residence of the Governor of the Poor Knights and the Military Knights, Garter House next door was the communal hall.

© The Royal Collection

327. John James   1753–1781

Admitted 18 May 1753 in succession to Edward Smart (317). Patent dated 5 May 1753. Died 1781. Succeeded by Mark Anthony Porny (364)

328. Andrew Glass   1753–1754

Admitted 4 December 1753 in succession to Robert Dixon (314). Patent dated 27 November 1753. Buried at St George's Chapel 20 September 1754. Succeeded by Richard Neville (329)

329. Richard Neville   1754–1769

Admitted 18 November 1754 in succession to Andrew Glass (328). Patent dated 13 November 1754. Died 1769. Succeeded by John Lamb (345)

330. Thomas Reeve   1755–1772

Admitted 27 March 1755 in succession to John Bowie (315). Patent dated 22 March 1755. Died 1772. Succeeded by James Watson (439).

331. Lieutenant George Hay   1758–1779

Admitted 8 May 1758 in succession to Henry Taylor (318). Patent dated 4 May 1758. Served in The Royal North British Fusiliers. Died 1779. Succeeded by William Tucker (363).

332. Sir William Wittewronge, Bart.   1760–1761

Admitted 2 July 1760 in succession to Pedro Pineda (311). Patent dated 17 June 1760. His family was of Dutch origin. Born 1697 at Stanton Barry, Bucks, he was entered at Rugby School in 1707. He succeeded as 5th and last Baronet in 1744 on the death of his brother Sir John Wittewronge. Sir John had been outlawed for murder and had died in Fleet prison from wounds received in an affray with a fellow prisoner He sold the property at Stanton Barry and became impoverished. The Baronetcy became extinct on the death of his only son. Died at Lambeth 20 January 1761. Succeeded by James Richardson (333).

333. James Richardson   1761–1787

Admitted 7 February 1761 in succession to Sir William Wittewronge, Bart (332). Patent dated 2 February 1761. Died 28 February 1787 aged 85. Buried at St George's Chapel 5 March. [Mon. Insc. outside the Chapel, South side pavement]. Succeeded by John Redman (371)

334. Thomas Coke   1761–1773

Admitted 4 April 1761 in succession to Samuel Chiswell (304). Patent dated 5 February 1761. Died 1765. Succeeded by Peter Hebrard (341)

335. Jonathan Maxted   1761–1773

Admitted 4 April 1761 in succession to Nicholas Budiani (326). Patent dated 30 March 1761. Buried at St George's Chapel 25 February 1773. Succeeded by James Lane (350)

336. Francis Howe   1761–1762

Admitted 25 September 1761 in succession to Lawrence Ainsworth (296). Patent dated 16 September 1761. Died 1762. Succeeded by Robert Rome (338)

337. Peter Papon   1761–1783

Admitted 16 December 1781 in succession to Joseph Walton (309). Patent dated 10 December 1761. Died 1783. Succeeded by Hanbury Potter (368).

338. Robert Rome   1762–1765

Admitted 25 May 1762 in succession to Francis Howe (336). Patent dated 111 May 1762. Died 1765. Succeeded by Thomas Richardson (340).

339. William Dick   1764 –1800

Governor of the Poor Knights 9 January 1778–1800

Admitted 1764 in succession to Strickland Lodge (324). Patent dated 15 November 1764. One of his Majesty's Messengers in 1745 and Clerk of the Papers in the Mint 1756. Appointed Governor of the Poor Knights 9 January 1778 in succession to Nathan Carrington (307). Patent dated 31 December 1777. Died 9 May 1800 aged 91. Buried at St George's Chapel 16 May. [Mon. Insc. Deans cloister East side pavement]. Succeeded by Samuel Smart (380) and by Charles Forrest (379) as Governor.

340. Thomas Richardson   1765–1774

Admitted 17 February 1765 in succession to Robert Rome (338). Patent dated 15 February 1765. Died 1774. Succeeded by Ludovick Loddiges (351)

341. Peter Hebrard   1765–1768

Admitted 29 July 1765 in succession to Thomas Coke (334). Patent dated 26 July 1765. Died 1768. Succeeded by James Sadlier (343).

342. John Morrison   1767–1798

Admitted 27 June 1767 in succession to Vincent Chateauvert (300). Patent dated 5 June 1767. Died 1798. Succeeded by Sir John Dineley, Bart (377).

343. James Sadleir   1768

Admitted 15 March 1768 in succession to Peter Hebrard (341). Patent dated 6 February 1768. Buried at St George's Chapel 23 1768. Succeeded by John Clark (344).

344. John Clark   1769–1776

Admitted 27 January 1769 in succession to James Sadlier (343). Patent dated 3 November 1768. Buried at St George's Chapel 16 September 1776. Succeeded by Jean Anneler (358)

345. John Lamb   1769–1787

Admitted 11 March 1769 in succession to Richard Neville (329). Patent dated 6 March 1769. Died 1787. Succeeded by Roderick Ogg (370).

346. George Steidel   1770–1771

Admitted 19 January 1770 in succession to John Bill (323). Patent dated 15 January 1770. Died 1771. Succeeded by Sir Evelyn Alston Bart (348)

347. Stephen Monnet   1771–1784

Admitted 22 June 1771 in succession to Wolf Hoffmaster (322). Patent dated 19 June 1771. Died 1784. Succeeded by Peter Bogoust (369).

348. Sir Evelyn Alston, Bart.   1771–1783

Admitted 4 July 1771 in succession to George Steidel (346). Patent dated 26 June 1771. He was the only son of Sir Evered Alston, Bart (320) whom he succeeded as 6th Baronet. At his death the baronetcy became extinct. Died 1783. Succeeded by Alexander Robertson (367).

349. James Watson   1772–1774

Admitted 3 April 1772 in succession to Thomas Reeve (330). Patent dated 24 February 1772. Died 1774. Succeeded by John Padmore (352).

350. James Lane   1773–1774

Admitted 5 May 1773 in succession to Jonathan Maxted (335). Patent dated 1 March 1773. Dismissed for non-residence 1 March 1774. Succeeded by john Beckett (353).

351. Ludovick Loddiges   **1774–1790**

Admitted 27 January 1774 in succession to Thomas Richardson (340). Patent dated 26 January 1774. Buried at St George's Chapel 13 October 1790. [Mon. Insc. Deanery Cloister south side pavement]. Succeeded by Thomas Creswell (373).

352. John Padmore   **1774–1802**

Admitted 27 January 1774 in succession to James Watson (349). Patent dated 26 January 1774. Died 1802, aged 82. Buried at St George's Chapel 7 December 1802. Succeeded by Percival Meggs (386)

353. John Beckett   **1774–1810**

Admitted 18 March 1774 in succession to James Lane (350). Patent dated 11 March 1774. Died 1810. Succeeded by Ingham Neale (393).

354. Lieutenant Thomas Gibbons   **1775–1775**

Admitted 7 January 1775 in succession to John Palairet (319). Patent dated 4 January 1775. Served as a lieutenant in The 23rd Regiment of Foot (or Royal Welch Fuzileers). Dismissed 22 May 1775, after three admonitions for not coming to Windsor to reside in his dwelling house. Succeeded by William Pollock (355)

355. William Pollock   **1775–1778**

Admitted 5 June 1775 in succession to Thomas Gibbons (354). Patent dated 2 June 1775. Buried at St George's Chapel 3 December 1778. Succeeded by Samuel Brooks (362)

356. Bernard Brooshooft1776–1781 Admitted 12 June 1776 in succession to Peter Palairet (319). Patent dated 7 June 1776. He was succeeded by John Edwards (366). He was called 'Baron Brooshooft'. Buried in St George's Chapel 7 June 1781. [Mon. Insc. Deans Cloister south side pavement.]

357. David Lauzun   **1777–1779**

Admitted 29 January 1777 in succession to John Gracieux (325). Patent dated 22 January 1777. Dismissed on 2 February 1779, after admonitions, for not coming to Windsor to reside in his dwelling house. Succeeded by Thomas Good (361)

358. James (Jean) Anneler   **1777–1800**

Admitted 29 January 1777 in succession to John Clark (344). Patent dated 22 January 1777. Buried at St George's Chapel 23 May 1800. Succeeded by Charles Forrest (379)

359. David MacCulloch   **1778–1778**

Admitted 6 February 1778 in succession to Nathan Carrington (307). Patent dated 31 December 1777. Died 1778. Succeeded by John Mark le Cointe (360).

360. John Mark le Cointe   **1779–1808**

Admitted 6 February 1779 in succession to David MacCulloch (359). Patent dated 17 January 1779. Died 1808. Succeeded by William Mansell (391).

361. Thomas Good   **1779–1791**

Admitted 4 March 1779 in succession to David Lauzun (357). Patent dated 27 January 1779. Died 1791. Succeeded by John Smith (374)

362. Samuel Brooks   **1779 –1807**

Admitted 5 April 1779 in succession to William Pollock (355). Patent dated 27 January 1779. Died 1 April 1807 aged 84. Buried at St George's Chapel 4 April 1807. [Mon. Insc. outside chapel, south side pavement]. Succeeded by Charles Jarman (388).

363. William Tucker 1779– 1820

Admitted 30 August 1779 in succession to George Hay (331). Patent dated 15 August 1779. Died 1820. Succeeded by Isaac Riches (407).

364. Mark Anthony Porny (Antoine Pyron du Martre) 1781–1802

Admitted 2 February 1781 in succession to John James (327). Patent dated 31 January 1781. Born at Caen, he had been badly treated by his family in Normandy and had run away to seek his fortune in England. He became French master at Eton College. Grammar and exercise books of his were published. He wrote a treatise on Heraldry that was published in 1765 that ran to at least two editions. He died leaving enough money, over £4000, after various legacies had been paid, to found a small charity school in Eton. Porny's Free School still exists in Eton High Street. He died 2 May 1802 and was succeeded by John Taylor (385). Buried at St George's Chapel 9 May. Mon. Insc. outside the Chapel, south side.

365. Francis Delavaux 1781–1806

Admitted 2 February 1781 in succession to John Fielding (316). Patent dated 31 January 1781. Died 1806. Succeeded by James burgess (387).

366. John Edwards 1781–1794

Admitted 11 June 1781 in succession to Bernard Brooshooft (356). Patent dated 8 June 1781. One of his Majesty's Messengers in ordinary [*Gentleman's Magazine*]. Died 6 August 1794 aged 71. Buried 8 August 1794 at St George's Chapel. [Mon. Insc. Deanery Cloister East side pavement]. Succeeded by Arthur Bellon (376).

367. Alexander Robertson 1783–1800

Admitted 19 April 1783 in succession to Sir Evelyn Alston (348). Patent dated 18 March 1783. Buried at St George's Chapel 3 June 1800. Succeeded by William Denman (382)

368. Hanbury Potter 1783 –1800

Admitted 11 June 1783 in succession to Peter Papon (337). Patent dated 4 June 1783. Died 19 June 1800 [*Gentleman's Magazine*]. Succeeded by James Gill (381).

369. Peter Bogoust 1784–1813

Admitted 16 April 1784 in succession to Stephen Monnet (347). Patent dated 14 April 1784. Died 16 November 1813. Buried at St George's Chapel 19 November 1813. Succeeded by James Mackay (398)

370. Roderick Ogg 1787–1801

Admitted 26 March 1787 in succession to John Lamb (345). Patent dated 23 March 1787. One of the King's Messengers. He was held up and robbed, between Kew Bridge and Gunnersbury Lane, whilst travelling in a post-chaise on 25th October 1779. At the trial at the Old Bailey on 8 December 1779 the accused was found guilty and sentenced to death. Died 28 December 1801. Succeeded by Charles Haynes (384).

371. John Redman 1787–1790

Admitted 9 April 1789 in succession to James Richardson (333). Patent dated 30 March 1787. Possibly Baptised at St Martins Salisbury 6 June 1724. Died 8 January 1790. Succeeded by John Duckett (372).

372. John Duckett 1790–1800

Admitted 25 January 1790 in succession to John Redman (371). Patent dated 22 January 1790. Died 1800 [*Gentleman's Magazine*]. Buried at St George's Chapel 23 August 1800. Succeeded by Thomas Zachariah Parsons (383).

373. Thomas Creswell   **1790–1792**

Admitted 2 November 1790 in succession to Ludovick Loddiges (351). Patent dated 24 October 1790. One of his Majesty's Messengers in ordinary. Died 7 December 1792 at his house in John Street, St James's Square London [*Gentleman's Magazine*]. Succeeded by Robert Harington Baudin (375)

374. John Smith   **1791–1807**

Admitted 22 August 1791 in succession to Thomas Good (361). Patent dated 19 August 1792. One of his Majesty's Messengers in ordinary. Died 23 April 1807 aged 78. Buried 30 April at St George's Chapel. [Mon. Insc. outside the Chapel, south side.] Succeeded by William Monsell (389).

375. Captain Robert Harrington Baudin (Beaudin)   **1792–1815**

Admitted 22 December 1792 in succession to Thomas Creswell (373). Patent dated 14 December 1792. He was a Captain Commissary of Horse in the Royal Artillery and the last surviving officer who had been present at the taking of Quebec. Died March 1815 in Dartmouth Street, Westminster, aged 83 [*Gentleman's Magazine*]. Succeeded by Joseph Barningham (401).

376. Arthur Bellon   **1794–1798**

Admitted 10 September 1794 in succession to John Edwards (366). Patent dated 1 September 1794. Died 1798. Succeeded by Reynier Tyler (378).

377. Sir John Dineley (Dineley–Goodere) Bart.   **1798 –1809**

Admitted 16 April 1798 in succession to John Morrison (342). Patent dated 1 April 1798. The Oxford Dictionary of National Biography gives a detailed account of this very eccentric man. He succeeded his brother Edward in 1761 as the 5th baronet. He dissipated his family estates to a point of near destitution. Lord North procured for him position as a Poor Knight of Windsor. Through the oddity of his dress, demeanour and mode of life he became one of the chief sights of Windsor. He was preoccupied with finding a wife whose wealth he hoped would allow him to establish his lineage. He died, aged 80, unmarried, on the 18th of October 1809 making the baronetcy extinct. Buried at St George's Chapel 21 October [Mon. Insc. outside the Chapel, south side pavement]. Succeeded by Edmund Taylor (392).

See Appendix for full text and picture

378. Lieutenant Reynier Tyler   **1798 –1829**

Admitted 26 October 1798 in succession to Arthur Bellon (376). Patent dated 22 October 1798. 'Late Lieutenant in our 19th Regiment of Foot (Later The Green Howards). Died 30 December 1829 aged 89. Buried 6 January 1830 at St George's Chapel. Succeeded by James McDermott (422).

379. Charles Forrest   **1800–1807**

Governor of the Poor Knights from 14 June 1800–1807.

Admitted 2 June 1800 in succession to James Anneler (358). Patent dated 30 May 1800. Of the 90th Foot. Died 1807. Succeeded by William Highmore (390) both as Poor Knight and Governor.

380. Samuel Smart   **1800–1818**

Admitted 14 July 1800 in succession to William Dick (339). Patent dated 8 July 1800. Died 1818. Succeeded by Touchet Campbell (405).

381. James Gill   **1800–1814**

Admitted 14 August 1800 in succession to Handbury Potter (368) Patent dated 15 July 1800. He obtained a letter of leave with his Patent and only once appeared in St George's Chapel [*The Windsor Express April 1814*]. Died 1814. Succeeded by William Thorne (399)

382.   William Denman   **1801–1810**

Admitted 7 November 1801 in succession to Alexander Robertson (367). Patent dated 19 October 1801.
Described as 'late of Willingdon, co, Sussex'. Died 17 November 1810. [Mon. Insc. Deanery Cloister North
side wall]. Succeeded by Samuel Moore (395).

383.   Thomas Zachariah Parsons   **1802–1816**

Admitted 26 January 1802 in succession to John Duckett (372). Patent dated 2 January 1802. Died 1816.
Succeeded by Edward Fuller (402).

384.   Charles Haynes   **1802–1830**

Admitted 26 April 1802 in succession to Roderick Ogg (370). Patent dated 16 April 1802. Died 8 July 1830.
'Old Haynes the Poor Knight died. His effigy was hung at the Market House at Williams' election for swearing
bribery'. This is a reference to the notorious Windsor Borough Election in 1802. He was a native of Windsor
and owned considerable property in the town. Succeeded by Thomas Varley (428)

385.   John Taylor   **1803–1811**

Admitted 11 January 1803 in succession to Mark Anthony Porny (364). Patent dated 5 January 1803. Died 11
January 1811 aged 74. Buried 17 January at St George's Chapel. [Mon. Insc. Deanery Cloister West side wall].
Succeeded by Richard Gideon Hand (394).

386.   Lieutenant Percival Meggs   **1803–1825**

Admitted 1 February 1803 in succession to John Padmore (352). Patent dated 5 January 1803. Of the 58th
Regiment of Foot. He was present at the siege of Gibraltar (Medal). Died at Dorchester 29 January 1825.
Succeeded by William Barber (416).

387.   James Burgess   **1806–1811**

Admitted 28 June 1806 in succession to Francis Delavaux (365).. Patent dated 18 June 1806. Died 2 May 1811
aged 82. Buried at St George's Chapel 9 May. [Mon. Insc. Deanery Cloister North side wall]. Succeeded by
John McLean (396)

388.   Charles Jarman   **1807–1812**

Admitted 5 May 1807 in succession to Samuel Brooks (362). Patent dated 23 April 1807. His original Patent
came into the possession of the Dean and Chapter in 1943 and is now in the Aerary. Died 1 January 1812.
Buried at St George's Chapel on 9 January. [Mon. Insc. Denary Cloister North side wall]. Succeeded by
Thomas Bassett (397).

389.   Lieutenant William Monsell   **1807–1837**

Admitted 9 May 1807 in succession to John Smith (374). Patent dated 25 April 1807. Of the 29th
(Worcestershire) Regiment. He lost his sight on active service in Canada. Eldest son Lieutenant Colonel
Monsell of the 29th Regiment [*Gentleman's Magazine*]. Died at Eton 6 August 1837 aged 64. Buried 12 August at
St George's Chapel. [Mon. Insc. Deanery Cloister East side pavement]. Succeeded by Thomas Fernyhaugh
(437).

390.   William Highmore   **1807–1822**

Governor of the Poor Knights from 23 December 1807–1822

Admitted 26 November 1807 in succession to Charles Forrest (379) and as Governor of the Poor Knights.
Patent dated 14 November 1807. Of the 8th, or The King's Regiment. Governor's Patent dated 16 December
1807. Died 9 September 1822. Buried at St George's Chapel on 15 September. Succeeded by William
McIntosh (412) and Thomas Bassett (397) as Governor.

391.   Captain William Mansell   **1808–1825**

Admitted 11 march 1808 in succession to John Mark le Cointe (360). Patent dated 27 February 1808. Of the 66th (Berkshire) Regiment of Foot. He served in the American War. Died 21 August 1825 aged 66. [*Gentleman's Magazine*]. Buried 27 August at St George's Chapel. Succeeded by William Betts (417).

392.   Edmund Taylor   **1810–1821**

Admitted 3 February 1810 in succession to Sir John Dineley (377). Patent dated 29 January 1810. Was for 41 years in the service of King George III and for some time Surgeon to the 15th Light Dragoons. [*Gentleman's Magazine*]. Died 13 April 1821, aged 84. Buried 24 April at St George's Chapel. Succeeded by William Stewart (408).

393.   Lieutenant Ingham Neale   **1810–1822**

Admitted 27 September 1810 in succession to John Beckett (353). Patent dated 21 September 1810. Of the 26th Light Dragoons. He was present at several actions in the Seven Years' War. Buried at St George's Chapel 2 August 1822 aged 81. Succeeded by Edward Skilton (411).

394.   Lieutenant Richard Gideon Hand   **1811–1836**

Admitted 21 March 1811 in succession to John Taylor (385). Patent dated 8 March 1811. Of the South Staffordshire Regiment of Militia. Died at Chelsea 24 February 1836. Succeeded by John Allen (432).

395.   Lieutenant Colonel Samuel Moore   **1811–1817**

Admitted 27 March 1811 in succession to William Denman (382). Patent dated 8 March 1811. Of the 56th Regiment of Foot and later as Barrack Master at Brighton [*Gentleman's Magazine*]. He was present at the siege of Gibraltar. Died 30 March 1817, aged 76. Buried the same day at St George's Chapel. Succeeded by Thomas Steel (404).

396.   Ensign John McLean   **1811–1822**

Admitted 26 July 1811 in succession to James Burgess (387). Patent dated - July 1811. Was for 40 Years in the 29th Regiment of Foot, and for many years in the Life Guards, and latterly as an Ensign in the 2nd Battalion of the Royal Veterans, making a total 68 years service [*Gentleman's Magazine*]. He served in the Peninsular War 1812-1814 and was present at the battle of Vittoria, the passage of the Bidassoa, Nivelle, Nive, and Toulouse (medal with five clasps). Died 26 August 1822, aged 81. Buried at St George's Chapel 3 September. Succeeded by John Allen Cooper (410).

Note: Ensign John McLean would appear to have fought in the Peninsular War after being admitted as a Poor Knight at the age of 70. (?)

397.   Lieutenant Colonel Thomas Basset   **1812–1842**

Governor of the Poor Knights from 4 November 1822–1842

Admitted 20 February 1812 in succession to Charles Jarman (388). Patent dated 14 February 1812. He joined the army in 1775 Served as a Major in the 5th (Northumberland) Regiment of Foot and saw much service in the American War in 1783. He was present at the battles of Brandywine, Monmouth, Court House and White Plains. He also served in the West Indies where he assisted in the capture of St Lucia In 1799 he served with the Duke of York in the Expedition to Holland and was present at the battle of Bergen and the affair at Winkel. He retired from the service after the peace of Amiens, but was again employed during the Peninsular War to organise a Spanish Force. Admitted as Governor of the Poor Knights 4 November 1822 in succession to William Highmore (390). He was of the family of Bassett of Beaupre, Glamorganshire. Died 7 January 1842 aged 84. Buried 13 January, At his funeral six Poor Knights acted as Pall Bearers 420, 437,438,439,440. Succeeded by Thomas Craddock (445) and by Captain John Johnstone Cumming (429) as Governor

398.   Lieutenant James Mackay   **1813–1818**

Admitted 22 December 1813 in succession to Peter Bogoust (369). Patent dated 1 December 1813. O f the 35th Regiment of Foot and Royal Independent Invalids. He served in the American War under Wolfe and was present at the capture of Quebec where he was severely wounded. Died at Chelsea 30 September 1818. Succeeded by John Hepburn (406).

399. Captain William Thorne   1814–1814

Admitted 30 April 1814 in succession to James Gill (381). Patent dated 6 April 1814. Served as a Captain in the 43rd (Monmouthshire) Regiment of Foot and Barrack Master at Manchester. He was present at the capture of Quebec and was wounded at the siege of Yorktown. Died 26 June 1814. Buried at St George's Chapel 2 July. [Mon. Insc. Denary Cloister South Side pavement]. Succeeded by William Brown (400).

400. Lieutenant William Browne   1814–1824

Admitted 5 August 1814 in succession to William Thorne (399). Patent dated 1 July 1814. He served with the 20th Regiment of Foot in the Seven Years War (severely wounded), later in the American Wars and was present at the siege of Charleston. He also served in the Royal Invalids. Died 7 November 1824 aged 89. Buried 12 Novembers at St George's Chapel. Succeeded by Richard O'Meara (415).

401. Captain Joseph Barningham   1815–1816

Admitted 20 May 1815 in succession to Robert Harrington Baudin (375). Patent dated 12 May 1815. Served as a Captain in the Duke of York's Own Banffshire Fencibles and as a Lieutenant in the 3rd Battalion Royal Veteran Corps. He saw service in the American War (wounded). Died at Kensington 30 September 1816. Succeeded by William Shaw (403).

402. Major Edward Fuller   1816–1827

Admitted 23 September 1816 in succession to Thomas Zachariah Parsons (383). Patent dated 9 September 1816. Of the 51st (Second Yorkshire West Riding) Regiment. He was present at the battle of Minden and at other actions in the Seven Years War. Died 9 March 1827 aged 95. Buried 17 March 1827 at St George's Chapel. Succeeded by Charles Hunt Lorimer (421).

403. Colonel William Shaw   1816–1826

Admitted 22 November 1816 in succession to Joseph Barningham (401). Patent Dated 10 October 1816. Served as Colonel of Colonial Forces, and was present at the capture of Martinique. Died at Nottingham 6 January 1826. Succeeded by Joseph Fowler (418).

404. Colonel Thomas Steel   1817–1839

Admitted 12 May 1817 in succession to Samuel Moore (395). Patent dated 2 April 1817. Served as Colonel in the 90th, Perthshire Volunteers (Later The Cameronian Scottish Rifles - 2nd Battalion). 'His Majesty allowed him an additional £50 a year, and a subscription has been set on foot for his widow, at the head of which stands the name of her Majesty for £10. ' [*Gentleman's Magazine*]. Died 24 December 1839 aged 85. Buried at St George's Chapel 31 December. Succeeded by Joseph Jocelyn Anderson (440).

405. Captain Touchet Campbell   1818–1827

Admitted 2 March 1818 in succession to Samuel Smart (380). Patent dated 23 February 1818. Served in the 3rd Royal Veteran Battalion. Died St Helier, Jersey, 10 November 1827. Succeeded by Samual Ragg (420).

406. Lieutenant John Hepburn   1819–1822

Admitted 1 March 1819 in succession to James Mackay (398). Patent dated 20 February 1819. Of the Royal Company of Invalids. He served under Burgoyne in the American War. Died at Portsea 23 May 1822, aged 75 [*Gentleman's Magazine*]. Succeeded by William Gillespie (409).

407. Lieutenant Isaac Riches   1820–1824

Admitted 6 March 1820 in succession to William Tucker (363). Patent dated 26 February 1820. Of the 29th (Worcestershire) Regiment. Died 14 September 1824. Succeeded by John Campbell (414).

408.   Captain William Stewart   1821–1826

Admitted 27 June 1821 in succession to Edmund Taylor (392). Of the Independent Company of Invalids. Died at Stepney 2 January 1826. Succeeded by William Hill (419)

409.   Quarter–Master William Gillespie   1822–1824

Admitted 23 July 1822 in succession to John Hepburn (406). Of the 29th (Worcestershire) Regiment. Served in the Expedition to Holland 1799 and in the Peninsular War 1808-11. Died 17 February 1824. Buried 25 February at St George's Chapel. Succeeded by John Everitt (413).

410.   Lieutenant John Allen Cooper   1822–1838

Admitted 2 November 1822 in succession to John McLean (396). He served with the 20th Regiment of Foot in the American War. Died 27 October 1838. Succeeded by Thomas McDermott (439) on the Lower Foundation.

411.   Captain Edward Skilton   1822–1842

Admitted 5 November 1822 in succession to Ingham Neale (393). Promoted to the Royal Foundation 3 April 1824. Served with the Yorkshire Fencibles during the Irish Rebellion in 1798. He was an amateur musician. A book of his dated 177-1822 is in the hands of the Dean and Chapter. It contains many small compositions, some of which were sung at the Chapel Services of his day. He died on 29 April 1842, aged 69. At his funeral on the 4 of May 100 men of the 15th or York, East Riding Regiment, preceded by the Regimental Band led the procession from his residence. He is buried on the green opposite the south entrance to St George's Chapel. Succeeded by Donald MacLachlan (446)

412.   Lieutenant William McIntosh   1822–1830

Admitted 20 December 1822 in succession to William Highmore (390). Of the 4th Battalion Royal Veteran Corps. Died 22 February 1830. Succeeded by David Williams (423).

413.   Lieutenant John Everitt   1824–1837

Admitted 14 May 1824 in succession to William Gillespie(409). Of the 2nd Battalion Royal Veteran Corps. Died 18 June 1837 aged 67. Buried 24 June at St George's Chapel. Succeeded by George Lawrence (435).

414.   Quarter–Master John Campbell   1824–1830

Admitted 11 November 1824 in succession to Isaac Riches (407. Of the 52nd (Oxfordshire) Regiment of Foot, Light Infantry. Served in the Peninsular War. Died at Canterbury 10 October 1830. Succeeded by Samuel Holmes (425).

415.   Captain Richard O'Meara   1824–1830

Admitted 29 December 1824 in succession to William Brown (400). Of the Royal Veteran Corps. Died 30 April 1830. Buried 5 May at St George's Chapel. Succeeded by William Jones (424)

416.   Lieutenant. & Adjutant William Barber   1825–1834

Admitted 21 March 1825 in succession to Percival Meggs (386). Died 16 November 1834 aged 72. Buried 22 November at St George's Chapel. Succeeded by Hugh Fleming (430).

417.   Captain William Betts   1825–1837

Admitted 8 November 1825 in succession to William Mansell (391). Of the 14th (Bedfordshire) Regiment. He served under the Duke of York in France (1793-94) and was present at actions at Valenciennes and Catteau. He also served under Sir Ralph Abercrombie in the West Indies 1796, at St Lucia, Porto Rico and Trinidad (wounded). Died in Kentish Town 17 March 1837 [*Gentleman's Magazine*]. Succeeded by Thomas Emans (434).

418.   Lieutenant Joseph Fowler   **1826–1835**

Admitted 5 April 1826 in succession to William Shaw (403). Of the Royal Veteran Battalion. Died at Edinburgh 5 August 1835. Succeeded by Alexander Strange (431).

419.   Quarter–Master William Hill   **1826–1837**

Admitted 28 April 1826 in succession to William Stewart (408). Died 9 June 1837 aged 64. Buried at St George's Chapel 12 June. Succeeded by Andrew Heartley (436).

The Military Knights of Windsor

The Garter Statute dated 17 September 1833 changed the title of the establishment to The Military Knights of Windsor. A new military style uniform was authorised. The dress was that of unattached officers, that is not attached to any particular regiment. The uniform is described in detail in the DressRegulations of 1834.
A specimen was made for the King's approval and presented to Lieutenant Samuel Ragg (420). It was worn by him at a Review in the Home Park. The first occasion when all the Military Knights appeared in their new uniforms was Christmas Day 1833.

420.   Lieutenant Samuel Ragg   **1827–1850**

Admitted 26 January 1827 in succession to Touchet Campbell (505). Of the Royal Veteran Battalion. He served in the campaigns in Flanders (1793-95 and Holland 1799 and was present in several actions at Valenciennes, , St Amand, Dunkirk, Lannoy and Catteau. He was the first to wear the uniform of a Military Knight; this was presented to him by William IV [*The Windsor and Eton Express 21 September 1833*]. Died 23 August 1850. Buried 29 August at St George's Chapel. Succeeded by Andrew Ellison (458).

421.   Lieutenant Charles Hunt Lorimer   **1827–1850**

Admitted 5 April 1827 in succession to Edward Fuller (402). Of the 1st (Royal) Dragoons. He was present at the battle of Corunna under Sir John Moore (wounded). He served also at Walcheren and the siege of Flushing (wounded). Died 25 November 1850 aged 70. Buried 3 December at St George's Chapel. [Mon. Insc. Deanery Cloister south side under arcading]. Succeeded by John Duncan King (459).

422.   Lieutenant Colonel James McDermott   **1830–1831**

Admitted 9 February 1830 in succession to Reynier Tyler (378). Of the 10th Light Dragoons. He served in the American War and was present at the relief of Quebec 1776 and actions at Three Rivers and Lake Champlain. Died 2 July 1831. Succeeded by Thomas Lalor (427).

423.   Quarter–Master David Williams   **1830–1831**

Admitted 22 May 1830 in succession to William McIntosh (412). Of the 43rd (Monmouthshire) Regiment of Foot, Light Infantry. He served in the West Indies and was present at the capture of St Lucia, Guadeloupe and Martinique (severely wounded). He was also in the Peninsular War and was present at Busaco, Ciudad Rodrigo, Badajoz, Salamanca, Vittoria, Nivelle and Toulouse. Died 28 June 1831 aged 58. succeeded by Charles Langford (426).

424.   Lieutenant William Jones   1830–1834

Admitted 31 July 1830 in succession to Richard O'Meara (415). Of the 50th (West Kent) Regiment. He served in the expedition to Walcheren (1809) and in the Peninsular War (1811-14). He was present at the actions at Fuentes d'Onor, the siege of Badajoz, Salamanca, Burgos, Vittoria (wounded), Nivelle and Orthes. He was present also at the battle of Waterloo. Died 24 June 1834. Succeeded by Johnstone Cumming (429).

425.   Captain Samuel Homes   1830–1840

Admitted 15 November 1830 in succession to John Campbell (414). Promoted to the Royal Foundation 20 July 1837. Of the 13th Light Dragoons. He served in the China War (1792), and also in the Peninsular War being present at the battle of Talavera (wounded). Died 27 December 1840 aged 72. Buried 2 January 1841 at St George's Chapel. Succeeded by Samuel Johnson (443).

426.   Captain Charles Langford   1831–1840

Admitted 26 July 1831 in succession to David Williams (423). Of the 1st (Royal) Dragoons. Only surviving son of Dr William Langford, Canon of Windsor (1787-1814). Died 12 October 1840 aged 63. Buried 20 October at St George's Chapel. Succeeded by George Wathen (441).

427.   Lieutenant Thomas Lalor   1831–1837

Admitted 28 July 1831 in succession to James McDermott (422). 'Served with honour and gallantry in the Peninsular War in the 43rd (Monmouthshire) Regiment of Foot, Light Infantry' [*Gentleman's Magazine*]. Previously he was a lieutenant in the 9th Dragoons. Died at St Omer 9 March 1837. Succeeded by John Powell (433) to the Lower Foundation.

428.   Quarter–Master Thomas Varley   1831–1841

Admitted 6 August 1831 in succession to Charles Haynes (384). He served as Quarter-Master in the Royal Horse Guards (Blue), and was present at the battle of Waterloo (severely wounded). Died 25 March 1841, aged 69. Buried 31 March at St George's Chapel. Succeeded by John Lamb (444).

429.   Captain John Johnstone Cumming   1834–1843
Governor Military Knights 19 March 1842–1843

Admitted 1 August 1834 in succession to William Jones (424). He served in the 8th West India Regiment, and was present at the action at Guadaloupe and at the capture of Martinique. He was present on the island of St Lucia during the hurricanes of 1817 and saved many lives. In 1822 he gave up the appointment of Deputy Assistant Quarter and Barrack Master. From March 1823 he was a Justice of the Peace in Aberdeenshire. Appointed Governor of the Military Knights 19 March 1842 in succession to Thomas Bassett (397). Died 11 June 1843, aged 57. Buried St George's Chapel on 17 June in the South Plot. Succeeded by Charles Moore (447) and by Thomas Fernyhaugh (437) as Governor.

Note: From this date forward it became the custom for appointments to be made in the first instance to the Lower, or Crane's Foundation. Promotion to the Royal Foundation followed, with a fresh Patent whenever a vacancy occurred. The dates are given for the admission to each foundation but the dates of the Patents are no longer quoted. L.F. and R.F. stand for Lower Foundation and Royal Foundation.

430.   Lieutenant Hugh Fleming   1835–1856

Admitted 28 January 1835 R.F. *vice* William Barber (416)(dec). He served in the campaign in Flanders 1793-95, in Holland 1799, in Germany in 1805, at Copenhagen in 1807, and in the Peninsular war 1809-14. He was present at the actions of St Amand, Famars, Lincelles, Dunkirk, Lannoy, Vaux, Cateau, Robaix, Moveaux, Tournay, Fort St Andre, Helder Zuyp, Walmenheuysen, Bergen (wounded), Oporto, Busaco, Espinhal, Fons d'Aronce, Fuentes d'Onor, Salamanca, Vittoria, Pyrenees, Ciudad Rodrigo, and Burgos. He was taken prisoner at Placentia 2 August 1809 but escaped ten days later and rejoined the army (war medal with eight clasps). Died 30 August 1856. Buried 5 September at St George's Chapel. At his death Captain Samuel Goddard (468) was appointed L.F.

Lower Ward, c. 1765 by Thomas and Paul Sandby
The figure in a long purple mantle is a Poor Knight of Windsor

438. Lieutenant George Sicker. 1838-1848. 11th Light Dragoons.
Carried the Regimental Standard at the battle of Waterloo

431. Paymaster Alexander Strange   1835–1840

Admitted 20 November 1835 in succession to Joseph Fowler (418) (dec). Admitted 17 April 1837 R.F. *vice* Thomas Lalor (427) (dec). Of the 15th (Yorkshire, East Riding) Regiment. He served at the siege of Fort Phillips in the Island of Minorca in 1782 (slightly wounded). Also in action against the Irish rebels near Clonakilty in 1798; and in the Peninsular, Flanders and France from 1811 till 1815 being present at the battle of Waterloo (medal). Died 16 December 1840, aged 83. Buried 22 December at St George's Chapel. At his death Major Robert Cochrane (442) was appointed L.F.

432. Captain John Allen   1836–1850

Admitted 16 March 1836 R.F. *vice* Richard Gideon Hand (394) (dec). Of the 84th Foot (York and Lancaster) Regiment. He served in the Peninsular War 1811-1812 and was present at the siege of Ciudad Rodrigo. Died 15 April 1850 aged 74. Buried 22 April 1850 at St George's Chapel in the Catacombs outside the West end of the Chapel [Mon. Insc. Denary Cloister, West side (wall). At his death colonel James FitzGibbon (457) was appointed L.F.

433. Quarter–Master John Powell   1837–1852

Admitted 24 April 1837 L.F. *vice* John Johnstone Cumming (429) (prom.). Admitted 7 December 1838 R.F. *vice* John Allen Cooper (410) (dec). Served as Quarter-Master in the 77th (East Middlesex) Regiment of Foot for nearly twenty years in India in the campaigns against Tippoo and Doondiah Wang; also in that of Wynaad (severely wounded). Subsequently he served at Cochin, Colombo, Sudasseer, Seringapatam, Pangalamcourchy, and the capture of Anakerry. He served throughout the Peninsular War 1811-14 (war medal with clasp). Died 27 December 1852 aged 83. Buried 30 December at St George's Chapel. At his death Sir John Milley Doyle (463) was appointed L.F.

434. Lieutenant Thomas Emans   1837–1837

Admitted 20 July 1837 L.F. *vice* William Betts (417) (dec). He served as adjutant of the 1st Regiment of Life Guards. Died 17 December 1837 aged 68. Buried 22 December at St George's Chapel. At his death Lieutenant George Sicker (438) was appointed L.F.

435. Major George Lawrence   1837–1847

Admitted 20 July 1837 L.F. *vice* John Everitt (413) (dec). Admitted 20 January 1840 R.F. *vice* Thomas Steel (404) (dec). Of the 13th Light Dragoons. Died 30 September 1847. Buried 5 October at St George's Chapel. At his death Quarter-Master James Whightman (452) was appointed L.F.

436. Lieutenant Andrew Heartley   1837–1861

Admitted 20 July 1837 L.F. *vice* Samuel Holmes (425) (prom.). Admitted 21 November 1840 R.F. *vice* Charles Langford (426) (dec). Of the Royal Horse Guards (Blue), and for twenty-five years Captain and Adjutant of the East Kent Regiment of Yeomanry Cavalry. He lost his hand in firing a canon at a review at Eastwell Park, Kent. His sad case was represented by Lord Winchelsea to William IV, who thereupon nominated him as a Military Knight. He served in the Peninsular War 1812-14 and was present at the battles of Vittoria and Toulouse (medal with two clasps). Also in the campaign of 1815 and was present at the battle of Waterloo. At his death, 13 February 1861, Captain Francis Collins (471) was appointed L.F.

437. Captain Thomas Fernyhaugh   1837–1844

Governor of the Military Knights 1843–1844

Admitted 16 September 1837 L.F. *vice* William Monsell (389) (dec.). Admitted 7 January 1841 R.F. *vice* Alexander Strange (431) (dec.). Succeeded John Johnstone Cumming (429) as Governor in 1843. Of the 40th (2nd Somersetshire) Regiment. He was well known as a genealogist, and was much employed by William Salt F.S.A., in forming his Staffordshire Collections [*Gentleman's Magazine*]. Died 8 January 1844 aged 67. Buried 15 January in the Catacombs at the West end of St George's Chapel. At his death Captain Arthur Wellesley Cassan (448) was appointed L.F. He was succeeded by Charles Moore (447) as Governor.

438. Lieutenant George Sicker   1838–1848

Admitted 9 February 1838 to the Lower Foundation vice Thomas Emans (434) dec. Admitted to the Royal Foundation 26 January 1841 vice Samuel Holmes (425) dec. Of the 11th Light Dragoons. Carried the Regimental Standard at the battle of Waterloo. Ordered to charge the fleeing French, they did so with their sabres sheathed out of humanity. They rode through the French, turned about and herded them back as prisoners. He accompanied Lord Macartney in his embassy to China in 1792. Died 13 January 1848 aged 89. Buried 21 January at St George's Chapel. On his death Henry Griffiths (453) was appointed to the Lower Foundation.

439. Lieutenant Thomas McDermott   1838–1862

Admitted 12 December 1838 L.F. *vice* John Powell (433) (prom.). Admitted 15 April 1841 R.F. *vice* Thomas Varley (428) (dec.). Of the 21st Light Dragoons and Staff Corps of Cavalry and 7th Royal Veteran Battalion. He served in the campaign to suppress the Irish Rebellion in 1798 and at the Cape of Good Hope. He also served in the Peninsular War and was present at the battles of the Pyrenees, Orthes and Toulouse (war medal with three clasps). Died 25 April 1862 aged 89, and was buried 3 May in the Catacombs at the West end of St George's Chapel. At his death Captain Francis Minchin (472) was appointed L.F.

440. Major Joseph Jocelyn Anderson K H   1840–1844

Admitted 20 January 1840 L.F. *vice* George Lawrence (435) (prom.). Admitted 30 March 1842 R.F. *vice* John Johnstone Cumming (429) (pro. Governor). Of the 10th (North Lincolnshire) Regiment. He was created a Knight of Hanover in 1837. He had been in active service both in the East and West Indies. Died in London 9 August 1844 aged 56. Buried in the Catacombs at the West end of St George's Chapel.

441. Major George Wathen   1840–1849

Admitted 17 November 1840 L.F. *vice* Charles Langford (426) (dec.). Admitted 31 May 1842 R.F. *vice* Edward Skilton (411) (dec.). Of the 14th (Bedfordshire) Regiment. He was one of the last survivors of those present at the siege of Gibraltar, where he served under General Elliott at the sortie on 27 November 1781 and the grand attack 13 September 1782. Died 21 April 1849, aged 87. Buried 27 April in the Catacombs at the West end of St George's Chapel. [Mon. Insc. Deanery Cloister, South side under arcading]. At his death Quarter-Master Samuel Rand (456) was appointed L.F

442. Major Robert Cochrane   1841–1864

Admitted 13 January 1841 L.F. *vice* Thomas Fernyhaugh (437) (prom.). Admitted 18 September 1843 R.F. Thomas Fernyhaugh (437) (promoted Governor). Of the 95th , The Rifle Brigade. Served in the Peninsular War from 1811 to 1814, including the defence of Cadiz, actions of the Aranjuaz, San Munos and San Milan; the battle of Vittoria, and the action of the bridge of Vera (severely wounded). He served in the campaign of 1815 and was present at the battle of Waterloo (slightly wounded). He was the first officer to enter Paris (war medal with two clasps). Died 27 May 1864 aged 69. Buried 2 June in the Catacombs at the West end of St George's Chapel. At his death John Leyburn Maclean (479) was appointed L.F.

443. Quarter–Master Samuel Johnson   1841–847

Admitted 1 February 1841 L.F. *vice* George Sicker (438) (prom.). Admitted 5 October R.F. *vice* Joseph Jocelyn Anderson (440) (dec.). Of the 48th (Northamptonshire) Regiment. He served in the Peninsular War (1809-14) and was present at many actions including the battle of Albuera. Died 24 July 1847. Buried 29 July at St George's Chapel. At his death Captain John Ledsam (451) was appointed L.F

444. Ensign John Lamb   1841–1853

Admitted 28 April 1841 L.F. *vice* Thomas McDermott (439) (prom.). Admitted 29 October 1847 R.F. *vice* Samuel Johnson (443) (dec.). Of the Royal Veteran Corps (see note after 398). He served in the Peninsular War and was present among other actions at the battles of Vimiera and Talavera (medal with three clasps). Died 13 August 1853 aged 67. Buried 18 August ay St George's Chapel. At his death Colonel Edward Anthony Angelo (464) was appointed L.F.

445.   Captain Thomas Cradock

1842–1851

Admitted 30 march 1842 L.F. *vice* Joseph Jocelyn Anderson (440) (prom.). Admitted 13 May 1848 R.F. *vice* George Lawrence (435) (dec.). Of the 27th (Enniskilling) Regiment of Foot. He served in the Peninsular War and also in the campaign in Flanders 1815, being present at the battle of Waterloo (wounded by being shot through the nose). At his death on 8 April 1851 Captain James Scott (460) was appointed L.F.

446.   Captain Donald MacLachlan

1843–1846

Admitted 27 May 1842 L.F. *vice* Edwaed Skilton (411) (dec.) Of the .57th (West Middlesex) Regiment of Foot. At his death in London 15 November 1846 Major John Clark (450) was appointed L.F.

447.   Major Charles Moore

1843–1865

Governor of the Military Knights 6 February 1844–1865

Admitted 19 September 1843 L.F. *vice* Robert Cochrane (442) (prom.). Appointed governor of the Military Knights 9 February 1844 *vice* Thomas Fernyhaugh (437) (dec.). Of the 5th (or Princess Charlotte of Wales's)Dragoon Guards, and later of the 67th (South Hampshire) Regiment of Foot. He was present at the siege of Cadiz and for five years was employed both at sea and on shore in the suppression of the African Slave Trade. Died 19 March 1865 aged 69. Buried 25 March in the Catacombs outside the West end of St George's Chapel [Mon. Insc. Deanery Cloister, West side wall] At his death Major Donald John MacQueen (183) was appointed L.F. Succeeded by Sir John Paul Hopkins (467) as Governor.

448.   Captain Arthur Wellesley Cassan

1844–1870

Admitted 19 February 1844 L.F. *vice* Charles Moore (447) (prom.). Admitted 9 March 1848 R.F. *vice* George Sicker (438) (dec.). Of the 65th, (2nd Yorkshire North Riding) Regiment. He served in the East Indies (1820) and was present at assault of Dwarka (severely wounded). At his death at Portsmouth 26 July 1870 Captain John James Watts (495) was appointed L.F.

449.   Lieutenant Richard Nantes

1844–1871

Admitted 5 October 1844 L.F. *vice* Samuel Johnson (443) (prom.). Admitted 31 May 1849 R.F. *vice* George Wathen (441) (dec.). Of the 7th Regiment of Foot (Royal Fusiliers). He served in the Peninsular and South of France from 1811 to the end of the war in 1814. He was present at the siege of Ciudad Rodrigo and commanded a company at the action of Guarena (slightly wounded) and at the battles of Salamanca (severely wounded) and Toulouse. He was accidentally hurt by one of his own men and carried off the field at the operations at the Nive (war medal with five clasps). At his death 4 April 1871 Lieutenant Colonel Anthony Ormsby (496) was appointed L.F.

450.   Major John Clarke

1846–1859

Admitted 13 April 1846 L.F. *vice* Donald MacLachlan (446) (dec.) Admitted 18 July 1850 R.F. *vice* John Allen (432) (dec.). Of the 66th (Berkshire) Regiment. He served in the Peninsular War (1811-1814) and was present at the actions of Talavera, Torres Vedras, Albuera, Badajoz, Nivelle, Nive, Orthes, and Toulouse (medal with eight clasps). At his death 21 March 1859 Major James Masterton Pennington (469) was appointed L.F.

451.   Quarter–Master John Ledsam

1847–1855

Admitted 18 December 1847 L.F. *vice* Thomas Cradock (445) (prom.). Admitted 28 January 1851 R.F. *vice* Charles Hunt Lorimer (421) (dec.). 7th Regiment of Foot (Royal Fusiliers). He served in the Expedition to Copenhagen in 1807; in the Peninsular from July 1810 until the end of the war, including the battles Busaco, Albuera, the siege and capture of Ciudad Rodrigo, Badajoz,, the battles of Salamanca, Vittoria, Pampeluna, Orthes and Toulouse. He was also present at the attack on New Orleans (war medal with seven clasps). Died 1 December 1855 aged 71. Buried 7 December at St George's Chapel. [Mon. Insc. deanery Cloister, Westside wall]. At his death Captain George Loggan (465) was appointed L.F.

452.   Quarter–Master James Wightman   **1848–1848**

Admitted 23 March 1848 L.F. *vice* Arthur Wellesley Cassan (448) (prom.). Of the Royal Regiment of Artillery.
He served in the Peninsular War (1811-14) and was present at the actions of Ciudad Rodrigo, Badajoz,
Salamanca, Vittoria, Nivelle, Nive, and San Sebastian. He was wounded at St Jean de Luz. He served in
Flanders in the campaign of 1815 and was wounded at the battle of Waterloo (war medal with seven clasps).
Died 20 April 1848. Buried 26 April 1848 at St George's Chapel. At his death Sir John Paul Hopkins (467) was
appointed L.F. but he resigned immediately. Hopkins was appointed again in 1856. Colonel Adam Gordon
Campbell (454) was appointed to the vacancy created by Hopkins.

453.   Lieutenant Henry Griffiths   **1848–1852**

Admitted 28 April 1828 L.F. *vice* John Lamb (444) (prom.). Admitted 1 October 1850 R.F. *vice* Samuel Ragg
(420). Of the 15th (King's) Light Dragoons (Hussars). He was present at the battle of Waterloo (medal). Died 2
October 1852 aged 70. Buried 8 October at St George's Chapel. At his death Major John William Henderson
(462) was appointed L.F

454.   Colonel Adam Gordon Campbell   **1848–1848**

Admitted 22 July 1848 L.F. *vice* Sir John Paul Hopkins (467) (resigned) *vice* James Wightman (452) (dec. on
L.F.). Of the 26th, The Cameronians. He served in the Egyptian Campaign (1801). He was present at the
retreat from Corunna in 1809. He took part in the Walcheren expedition and served in the Peninsular War
(1811-12). Died 21 December 1848 aged 65. Buried in the Catacombs outside the West end of St George's
Chapel. [Mon. Insc. Deanery Cloisters, South wall under the arcading.] At his death Lieutenant Colonel
William Sall (455) was appointed L.F.

455.   Lieutenant Colonel William Sall K H   **1849–1862**

Admitted % February 1849 L.F. *vice* Adam Gordon Campbell (454) (dec. on L.F.). Admitted 14 May 1851 R.F.
vice Thomas Cradock (445) (dec.). Of the 47th (Lancashire) Regiment. He was present at the capture of
Moldonodo and Monte Video in 1807. He served in the Peninsular War from 1813 till the end of the war in
1814 being present at the sortie from Bayonne. He commanded the troops for some years in Newfoundland
and acted as Lieutenant Governor of that Colony. He was created a Knight of Hanover (see note after 440) in
1837. At his death, 5 May 1862, aged 90, Captain Alexander Hendry (473) was appointed L.F.

456.   Quarter–Master Samuel Rand   **1849–1851**

Admitted 31 May 1849 L.F. *vice* Richard Nantes (449) (prom.). Of the 43rd (Monmouthshire) Regiment of
Foot, Light Infantry. He served in the Peninsular in 1809 and was present at the battle of Vimiera and the retreat
from Corunna. He took part in the expedition to Walcheren (1809), and served again in the Peninsular from
1811 till 1814 being present at the siege of Badajoz (severely wounded), the battles of Salamanca, Vittoria,
Nivelle, Nive, and Toulouse (war medal with nine clasps). Died 31 December 1851 aged 70. Buried at St
George's Chapel 17 December. At his death Captain Henry Hollingsworth (461) was appointed L.F.

457.   Colonel James FitzGibbon   **1850–1863**

Admitted 12 June 1850 L.F. *vice* John Clark (450) (prom.). Admitted 21 January 1853 R.F. *vice* Henry Griffiths
(453) (dec.). With the 49th (Hertfordshire) Regiment acting as Marines he was present on board H.M.S.
Monarch at the battle of Copenhagen. He served later in the American War 1812-14 and was present at the
actions of Stony Creek, Fort St George, the siege of Fort Erie and the Weaver dams. Died 13 December 1863
aged 83. Buried 17 December in the Catacombs outside the West end of St George's Chapel. At his death
Captain Samuel Scotlock (478) was appointed L.F

458.   Captain Andrew Ellison   **1850–1862**

Admitted 24 October 1850 L.F. *vice* Henry Griffiths (453) (prom.). Admitted 21 July 1853 R.F. *vice* John Powell
(433) (dec.). Of the 60th (The Duke of York's Rifle Corps and Light Infantry) Regiment. Died 16 July 1862
aged 69. Buried 21 July in the Catacombs outside the West end of St George's Chapel. At his death Lieutenant
Colonel Anthony Gardiner Sedley (475) was appointed L.F.

**459.	Captain John Duncan King**	1851–1863

Admitted 28 January 1851 L.F. *vice* John Ledsam (451) (prom.). Admitted 23 March 1854 R.F. *vice* Andres Heartley (436) (dec.). Of the 8ᵗʰ (The King's) Regiment. He served in the Netherlands and he was present at the capture of Walcheren and the siege of Flushing. In the Peninsular War He was present at the battle of Busaco, the ction at Fuente Guinaldo, the affair at Aldea de Ponte, the action of Osma, the battles of Vittoria and the Pyrenees (severely wounded). He was also present at the capture of Paris (war medal with three clasps) Captain King was an excellent artist in water-colour. Several of his paintings were exhibited at the Royal Academy. Eight of his water-colour drawings, some of them representing subjects in the Peninsular War, were presented by his grandson, Paul King to King George V in 1931. These are now in the Royal Library in Windsor Castle.At his death 21 August 1863, Captain Robert Cochrane (476) was appointed L.F. He is buried in the Catacombs outside the West end of St George's Chapel

**460.	Quarter–Master (Hon. Capt.) James Scott**	1851–1863

Admitted 29 July 1851 L.F. *vice* William Sall (455) (prom.). Admitted 23 March 1854 R.F. *vice* John Lamb (444) (dec.). Of the 9ᵗʰ (East Norfolk) Regiment. He served in Holland in 1799 and was present at the action of 19 September. Also in the Peninsular 1808-09 and again from 1813 to the end of the war. He was present at the battle of Vimiera, the capture of Oporto, the battle of Vittoria, the siege of San Sebastian and the battles of the Nive (war medal with five clasps). At his death on 18 November 1863 Lieutenant Colonel Joseph Robert Raines (477) was appointed L.F

**461.	Captain Henry Hollinsworth**	1852–1865

Admitted 10 February 1852 L.F. *vice* Samuel Rand (456) (de c.). Admitted 2 November 1857 R.F. *vice* John Ledsam (451) (dec. 1855). His admission was delayed because of his absence on foreign service with the 2ⁿᵈ Regiment of Yorkshire Militia. Of the 56ᵗʰ (West Essex) Regiment, and formerly of the 20ᵗʰ (East Devonshire) Regiment of Foot. He served in the campaign of 1799 in Holland including the actions of 10 September, 2 and 6 of October. Also in the Egyptian campaign of 1801, including the actions of 17 and 25 August. He was present at the battle of Maida. He served in the Peninsular 1808-09 including the battles of Vimiera and Corunna. He took part in the Walcheren expedition 1809. He was again in the Peninsular 1812-14 being at the battle of Vittoria and the actions at Roncesvalles in the Pyrenees, on entering France and the battle of Orthes (severely wounded) (war medal with nine clasps). Died 14 September 1865 aged 78. He was buried 18 September in the Catacombs outside the west end of St George's Chapel. At his death Major Aylmer Dowdall (484) was appointed L.F..

**462.	Major John William Henderson K.H.**	1853–1855

Admitted 21 January 1853 L.F. *vice* James FitzGibbon (457) (prom.). Of the 8ᵗʰ West India Regiment. He served at the capture of the Danish West Indian Islands (now the American Virgin Islands) in 1801. He was afterwards present at suppression of the mutiny of that regiment at Prince Rupert in Dominica. He served with the 3ʳᵈ West India Regiment, at the storming and capture of Morne Fortunee in San Lucia and at the Capture of Tobago. He joined the 50ᵗʰ, or West Kent Regiment after the storming of Almaraz and served in the Peninsular and France until the peace in 1814. He was severely wounded at the capture of Aire 1814 (war medal with four clasps for the Pyrenees, Nivelle, Nive and Orthes). He was created a Knight of Hanover in 1837 (see note after 440). At his death, in London, 14 December 1855, Captain Joseph Douglas (466) was appointed L.F.

**463.	Colonel Sir John Milley Doyle, KCB**	1853–1856

Admitted 21 July 1853 L.F. *vice* Andrew Ellison (458) (prom). Commissioned ensign May 1794 into the 107ᵗʰ Regiment and promoted lieutenant into the 108ᵗʰ in June. He accompanied his uncle Brigadier-General John Doyle as his ADC throughout the expedition to Egypt being present at the battles of 8, 13 and 21 March 1801 and at the capture of Alexandria. He eventually exchanged as a captain into the 87ᵗʰ (The Prince of Wale's) Irish Regiment of Foot in 1804. He joined his uncle in Guernsey where he acted as ADC and as inspector-general of the Guernsey Militia. In 1809 he was one of the officers selected to assist Beresford in reorganizing the Portuguese army, and was promoted Major in the British army and Lieutenant Colonel in the Portuguese army. He was placed in command of the 16ᵗʰ Portuguese Regiment of Infantry which he led at the battles of Fuentes de Onoro and the storming of Ciudad Rodrigo. He was made Colonel in the Portuguese service and place in command of the 17th Regiment at the battles of Vittoria and the Pyrenees. He was made a Knight of the Tower and Sword (Portugal). In 1813 he took command of the 6th Portuguese Brigade at the battles of Nivelle and Orthes and the march on Bordeaux. He was made KCB on 28 January 1814. He continued to take an interest in Portugal taking despatches for Dom Pedro to Cadiz. He was arrested by Dom Miguel. Eventually released he became MP for county Carlow 1831-32. He continued to assist Dom Pedro and acted as his ADC as a Major-General in the defence of Oporto (1832). At the end of the war he was disgracefully treated and made to resign his commission on the promise of being paid in full for his expenditure. He was never paid and for many years was engaged in lawsuits to obtain his money. He gave up and became a Military Knight of Windsor and a Sergeant-at-Arms to the Queen. Died 9 August 1856 aged 78. Buried 13 August with full military honours on the green on the south side of St George's Chapel. At his death Sir John Paul Hopkins (467) was appointed L.F.

464.   Colonel Edward Anthony Angelo K H   1854–1868
Admitted 30 May 1854 L.F. *vice* James Scott (460) (prom.). Admitted 31 October 1856 R.F. *vice* Hugh Flemming (430) (dec.). Of the 30th, (Cambridgeshire) Regiment. He served in the expedition to Egypt in 1807; on the coast of Calabria in 1808; in the expedition to Walcheren in 1809. He went with the army to Catalonia in 1812-13 serving as Assistant Adjutant-General. Attached to the Austrian Army he acted as ADC to Major-General Count Nugent in the campaign against the Viceroy of Italy. He was present at the siege of Trieste, Cattaro and Ragusa and saw service in the Adriatic. He was created a Knight of Hanover in 1827 (see note after 440). At his death 27 August 1869 Captain Robert Nairne Boyes (493) was appointed L.F.

465.   Captain George Loggan   1856–1860
Admitted 13 February 1856 L.F. *vice* Henry Hollingsworth (461) (prom.). Admitted 12 August 1859 R.F. *vice* John Clarke (450) (dec.). of the 7th Regiment of Foot (Royal Fusiliers). He served in the Peninsular War and was present at the battles of Busaco, Salamanca, Vittoria and Pamplona (severely wounded). At his death 1 March 1860 Major Francis Gee (470) was appointed L.F.

466.   Captain Joseph Douglas   1856–1866
Admitted 13 February L.F. *vice* John William Henderson (462) (dec. L.F.). admitted 13 April 1860 R.F. *vice* George Loggan (465) (dec.). Served as 2nd Lieutenant of Royal Marines on board H.M.S. *Hindostan* in the North Sea off Texel in 1804, watching the movements of the Dutch Fleet. On 4 June 1805 he was employed in the boats of the *Loire* cutting out the boats of the *Confiance* off the coast of Spain, and storming the batteries under Sir James Yeo. He was present on 24 November 1805 on board the *Loire* during the engagement with the French frigate *Libre* off Rochefort. In 1808 he was gazetted to an ensigncy in the 32nd (Cornwall) Light Infantry and served in the Walcheren expedition, the siege of Flushing and the ascent of the Sheldt. In December 1810 he was promoted Lieutenant in the 45th (Nottinghamshire) Regiment, and served in the Peninsular at the battles of Nivelle, Nive, Orthes and Toulouse, where he was wounded carrying the King's Colour (war medal with four clasps). Died 11 May 1866 aged 80. Buried 15 May in the Catacombs outside the West end of St George's Chapel. At his death Major John Milliquet Hewson (487) was appointed L.F

467.   Major Sir John Paul Hopkins K H   1856–1875
Governor of The Military Knights 29 April 1865–1875
Admitted 31 October 1856 L.F. *vice* Sir John Milley Doyle (463) (dec.). Admitted 3 July 1862 R.F. *vice* Thomas McDermott (439) (dec.). Admitted Governor of the Military Knights 29 August 1865 in succession to Charles Moore (447). Of the 43rd (Monmouthshire) Regiment of Foot, Light Infantry. He served during the campaign in Denmark in 1807, including the siege and surrender of Copenhagen and the battle of Kioga. In 1808 he landed at Corunna with Sir David Baird's expedition. In 1809 in Portugal with the Light Division he was present at the affair at Almaraz, and the crossing of the Tagus. In 1810 he took part in the actions at Almeida and Ciudad Rodrigo, the action at Coo (severely wounded) and the battle of Busaco. In 1811 he was engaged at Pobbal, Redinha, Condeixa, Miranda, de Coorg, Sabal and Fuentes d'Onor. In 1812 he was present at the storming of Ciudad Rodrigo and Badajoz and the reduction of the forts at Salamanca, the action at Castrajon,

the battle of Salamanca and the surrender of the Retiro in Madrid. In 1813 he was at the action of San Milan, the battles of Vittoria and Pyrenees, the attack on the heights of Santa Barbara and the capture of San Sebastian. He served in the campaign of 1815 and at the capture of Paris (war medal with seven clasps). He was created a Knight of Hanover in 1836 (see 440) and was knighted in 1867. Died 7 March 1875 aged 90. Buried 13 March in the Catacombs outside the West end of St George's Chapel. [Mon. Insc. in the Rutland Chapel. Succeeded by Lieutenant Colonel Anthony Gardner Sedley (475).

468. Quarter–Master (Hon. Captain) Samuel Goddard 1856–1869
Admitted 31 October 1859 L.F. *vice* Edward Anthony Angelo (464) (prom.). Admitted 3 July 1862 R.F. *vice* William Sall (455) (dec.). Of the 14th, (Buckinghamshire) Regiment. He served in the campaign of 1815, including the battle of Waterloo and the storming of Cambrai. In 1817 he was present at the siege of Hattras and served in the campaign of 1817-18 in the Deccan. He was also present at the siege of Bhurtpore in 1825-26 (medal). At his death, 3 January 1869, Colonel Giles Vandeleur Creagh (491) was appointed L.F.

469. Major James Masterson Pennington 1859–1862
Admitted 12 August 1859 L.F. *vice* George Loggan (465) (prom.). Of the 5th, or Northumberland Fusiliers. He served in the Peninsular from 1809 to the end of the war in 1814, including the battle of Busaco, actions at Torres Vedras, Leria, Redhina. Pombal, Robleda, Condeixa, Fons d'Aronce, Guarda and Sabugal, the battle of Fuentes d'Onor, the first siege of Badajoz (with one sergeant and thirty men he drove the enemy from the foot of the breach); actions at Capo Mayor, El Bodon, and Fuente Guinaldo; siege and storm of Ciudad Rodrigo (wounded), siege and storm of Badajoz, battle of Salamanca, capture of Madrid, battles of Vittoria, Pyrenees, Nivelle, Nive, Orthes and Toulouse (war medal and eleven clasps). At his death, 11 May 1862 Lieutenant Colonel Park Percy Neville (474) was appointed L.F.

470. Major Francis Gee 1860–1883
Admitted 13 April 1860 L.F. *vice* Joseph Douglas (466) (prom.). Admitted 30 September 1862 *vice* Andrew Ellison (458) (dec.). Occupied No 8 Military Knights Row. Of the 39th (Dorsetshire) Regiment. He enlisted on the 16th of August 1806 at the age of seven years and for monthe as a Drummer Boy. His father was serving in the same regiment Served in the Peninsular from 1811 until the end of the war in 1814. Was present at the battle of Vittoria, Stewart's Rock near Maya, Pyrenees, Pamplona, Nivelle, Nive, Bayonne, Garris, Orthes, and Toulouse (war medal with six clasps). He was promoted to sergeant in 1825. He accompanied his regiment to India. He was commissioned as an ensign on 18th Sepotember 1840. He was also present at the battle of Maharajpore, December 1843 (medal). He served in the same regiment for 47 years. Died 11 April 1883 aged 84. At his death Captain George Lewis Dive Amiel (524) was appointed L.F.

471. Quarter–Master (Hon. Captain) Francis Collins 1861–1873
Admitted 20 April 1861 L.F. *vice* John Duncan King (459) (prom.). Admitted 24 December 1863 *vice* John Duncan King (459) (dec.). Of the 11th Light Dragoons. He served in the Peninsular from 1809 until the end of the war in 1814. He was present at the battle of Busaco, the retreat to the lines of Torres Vedras and subsequent advance, the battle of Fuentes d'Onor, the siege of Ciudad Rodrigo, the battle of Salamanca, the capture of Madrid, the siege of Burgos, the retreat to the frontiers of Portugal. Also at he battle of Vittoria , the siege of San Sebastian, the crossing of the Bidassoa, the battle of Nive, the passage of Adowa, investment of Bayonne and repulse of the sortie (severely wounded) (war medal with six clasps). At his death at Penge 23 August 1873 Captain Peter McInnis (505) was appointed L.F

472. Captain Francis Minchin 1862–1865
Admitted 8 July 1882 L.F. *vice* Sir John Paul Hopkins (467) (prom). Admitted 24 December 1863 R.F. *vice* James Scott (460) (dec.). Of the 51st King's Own Light Infantry (Second Yorkshire West Riding). Served in the Peninsular War and was present at the battle of Corunna; he took part in the expedition to Walcheren and was at the siege of Flushing. He embarked with the regiment to Lisbon in 1811 and was present at the battle of Fuentes d'Onor, the siege of Ciudad Rodrigo, the two sieges of San Cristoval, the second siege of Badajoz, the battle of Salamanca, the capture of Madrid and the Retiro, the siege of Burgos. actions of Monasterio and

Quintana Pulla, the retreat into Portugal, the battles of Vittoria and the Pyrenees and the siege of San Sebastian. He was severely wounded in the action of Lesaca and the occupation of Bordeaux. He also served in campaign of 1815 including the battle of Waterloo, the capture of Cambrai and the capitulation of Paris (War Medal with five clasps). He died 5 March 1865 aged 77. Buried 11 March in the Catacombs outside the West end of St George's Chapel. At his death Captain George Copeland (482) was appointed L.F.

473.   Quarter–Master (Hon. Captain) Alexander Hendry   1862–1865
Admitted 18 September 1862 L.F. *vice* Samuel Goddard (468) (prom.). Admitted 13 February 1864 R.F. *vice* James Fitzgibbon (457) (dec.). Served in the campaign of 1815 and was present at the battles of Quatre Bras, Waterloo and the capture of Paris (medal). At his death at Great Malvern 16 February 1865 Colonel Richard Blacklin (481) was appointed L.F.

474.   Lieutenant Park Percy Neville   1862–1875
Admitted 30 September 1862 L.F. *vice* James Masterton Pennington (469) (dec.). Admitted 11 1864 R.F. *vice* Robert Cochrane (442) (dec.). He served in the Peninsular with the 2nd Battalion of the 30th (Cambridgeshire) Regiment from 1810 to 1813;; also in the campaign of 1814 in Holland and that of 1815 in the Netherlands. He was present at the defece of Cadiz, the occupation of Torres Vedras, the battle of Fuentes d'Onor, The siege of Rodrigo, the siege and storm of Badajoz (severely wounded). He was present at the bombardment of Antwerp, the assault on Bergen op Zoom, the battle of Waterloo and the capture of Paris. In 1817 -19 he served in the Mahratta war from the battle of Mahipore (as a volunteer) to the siege of Asseerghur. In 1820 he was attached to the Nizam's troops at the capture of a predatory force. After serving 22 years in India with the 30th and the 13th Light Dragoons and the 26th, The Cameronians and the 63rd, Wesr Suffolk Regiment of Foot his health failed (war medal with four clasps, India war medal with two clasps, cross of the Legion of Honour for services rendered on board the French ship *Bengalie* 1831). Died 6 February 1865. Buried 11 February in the Catacombs outside the West end of St George's Chapel. At his death Major George Frederick Berkley St John (480) was appointed L.F.

475.   Lieutenant Colonel Anthony Gardiner Sedley   1862–1876
Governor of the Military Knights 10 may 1875 to 22 March 1876.
Admitted 30 September 1862 L.F. *vice* Francis Gee (470) (prom.). Admitted 20 March 1865 R.F. *vice* Park Percy Neville (474) (dec.). Admitted Governor of the Military Knights 10 May 1875 in succession to Sir John Paul Hopkins (467). Of the 63rd (West Suffolk) Regiment of Foot, and previously of the 23rd Royal Welsh Fusiliers, 8th, or King's Regiment (half pay), Royal Veteran Battalion, and the 45th, or 1st Nottinghamshire Regiment. He served in the Peninsular War from 1812 to December 1813, including the taking of the Forts and the affair of Guarena, the battle of Salamanca, the actions at Osma, Babuganna de Morilla (severy wounded) and the Pyrenees. He was in the campaign of 1815 including the battle of Waterloo (wounded). He served in the Burmese War under Sir Archibald Campbell (war medal with three clasps). At his death 22 March 1876, Major James Powell (513) was appointed L.F. Succeeded by Major Rollo Gillespie Burselm (494) as Governor.

476.   Captain Robert Cochrane   1864–1878
Admitted 14 January 1864 L.F. *vice* Francis Collins (471) (dec.). Admitted 20 March 1865 R.F. *vice* Alexander Hendry (473) (dec.) Of the 47th (Lancashire) Regiment. He served in the Peninsular War and was present at the defence of Cadiz, the retreat from Burgos, the occupation of the lines of Torres Vedras, the battle of Vittoria, the siege and taking of San Sebastian, the passage of the Bidassoa, the battle of Nive and the investment of Bayonne (war medal and six clasps). At his death 26 March 1878, Major James Stillman (516) was appointed L.F.

477.   Lieutenant Colonel Joseph Robert Raines   1864–1874
Admitted 4 February 1864 L/F. *vice* Francis Minchin (472) (prom.). Admitted 3 April 1865 R.F. *vice* Francis Minchin (dec.). Of the 8th West India Regiment and the 77th (East Middlesex) Regiment. He served in the Peninsular War and was present at the battles of Roleia, Vimiera and Corunna, besides minor affairs during the

retreat. He was also in the expedition to Walcheren (war medal and two clasps). Died 14 June 1874 aged 84. [Mon. Insc. in the Rutland Chapel]. At his death Colonel Henry Gahan (508) was appointed L.F.

478. Quarter–Master (Hon. Captain) Samuel Scoltock 1864–1868

Admitted 26 February 1864 L.F. *vice* Alexander Hendry (473) (prom.). Admitted 29 April 1865 R.F. *vice* Sir John Paul Hopkins (476) who had been promoted to Governor. Of the 46th (South Devonshire) Regiment. He was present at the capture of Kiltoor in December 1824. At his death, 23 May 1868, Captain Laurence William Desborough (490) was appointed L.F.

479. Captain John Leyburn Maclean 1864–1873

Admitted 11 July 1864 L.F. *vice* Park Percy Neville (474) (prom.). Admitted 11 November 1865 R.F. *vice* Henry Hollinsworth (461) (dec.). Of the 43rd (Monmouthshire) Regiment of Foot, Light Infantry. He served in the Peninsular War, including the battles of Vittoria, the passage iof the Bidassoa, Nivelle, Nive and Toulouse (war medal with five clasps). Later he served in the American War and was present at New Orleans. At his death 4 July 1873 Lieutenant Colonel Joseph Sanderson (503) was appointed L.F.

480. Major George Frederick Berkeley St John 1865–1866

Admitted 20 March 1865 L.F. *vice* Robert Cochrane (442) (prom.). Of the 52nd (Oxfordshire) Regiment of Foot, Light Infantry. He served in the *campaign* of 1815 acting as Orderly Officer to Sir Henry Clinton at the battle of Waterloo. Died 24 July 1866 aged 68. At his death Lieutenant Colonel William Rainforth (486) was appointed L.F.

481. Colonel Richard Blacklin 1865–1867

Admitted 3 April 1865 L.F. *vice* Anthony Gardiner Sedley (475) (prom.). Admitted 30 August 1866 R.F. *vice* Joseph Douglas (466) (dec.). He served with the 3rd Battalion, 1st Royal Scots at Quatre Bras 16 June, the retreat on the 17th and carried the King's Colour, after four officers had been killed from it, at Waterloo (wounded). He was present at the capture of Paris and was one of only surviving 5 officers out of thirty nine who marched with his regiment to Paris. He was with the army of occupation in France 1815-16. Later he joined the 2nd Battalion in the East Indies, and served in the Deccan campaign of 1817-19, including the pursuit of Nagpore Rajah, the battle of Nagpore and minor skirmishes. He served with Sir John Doveton's Force in pursuit of the Peishwa and was present at the siege of Asseerghur in 1819. He also served in the West Indies and Turkey (Indian War Medal with clasp). Died 18 May 1867 aged 71. Buried 23 May in the Catacombs outside the West end of St George's Chapel. At his death Lieutenant Alexander Innes (489) was appointed L.F.

482. Quarter–Master (Hon. Captain) George Copeland 1865–1871

Admitted 29 April 1865 L.F. *vice* Samuel Scotlock (478) (prom.). Admitted 9 July 1867 R.F. *vice* Richard Blacklin (481) (dec.). Of the Scots Fusilier Guards. He served in the Peninsular War from 1813 until the end of the war in 1814, including the battle of Vittoria, the siege of San Sebastian, the passage of the Bidassoa, the Nive, and the Adowa, the investment of Bayonne and the repulse of the sortie. He took part in the campaign of 1815 including the battles of Quatre Bras and Waterloo (war medal with two clasps for Vittoria and the Nive). At his death 13 April 1871 Captain John Edward Knox Grogan (497) was appointed L.F.

483. Major Donald John MacQueen K.H. 1865–1866

Admitted 29 May 1865 L.F. *vice* Joseph Robert Raines (477) (prom.). Of the 74th (Highlanders) Regiment. He served in the Peninsular War on Picton's Division from February 1810 until the end of the war in 1814. He was present at the battle of Busaco, the retreat to the lines of Torres Vedras, the actions of Porbal, Redinha, Casal Novo, Fons d'Aronce, Sabagul, the battles of Fuentes d'Onor(severely wounded) and Salamanca, the capture of Madrid and the Retro, affairs on the retreat to Portugal, the battles of Vittoria(three times wounded) , the Pyrenees, Nivelle and Orthes; actions of Vic Bigorre and Tarbes, and the battle of Toulouse (severely wounded) (silver war medal with nine clasps). At his death on 20 January 1866 Captain Loraine White (485) was appointed L.F.

484.   Major Aylmer Dowdall   **1866–1873**

Admitted January 1866 L.F. *vice* John Leyburn Maclean (479) (prom.). Admitted 23 June 1868 R.F. *vice* Samuel Scotlock (478) (dec.) Of the 89th Regiment of Foot. He served in the Mahratta campaigns of 1818-19, including the capture of Loghur, Isapoor, Kooaree, Rhygur, Raree (severely wounded) and several small forts. Also in the Burmese War under Sir Archibald Campbell, and was severely wounded in storming the Dalla stockades near Rangoon. He commanded the Light Company at five different stormings.   At his death 10 April 1873 Lieutenant Colonel Joseph Webster (502) was appointed L.F.

485.   Captain Loraine White   **1866–1879**

Admitted 5 April 1866 L.F. *vice* Donald John MacQueen (483) (dec.). Admitted 16 February 1869 R.F. *vice* Samuel Goddard (468) (dec.). Of the 55th (Westmoreland) Regiment. He served in the expedition to the Elbe and Weser under Lord Cathcart, and in the Peninsular War, including operations on the Coa during the siege and battle of Almeida, the siege of Ciudad Rodrigo, the siege and storming of Badajoz, the battle of Salamanca, the capture of Madrid and the Retiro, the siege of Burgos and the affair at Muriel. Also in the campaigns in Flanders and France, including the attack on Merxem, the bombardment of Antwerp, the affairs at Fort Frederick, Hendrick, and the siege of Bergen op Zoom; the battle of Waterloo and the storming of Cambrai, and the capitulation of Paris (war medal with three clasps). At his death in London 13 March 1879 Captain John Atkin Pickworth (517) was appointed L.F.

486.   Lieutenant Colonel William Rainforth   **1866–1870**

Admitted 30 August 1866 L.F. *vice* George Frederick Berkeley St John (480) (dec.). Admitted 2 October 1869 R.F. *vice* Edward Anthony Angelo (464) (dec.). Of the 35th (Royal Sussex) Regiment. He was present at the battle of Waterloo. He later saw service in the West Indies in 1829. At his death on 19th March 1870 Major Rollo Gillespie Burselm (494) was appointed L.F.

487.   Major John Milliquet Hewson   **1866–1869**

Admitted 30 August 1866 L.F. *vice* Richard Blacklin (481) (prom.). Of the 89th Regiment of Foot. He served in the American War and was engaged at the battle of Niagara and the siege of Fort Erie. He also served in the Burmese War (medal). At his death 7 June 1869 Captain Richard Leal Shaw (492) was appointed L.F.

488.   Captain Lambert Cowell   **1867**

His Patent was dated 13 July 1867; but his death took place on 24 September 1878 before he could be admitted. Of the 73rd Regiment of Foot. He served in the Khandian campaigns of 1817-19.

489.   Lieutenant Alexander Innes   **1867–1875**

Admitted 22 October 1867 L.F. *vice* George Copeland (482) (prom.). Admitted 9 April 1870 R.F. *vice* William Rainforth (486) (dec.). Of the 42nd (The Royal Highland) Regiment of Foot. He served in the Peninsular War and was present at the battle of Toulouse (war medal with one clasp). He also seved in the Netherlands in 1815 and was present at the battle of Waterloo. At his death 23 September 1875 Colonel James John Graham (512) was appointed L.F.

490.   Captain Laurence William Desborough   **1868–1874**

Admitted 29 June 1868 L.F. *vice* Aylmer Dowdall (484) (prom.). Admitted 23 September 1870 R.F. *vice* Arthur Wellesley Cassan (448) (dec.). Of the 27th (Inniskilling) Regiment. At his death 10 July 1874, Captain William Maloney (509) was appointed L.F.

491.   Colonel Giles Vandeleur Creagh   **1869–1871**

Admitted 11 March 1869 L.F. *vice* Loraine White (485) (prom.). Admitted 22 May 1871 R.F. *vice* Richard Nantes (449) (dec.). Of the 81st Regiment (Loyal Lincoln Volunteers) He distinguished himself whilst serving with the Anglo-Spanish Legion and was engaged at the heights of Arlaban 1836, besides other affairs. He was also employed on a particular service in Canada at the outbreak of the Rebellion in 1837. He received a gold medal from the Sultan of Turkey for his services on the Danube. At his death in London, 24 July 1871, Colonel Paris William Augustus Bradshaw (498) was appointed L.F.

492. Captain Richard Leal Shaw 1869–1872

Admitted 7 September 1869 L.F. *vice* John Milequet Hewson (487) (dec.). Admitted 20 June 1871 R.F. *vice* George Copeland (482) (dec.). Of the 103rd Royal Bombay Fusiliers. He served in the Indian campaign against the mutineers 1858-59 (medal). At his death, Major William Young (499) was appointed L.F.

493. Captain Robert Nairn Boyes 1870–1872

Admitted 16 February 1870 L.F. *vice* William Rainforth (486) (dec.). Admitted 24 August 1871 R.F. *vice* Giles Vandeleur Creagh (491) (dec.). Of the 55th (Westmoreland) Regiment. He served in the American War, and was present at the battle of Bladensburg 1814 and the capture of Washington, Baltimore and New Orleans. At his death 26 November 1872 aged 77 Captain John Buckley (501) was appointed L.F.

494. Major Rollo Gillespie Burslem 1870–1896
Governor Military Knights 3 May 1876–1896

Admitted 25 May 1870 L.F. *vice* Alexander Innes (489) (prom.) Admitted 13 February 1872 R.F. *vice* Richard Leal Shaw 492) dec.). Appointed Governor of the Military knights 3 May 1876 in succession to Anthony Gardiner Sedley (475) (dec.). Of the 13th (1st Somersetshire) Light Infantry. Occupied No 13 Military Knights Row (Mary Tudor Tower). He served in the Afghan Campaign 1838-40, and was present at the storming and capture of Ghuzee (medal), the capture of the fortress of Tootumdurrah, the storming of Joolghur, the night attack on Baboo Koosh Ghur, the destruction of Khardurrah, and the assault of Perwandurrah. In 1839 he accompanied the force under Sir Robert Sale to Girisk. In 1840 he, with Lieutenant Stuart, of the Bengal Engineers, proceeded on a survey of the defiles through the Hindu Koosh, 200 miles in extent, to Koollum. At his death 26 March 1896, Lieutenant Colonel Montagu McPherson Battye (545) was appointed L.F. Succeeded by Captain William Maloney (509) as Governor.

495. Captain John James Watts 1870–1873

Admitted 23 September 1870 L.F. *vice* Lawrence William Desborough (490) (prom.). Admitted 23 December 1872 R.F. *vice* Robert Nairne Boyes (493) (dec.). Of the 85th (Bucks Volunteers) King's Light Infantry. He served in the Peninsular War, and was present at the siege of San Sebastian, the passage of the Bidassoa, Nivelle, Nive, and the siege of Bayonne (medal with three clasps). He was also in the American War in 1814, and was present at the battle of Bladensburg and the capture of Washington and Baltimore, operations in front of New Orleans and the taking of fort Bowyer. At his death 2 October 1873 aged 78 Captain Charles Donovan (504) was promoted L.F.

496. Lieutenant Colonel Anthony Ormsby 1871–1872

Admitted 21 June 1871 L.F. *vice* Giles Vandeleur Creagh (491) (prom.). Of the 80th, (Staffordshire Volunteers) Regiment. He served during the Sutlej Campaign of 1846 and was present at the affair of Buddiwal, and the battles of Aliwal and Sobraon (medal and one clasp). Also during the Burmese War of 1852-53, and was present at the assault and capture of Pegu where he commanded the storming party; he commanded at the Pagoda Hill stockade at Martaban, and was at the capture of Prome (medal). At his death 26 February 1872 Captain john Godwin (500) was appinted L.F.

497. Captain John Edward Knox Grogan 1871–1874

Admitted 21 June 1871 L.F. *vice* Richard Leal Shaw (492) (prom.). Admitted 4 August 1873 R.F. *vice* Aylmer Dowdall (484) (dec.). Of the 2nd West India Regiment. At his death 17 January 1874 Major Patrick Cahill (506) was appointed L.F.

498. Colonel Paris William Augustus Bradshawe 1871–1885

Admitted 7 October 1871 L.F. *vice* Robert nairne Boyes (493) (prom.). Of the 77th (East Middlesex) Regiment of Foot. Admitted 27 September 1873 R.F. *vice* John Leyburn Maclean (479) (dec.). Occupied No 7 Military

Knights Row. At his death in Malta, 28 December 1885, Lieutenant Colonel Charles Rowley Platt (527) was appointed L.F.

499.   Major William Young   1872–1881

Admitted 23 April 1872 L.F. *vice* Rollo Gillespie Burslem(494) (prom.). Admitted 27 September 1873 R.F. *vice* Francis Collins 471) (dec.). Of the 49th (Princess Charlotte of Wales's Hertfordshire) Regiment. Occupied No 18 Military Knights Row. He served in the Crimean Campaign 1854-55, and was present at the battle of Inkerman, the siege and fall of Sebastopol and the capture of the Quarries (severely wounded) with the storming party assaults of the Redan (medal and clasp). He was also awarded the Sardinian medal. At his death 14 May 1881, Captain William Percy (522) was appointed L.F.

500.   Captain John Godwin   1872–1879

Admitted 23 April 1872 L.F. *vice* Anthony Ormsby (496) (dec.). Admitted 1 December 1873 R.F. *vice* John James Wade (495) (dec.). Of the 20th (East Devonshire) Regiment. He served in the Ashanti Expedition 1824, including the action near Cape Coast Castle. Later during the Crimean War with the Turkish contingent. At his death, 25 April 1879 Colonel George Frederick de Rottenburg (518) was appointed L.F.

501.   Captain John Buckley   1873–1875

Admitted 8 February 1873 L.F. *vice* John James Watts (495) (prom.) Admitted 16 February 1874 R.F. *vice* John Edward Knox Grogan (497) (dec.) Of the 92nd (Highland) Regiment of Foot. He left Windsor in September 1874 and never returned. He died at Chatham 25 April 1875 when Major William Stevens (511) was appointed L.F.

502.   Lieutenant Colonel Joseph Webster   1873–1877

Admitted 27 September 1873 L.F. *vice* John James Knox Grogan (497) (prom.). Admitted 11 August 1874 R.F. *vice* Joseph Robert Raines (477) (dec.). He served as Paymaster with the 78th Highland Regiment (Ross-shire Buffs). He was present at the battle of Plattsburg and various skirmishes in 1814. Also in the Persian War 1857, including the bombardment of Mohumrah (medal and clasp). Also in the Rohilcund campaign in 1858 and the capture of Bareilly (medal). At his death 25 March 1877 Major Patrick Geraghty (415) was appointed L.F

503.   Lieutenant Colonel Joseph Sanderson   1873–1893

Admitted 27 September 1873 L.F. *vice* Paris William Bradshaw (498) (prom.). Admitted 1 October 1874 R.F. *vice* Laurence William Desborough (490) (dec.). Of the 62nd (Wiltshire) Regiment. Occupied No 14 Military Knights Row. He served in the Sutlej Campaign of 1845-46, including the battles of Ferozeshah and Sabraon (medal and clasp). At his death, 6 March 1893, Captain Maurice George Beaufoy Fitzgerald was appointed L.F.

504.   Captain Charles Donovan   873–1874

Admitted 1 December 1873 L.F. *vice* William Young ($99) (prom.). Of the 9th (Queen's Royal) Light Dragoons (Hussars). He served in the Sutlej Campaign of 1845-46 and was present at the battle of Sabraon. Also in the Punjab Campaign 1848-49 and was present at the battles of Chillianwallah and Goojerat (medal). At his death 2 April 1874 Lieutenant Colonel Frederick Percy Lea was appointed L.F.

505.   Captain Peter McInnis   873–1880

Admitted 1 December 1873 L.F. *vice* John Godwin (500) (prom.). Admitted 11 June 1875 R.F. *vice* Anthony Gardiner Sedley (475) (promoted Governor). Of the 44th (East Essex) Regiment. He served in the Crimean War (medal with clasp). He was subsequently crippled for life by a fall from his horse. His son, Lieutenant Colonel E. B. McInnis C.M.G. was appointed a Military Knight in 1915. At his death, 16 February 1880. Lieutenant Colonel Henry Frederick Saunders (519) was appointed L.F.

506.   Major Patrick Cahill   1874–1881

Admitted 20 March 1874 L.F. *vice* John Buckley (501) (prom.). Admitted 11 June 1875 R.F. *vice* John Buckley (501) (dec.). Of the 49th (The Princess Charlotte of Wales's Hertfordshire) Regiment. Occupied No 11

Military Knights Row. He served throughout the operations in China (1840-42) from the first capture of Chusan until the demonstration before Nankin, including the storming and capture of the heights above Canton (wounded), the capture of Amoy, the second capture of Chusan, the capture of the heights of Chinhae, the occupation of Ningpo, the capture of Chapoo, Woosung, Shanghae and Chin Kiang Foo. He served in the Crimean War 1845 and was present at the battle of Alma (carried the Regimental Colour), the siege of Sebastopol, and was severely wounded at the repulse of the sortie 26 October 1854 (medal and clasp). At his death, 24 March 1881, Captain Louis James Versturme (521) was appointed L.F.

507.   Lieutenant Colonel Frederick Percy Lea   1874–1892

Appointed 1 October 1874 L.F. *vice* Charles Donovan (504) (dec.). Appointed 6 November 1875 R.F. *vice* Peter McInnis (505) (dec.). Of the 57th (West Middlesex)Regiment of Foot. Occupied No 16 Military Knights Row. He served in the Crimean War 1854-55, including the siege of Sebastopol and the assault on Redan 18 June (severely wounded). He was previously wounded in the Trenches (medal and clasp, 5th class of the Medijeh and the Turkish medal), Died 25 April 1892. [Mon. Insc. Rutland Chapel]. At his death Lieutenant Colonel Charles Courtney Villiers (535) was appointed L.F.

508.   Colonel Henry Gahan   1874–1880

Admitted 1 October 1874 L.F. *vice* Joseph Webster (502) (prom.). Admitted 3 May 1876 R. F. *vice* Rollo Gillespie Burslem (494) (promoted Governor). Of the 5th West India Regiment. At his death, 26 May 1880, Captain Walter Niell Dyett (520) was appointed L.F

509.   Quarter–Master (Hon. Captain) William Maloney   1874–1905
Governor of the Military Knights 24 April 1896–1905

Admitted 5 December 1874 L.F. *vice* Joseph Sanderson (503) (prom.). Admitted 23 April 1877 R.F. *vice* Joseph Webster (502) (dec.). Appointed Governor of the Military Knights 24 April 1896 In succession to Rollo Gillespie Burslem (494) (dec.). Of the 80th (Staffordshire Volunteers)' Regiment. Occupied Mary Tudor Tower. He served in the Sutlej campaign of 1845-46, including the battles of Moodkee, Feroeshaw and Sabraon (medal with two clasps). Also in the Burmese War 1852-53, including the capture of Martaban, operations before Rangoon and the capture of Prome (medal with clasp for Pegu). Also in the Indian Campaign of 1858-59, including the affairs of Hurra, Simree, Bera, Dhoondeakeira and Busingpore (medal with clasp). At his death, 9 August 1905, Mahor General Edward Courtney (560) was appointed R.F and Governor of the Military Knights.

510.   Quarter–Master (Hon. Captain) James Menzies   1875–1891

Admitted 12 July 1875 L.F. *vice* Peter McInnis (505) (prom.). Admitted 9 April 1878 R.F. *vice* Robert Cochrane (476) (dec.). Of the 96th Regiment of Foot. Occupied No 9 Military Knights Row. At his death 14 september 1891, aged 90, Lieutenant Colonel William Edward Durand deacon (533) was appointed L.F.

511.   Major William Stevens   1875–1890

Admitted 10 August 1875 L.F. *vice* Patrick Cahill (506) (prom.). Admitted 31 March 1879 R.F. *vice* Loraine White (485) (dec.). Of the 49th (Princess Charlotte of Wales's Hertfordshire) Regiment. Occupied No 10 Military Knights Row. He served throughout the operations in China (1840-42) (medal), from the capture of Chusan until the landing before Nankin, including the storming and capture of the heights of Canton, the capture of Amoy, the second capture of Chusan, the capture of the height of Chinhae, the occupation of Ningpo, the capture of Chapoo, Woosung, Shanghae and Chinkiangfoo. At his death, 13 September 1890, Captain Harry Dyke Marsh (531) was appointed L.F.

512.   Colonel James John Graham   1875–1883

Admitted 22 December 1875 L.F. *vice* Frederick Percy Lea (507) (prom.). Admitted 10 May 1879 R.F. *vice* John Godwin (500) (dec.). Of the 70th (The Surrey) Regiment . Occupied No 19 Military Knights Row. He received the 3rd class of the Medjedie and the Turkish medal for services with the Turkish contingent. At his death, 3 July 1883, Major Robert Vaughan Dickens (525) was appointed L.F.

November 1899

Maj H F S Bolton
(538)

Col D D Muter
(547)

Col H Somerset
(546)

Col F H Swinfen
(537)

Col F C Maud VC
(540)

Lt Col M M Battye
(545)

Capt W Maloney (509)

1930

Ma A W Waitw
(574)

Lt Col J F Plunkett
(583)

Brig C C Onslow
(582)

Lt Col J H Martin
(580)

Brig C B Norton
(577)

Maj Gen C W Carey
(568)

Maj A F R Colquhon
(581)

Lt Col A C Money
(565)

Lt Col H H Rogers
(579)

Lt Col W E Webb
(578)

91

513. Major James Powell   **1876–1892**

Admitted 1 August 1876 L.F. *vice* Henry Gahan (508) (prom.). Admitted 2 March 1880 R.F. *vice* Peter McInnis (505). Of the 39th (Dorsetshire) Regiment. Occupied No 15 Military Knights Row. He took part in the Kernool Expedition in 1839, and was present at the capture of Kernool. He served in the Crimean War, including the siege of Sebastopol. He subsequently organized and commanded trhe 8th Battalion of the Land Transport Corps (medal with clasp and Turkish medal). At his death, 1 January 1892, Captain John Purcell (534) was appointed L.F.

514. Major Patrick Geraghty   **1877–1877**

Admitted 15 June 1877 L.F. *vice* William Maloney (509) (prom.). Of the 20th (East Devonshire) Regiment of Foot. He served in the Crimean War 1854-55, including the battles of Alma, Balaclava and Inkerman, and the siege of Sebastopol (medal and four clasps). Also in the Indian Campaign of 1857-58, including the actions of Chanda, Umeerpore and Sultampore, and at the siege and capture of Lucknow (medal and clasp). At his death. 25 October 1877, Captain James Baird (515) was appointed L.F.

515. Captain James Baird   **1877–1896**

Admitted 13 December 1877 L.F. *vice* Patrick Geraghty (514) (dec.). Admitted 10 July 1880 R.F. *vice* Henry Gahan (508) (dec.). Of the 41st (The Welsh) Regiment of Foot. Occupied No 6 Military Knights Row. He served in the Crimean War 1854-55, including the battles of Alma and Inkerman, and the siege and fall of Sebastopol (wounded), the sortie of 26 October and the assaults of the Redan 18 June and 8 September (medal with clasp and Turkish medal). At his death, 9 February 1896, Captain John Augustus Tighe (544) was appointed L.F.

516. Major James Stillman   **1878–1886**

Admitted 6 May 1878 L.F. *vice* James Menzies (510) (prom.). Admitted 26 April 1881 R.F. *vice* Patrick Cahill (506) (dec.). Of the 6th Regiment of Dragoon Guards (the Carbineers). Occupied No 3 Military Knights Row. He served in the Crimean War 1855, including the battle of the Tchernaya, the siege and fall of Sebastopol and the operations near Eupatoria (medal with clasp and Turkish medal). He was present at Meerut during the Sepoy mutiny 10 May 1857, and served in the campaign of that year, including the battle of Hindun, the siege and fall of Delhi, and the subsequent operations under Brigadier Showers (medal with clasp). At his death, 3 November 1886, Sir Edward Henry John Meredyth, Bart., (528) was appointed L.F

517. Riding–Master (Hon. Captain) John Attkin Pickworth   **1879–1901**

Admitted 24 April 1870 L.F. *vice* William Stevens (511) (prom). Admitted 11 June 1881 R.F. *vice* William Young (499) (dec.). Of the 8th (The King's Royal Irish) Light Dragoons (Hussars). Occupied No 1 Military Knights Row, Salisbury Tower. He served in the Crimean War 1854-55, including the reconnaissance to Silistria, the battles of Alma, Balaclava (was in the charge of the Light Brigade), Inkerman, and the Tchernaya, the affairs of Bulganak, and McKenzie's Farm, and the siege and fall of Sebastopol (war medal with four clasps, French war medal and Turkish medal). Also in the Indian Campaign of 1858-59, and was present at the capture of Kotah, the re-occupation of Chundaree, the battle of Kota Ke Serai, the capture of Gwalior and the action of Boordah (medal with clasp). At his death, 22 February 1901, Major Charles Grantley Campbell Norton (551) was appointed L.F.

518. Colonel (Baron) Frederick George de Rottenburg CB   **1879–1894**
(George Fredrick Bernard de Rattenbury)?

Admitted 7 June 1879 L.F. *vice* James John Graham (512) (Prom.) Admitted to R.F. *vice* Francis Gee (470) (dec.). He entered the British Army as a cornet in 1825, and in 1837 served in Canada during the rebellion, and received the brevet rank of Major. Subsequently he served in the 46th (South Devonshire) Regiment, and was nominated as assistant Adjutant General in Canada. In July 1855, he was appointed Adjutant General of the Militia of Upper Canada, which rank he retained until June 1858, when he was appointed to the Lieutenant Colonelcy of the 100th (Price of Wales's Royal Canadian) Regiment, recently organized and embodied in the

British Army. At his death 11 February 1894, Major Henry Francis Somerset Bolton (538) was appointed L.F. Occupied No 5 Military Knights Row.

519.   Lieutenant Colonel Henry Frederick Saunders   1880–1899

Admitted 20 March 1880 L.F. *vice* James Powell (513) (prom.). Admitted 21 July 1883 R.F. *vice* James John Graham (512) (dec.). Of the 3rd West Indian Regiment. Occupied No 2 Military Knights Row, Salisbury Tower. He served at Sierra Leone and the Gambia 1836-41, and went with the expeditionary force into the interior in 1837. He was employed on a special mission to convey dispatches to the French at Senegal in 1838, and commanded the troops at a riot in the Gambia 1838. He also served in the Indian campaign 1857-58 (Brevet Major and medal). At his death at Clapham, 16 January 1899, Colonel Dunbar Douglas Muter (547) was appointed L.F.

520.   Captain Walter Neill Dyett   1880–1894

Admitted 10 July 1880 L.F. *vice* James Baird (515) (Prom.). Admitted 23 January 1886 R.F. *vice* Paris William Augustus Bradshaw (498) (dec.) Of the Indian Army. Occupied No 4 Military Knights Row. He served in the Scinde War of 1843. Also in the Indian Campaign 1857-58 against the mutineers. At his death, 21 March 1894, Major Stephen Watson was appointed L.F.

521.   Captain Louis Robert James Versturme   1881–1881

Admitted 14 May 1881 L.F. *vice* James Stillman (516) (prom.). Of the 27th (Enniskilling) Regiment of Foot. It is stated in Fellows book that he was present at the battle of Waterloo. If so, he was not in the 27th fighting in the battle. At his death at Cheltenham, 4 December 1881, Lieutenant Colonel George James Ivey was appointed L.F.

522.   Captain William Percy   1881–1852

Admitted 16 July 1881 L.F. *vice* John Attkin Pickworth (517) (prom.). Of the 9th (Queen's Royal) Lancers. He served in the Crimean War 1854-55, and was present at the battles of Balaclava (severely wounded) and Inkerman, the attack on the Russian outposts 19 February 1855, battle of Tchernaya, siege and fall of Sebastopol (medal with three clasps, the Turkish medal, medal and gratuity of £15 for distinguished conduct in the field, and Chevalier of the Legion of Honour). At his death, 31 July 1885, Colonel Samuel Percy Lea (526) was appointed L.F.

523.   Lieutenant Colonel George James Ivey   1882–1896

Admitted 9 March 1882 L.F. *vice* Louis Robert James Versturme (521) (dec.). Admitted 6 December 1886. R.F. *vice* James Stillman (516) (dec.). Of the 4th West Indian Regiment. He commanded the force during the insurrection of the Negroes in San Lucia I 1849. He also commanded the expeditionary force employed against the native chiefs in the Burra Kingdom, West Coast of Africa, May 1862. He served in the Ashanti War 1863-64 in command of the Left Division. At his death, 15 January 1896, Major Richard Molesworth (543) was appointed L.F.

524.   Captain George Lewis Dive Amiel   1883–1890

Admitted 16 June 1883 L.F. *vice* Frederick George de Rottenburg (518) (prom.). Of the 10th (North Lincolnshire) Regiment. He served in the Sutlej Campaign of 1845-46, including the battle of Sobraon (medal). Also In the early part of the siege operations against Mooltan in 1848, and in the action of Soorikoond (medal). At his death, 22 June 1890, Captain Thomas Charles French (530) was appointed L.F.

525.   Major Robert Vaughan Dickens   1883–1904

Admitted 4 September 1883 L.F. *vice* Henry Frederick Saunders (519) (prom.). Admitted 18 October 1890 R.F. *vice* William Stevens (511) (dec.). Of the 64th (the 2nd Staffordshire) Regiment of Foot. Occupied No 10 U F (Upper Foundation?). He served in the Persian Campaign of 1856-57, including the storm and capture of Reshire, the surrender of Bushire and the bombardment of Mohumrah (medal with clasp). Also in Bengal and in the N.W. Province in suppressing the mutiny of 1857-58, being present with Havelock's column in the actions of Futtehpore, Aoung, Pandoo, Nuddee, Cawnpore (wounded) and Bithoor; also in an affair at Shirazpore with Brigadier Wilson and was Assistant Engineer during the defence of Cawnpore (medal). At his death, 2 August 1904. Major Ernest Gordon Bedingfeld (559) was appointed L.F.

526. Colonel Samuel Percy Lea   1885–1895
Admitted 10 October 1885 L.F. *vice* William Percy (522) (dec.).. Admitted 19 October 1891 R.F. *vice* James Menzies (510) (dec.). He served in the 87th The Royal Irish Fusiliers, the 25th (The King's Own Borderers) Regiment of Foot and commanded the South Mayo Militia. He was brother of Lieutenant Colonel Frederick Percy Lea (507). Died 28 February 1895. [Mon. Insc. Rutland Chapel] At his death Captain William Atkinson (541) was appointed L.F.

527. Lieutenant Colonel Charles Rowley Platt   1886–1890
Admitted 20 February 1886 L.F. *vice* Walter Neill Dyett (520) (prom.). He commanded a wing of the 6th (Royal 1st Warwickshire) Regiment during the operations in Sikkim in 1861. At his death, 16 April 1890, the Hon. Frederick Nathaniel Twisleton-Wykeham_Fiennes (529) was appointed L.F.

528. Captain Sir Edward Henry John Meredyth, Bart.   1886–1904
Admitted 22 December 1886 L.F. *vice* George James Ivey (523) (prom.) Admitted 18 February 1892 R. F. *vice* James Powell (513) (dec.). Of the 87th The Royal Irish Fusiliers. Occupied No 15 U F. His sister Elizabeth, was the wife of Lieutenant Colonel Frederick Percy Lea (507). At his death, 8 October 1904, Captain Richard Edward Brookes (558) was appointed L.F

529. Captain the Hon. Frederick Nathaniel Twisleton–Wykeham–Fiennes   1890–1896
Admitted 5 June 1890 L.F. *vice* Charles Rowley Platt (527) (dec.). Admitted 9 June 1892 R.F. *vice* Frederick Percy Lea (507) (dec.). Of the 23rd Royal Welsh Fusiliers. He served in the Crimean War, 1855, and was present at the siege of Sebastopol and the storming of the Redan 6 June and 8 September (slightly wounded; medal with clasp and Turkish medal). At his death, 26 September 1896, Colonel Henry George Edward Somerset (546) was appointed L.F.

530. Captain Thomas Charles French   1890–1895
Admitted 9 August 1890 L.F. *vice* George Lewis Dive Amiel (524) (dec.). Admitted 3 April 1893 R.F. *vice* Joseph Sanderson (503) (dec). Of the 53rd (Shropshire) Regiment of Foot. He served in the Indian Mutiny Campaign 1857-58, including the relief of Lucknow (wounded), the battle of Cawnpore and the pursuit of the Gwalior contingent to Serai Ghat, the action of Khodagunge and the entry into Futtehghur, the capture of Meangunge the siege and fall of Lucknow and the affair of Koorsie. He served later with the Oude military Police against a force at Raheemabad, and was present at the attack on the Fort of Birwah (medal with two clasps). At his death, 22 February 1895, Lieutenant Colonel John Thomas Maguire (542) was appointed L.F.

531. Captain Henry Dyke Marsh   1890–1907
Admitted 10 December 1890 L.F. *vice* Robert Vaughan Dickens (525) (prom.). Admitted 7 March 1894 R.F. *vice* Frederick George de Rottenburg (518) (dec). Of the 82nd (The Prince of Wales's Volunteers) Regiment of Foot. Occupied No 8 U F. He served in the Crimean War from 2 September 1855, and was present at the siege and fall of Sebastopol (medal). Also in the North West Provinces in suppressing the Indian Mutiny 1857-58, and was present at the operations at Cawnpore and the defeat of the Gwalior contingent, actions of Kala Nuddee, Khankur, and Bunkgaon, the capture of Bareilly, relief of Shajehanpore, and the affairs of Mahomdee and Shahabad (medal). Died 17 August 1907. [Mon. Insc. South Choir Aisle (wall)]. At his death Captain Edward Gould Hasted (563) was appointed L.F.

532. Lieutenant Colonel Edmund Henry Lenon VC   1892/3
Of the 67th Regiment (South Hampshire)Regiment of Foot 21 August 1860. Taku Fort, China. (Lieutenant). With two men entered the Fort by an embrasure and were the first men to mount the walls

His name is found among the Military Knights in the Official Army List for the two years 1892, 1893. He was never admitted. A note in the hand of the Chapter Clerk, Richard Cope, states that although Letters Patent were issued for his appointment, the authorities were satisfied that his character justified a refusal to grant his admission

Died 15th April 1893 aged 54 at St Thomas's Hospital, Lambeth from aortic stenosis and dropsy. Buried Kensal Green Cemetery, West London

533. Lieutenant Colonel William Edward Durand Deacon   1892–1901

Admitted 23 March 1892 L.F. *vice* Samuel Percy Lea (526) (prom.). Admitted 23 April 1894 R.F. *vice* Walter Neill Dyett (5200 (dec.). Of the 61st ,South Gloucestershire Regiment. He served in the Punjab Campaign of 1848-49, and was present at the passage of the Chenab and at the battles of Sadoolapore, Chillianwallah and Goojerat, and with the Field Force in pursuit of the enemy to the Khyber Pass (medal and two clasps). Also at the siege and assault of Delhi (deverely wounded), and the action of Nujjufghur. (Brevet Major, medal and clasp) At his death 10 January 1901, Major Charles George Clark (550) was appointed L.F.

534. Captain John Purcell   1892–1893

Admitted 23 March 1892 L.F. *vice* Sir Edward Henry John Meredyth (528) (prom.). With a detachment of the 50th (The Queen's Own) Regiment he was wrecked on the Andaman Islands in November 1844, where he remained for fifty-five days, suffering great privations. He served in the Sutlej Campaign (medal), and was present at the action of Buddiwal and severely wounded at Aliwal while carrying the colours. At his death, 23 June 1893, Colonel Frederick Hay Swinton (537) was appointed L.F.

535. Lieutenant Colonel Charles Courtenay Villiers   1892–1895

Admitted 25 June 1892 L.F. *vice* Frederick Nathaniel Twisleton Wykeham Fiennes (529) (prom.). Of the 47th (Lancashire) Regiment. He served throughout the Crimean War, 1854-55, including the battles of Alma and Inkerman, the capture of Balaclava, the siege and fall of Sebastopol and the sortie of 26 October (medal with three clasps, Brevet Major, Chevalier of the Legion of Honour, 5th Class of the Medjidie and Turkish medal). At his death, 5 February 1895 Colonel Francis Cornwallis Maude (540) was appointed L.F.

536. Captain Maurice George Beaufoy FitzGerald   1893–1901

Admitted 1 June 1893 L.F. *vice* Thomas Charles French (530) (prom.). Admitted 16 April 1895 R.F. *vice* Thomas Charles French (530) (dec.). Of the 97th (the Earl of Ulster's) Regiment, later of the 16th Lancers. Occupied No 9 U F. He served in the Crimean War, and was present at the siege of Sebastopol, he was of the ladder party at the assault on the Redan on 8 September (wounded) (medal and clasp; and Turkish medal). He served also in Bengal in surpressing the Mutiny in 1857-58, with the Jounpore Field Force in the actions of Nusrutpore, Chanda, Ummeerpore and Sultanpore; was one of the stormers at Fort Dhowrara and was present at the siege and capture of Lucknow. He commanded a detachment of the 97th Regiment in pursuit of Rummut Sing and Fuzand Ally in Bundlecund in March 1859 (medal and clasp). He died at Rothsay Lodge, Kings Road, Windsor and is buried in Windsor Cemetery. At his death, 14 August 1901, Major Charles Henry Strutt (553) was appointed L.F.

537. Colonel Frederick Hay Swinfen   1893–1914

Admitted 6 September 1893 L.F. *vice* John Purcell (534) (dec.). Admitted 16 April 1895 R.F. *vice* Samuel Percy Lea (526) (dec.). Of the 5th (Princess Charlotte of Wales's) Dragoon Guards. Occupied No 14 U F. He served in the Crimean War 1845-55, including the Battle of Balaclava and the Charge of the Heavy Brigade (wounded) and was present at the siege of Sebastopol (medal and two clasps and the Turkish medal). At his death, 22 June 1914, Captain John Coley Coley-Bromfield (570) was appointed L.F

538. Major Henry Francis Somerset Bolton   1894–1921

Admitted 30 March 1894 L.F. *vice* Henry Dyke March (531) (prom.). Admitted 20 February 1896 R.F. *vice* George James Ivey (523) (dec.). Of the 72nd (Duke of Albany's Own Highlanders) and 18th Royal Irish Regiment, Occupied No 11 U F. He took part in operations on the West Coast of Africa in 1867, and in the

Mumford and Pram Pram Expeditions; also in operations in British Honduras in 1870 and 1872. He served in the Ashanti War in 1873-74 and was present at the capture of Coomasie (medal and clasp). In the Afghan War of 1880 he took part in the operations in the Khyber Pass ()medal with clasp).

At his death, 18 March 1921, Albert William Waite (574) was promoted to the Royal Foundation, and no appointment was made to the Lower Foundation, which had been absorbed into the Royal Foundation. The Number of military Knights was thus reduced gradually from eighteen to thirteen by the process of leaving five vacancies unfilled.

539. Major Stephen Watson   1894–1911

Admitted 5 june 1894 L.F. *vice* William Edward Durand Deacon (533) (prom.). Admitted 7 March 1896 R.F. *vice* James Baird (515) (dec.). Of the 29th (Worcestershire) Regiment. Occupied No 6 L F. He served in the Afghan War 1879-80, and was present at the action of Ahmed Kheyl (medal and clasp). Died 27 February 1911, aged 72. [Mon. Insc. South choir aisle (wall)]. At his death, Major Edward Hampton was appointed L.F.

540. Colonel Francis Cornwallis Maude VC CB   1895–1900

Admitted 2 May 1895 L.F. *vice* Charles Courtney Villiers (dec)(535). Admitted 16 February 1899 R.F. *vice* Henry Frederick Saunders (dec) (519). Of the Royal Regiment of Artillery. He commanded the Royal Artillery throughout the operations with general Havelock's Column in India in 1857, including the defeat of the rebels at Futtehpore, actions at Aoung, Pandoo Nuddee, Cawnpoor, Oonao, Buseerutgunge, Mungarwar and the relief and defence of the Residency of Lucknow. He was with Outram's Force at the Alumbagh, also at the siege and capture of Lucknow. He was awarded Brevets of Major and Lieutenant Colonel, the C.B., Victoria Cross, medal with clasps and a year's service. He died 19 October 1900 aged 72, there is a monument on the wall of the South Choir aisle and he is buried in Windsor Town Cemetery, St Leonards Road, Windsor, with a cross headstone. At his death Captain Edward le Breton Butler (549) was appointed L.F

At Char Bagh, Lucknow,   'This Officer steadily pushed on with his men and bore down the desperate opposition of the enemy, though with the loss of one third of his artillery men. But for Captain Maude's nerve and coolness the army could not have advanced. 76 Battery Royal Artillery in named 'Maude's Battery' in his honour

541. Captain William Atkinson   1895–1901

Admitted 3 May 1895 L.F. *vice* Frederick Hay Swinfen (537) (prom.). Admitted 23 June 1896 R.F. *vice* William Maloney (509) (Prom. Governor). Of the 13th Light Dragoons. Occupied No 17 U F. He served in the Indian Mutiny Campaign 1857-58, and was present at the siege of Delhi (wounded; medal and clasp). At his death, 29 November 1901, Major Charles John Burgess (5550 was appointed L.F.

542. Lieutenant Colonel John Thomas Maguire   1895–1904

Admitted 25 June 1895 L.F. *vice* Maurice George Beaufoy FitzGerald (536) (prom.). Admitted 27 October 1896 R.F. *vice* Frederick Nathaniel Twisleton-Wykeham-Fiennes (529) (dec.). Of the 55th (Westmoreland) Regiment. He served in the China War 1839-41, including the attack and capture of Amoy, the second capture of Chusan, the attack and capture of Chinhoe and the operations up the Yangtsekiang (medal). Served with the 60th (The King's Royal Rifle Corps) Regiment throughout the Punjab Campaign 1848-49, including the siege and capture of Mooltan, the battle of Goojerat, the pursuit of the Sikh army till its surrender at Rawalpindee, the occupation of Attock and Peshawar, and the expulsion of the Afghan Force from the Khyber Pass (medal with two clasps). Also throughout the campaign of Rohilkund in 1858, including the actions at Bugawalla and Nugena, the relief of Moradabad, the action in the Dojura, the assault and capture of Bareilly, the bombardment of Shahjehanpore, the capture of the Fort of Bunnal, the pursuit of the enemy across the river Goomtee, and the destruction of the Fort of Mahomdee: he commanded a wing of the 1st Battalion of the 60th Rifles at the attack and destruction of Shahabad (Brevet of Major), amd command of the Battalion in the action of Bunkagong (medal). At his death, 11 January 1904, Lieutenant Colonel William Henry Moffatt (557) was appointed L.F.

543. Major Richard Molesworth   1896–1900

Admitted 19 March 1896 L.F. *vice* Henry Francis Somerset Bolton (538) (prom.). Of the 19th (1st Yorkshire North Riding, Princess of Wales Own Regiment). He served in the Crimean War 1855, and was engaged in the attack on the Quarries 7 June, and in the attack on the Redan 18 June and 8 September (severely wounded; medal and clasp). At his death 2 April 1900, Major Clement Headington Dale (548) was appointed L.F.

544. Captain John Augustus Tighe   1896–1901
Admitted 14 April 1896 L.F. *vice* Stephen Watson (539) (prom.). Admitted 28 February 1901 R.F. *vice* William Edward Durand Deacon (533) (dec.). Of the 70th (Surrey) Regiment. Occupied No 1 Salisbury Tower. He served in the New Zealand campaign of 1863-65, including the actions at Taranaki, Waiaru, Hourini, Rangiawhai and Orakau. Commanded for fifteen months the whole of the Transport Corps in the Waikato country (medal). At his death, 9 June 1901, colonel Thomas George O'Donaghue Hervey (552) was appointed L.F.

545. Lieutenant Colonel Montagu McPherson Battye   1896–1929
Admitted 11 July 1896 L.F. *vice* William Atkinson (541) (prom.). Admitted 24 November 1900 R.F. *vice* Francis Cornwallis Maude (540) (dec.). Of the 10th (North Lincolnshire) Regiment. Occupied No 19 U F. He served in the Indian campaign of 1857-58, and was present at the Mutiny at Dinapore and the attempt to relieve Arrah; also at the capture of Atrowleea, the advance to Lucknow and the actions at Chandra, Umeerpore, Sultanpore and Douraha, the siege and capture of Lucknow and the stormimg of Emaumbara and Kaisabagh (medal with clasp). He was present at Headquarters at Versailles during the siege of Paris. At his death, 7 May 1929, Major Arthur Frederick Rowan Colquhoun (581) was appointed R.F.

546. Colonel Henry George Edward Somerset   1896–1920
Admitted 17 November 1896 L.F. *vice* John Thomas Maguire (542) (prom.). Admitted 11 April 1901 R.F. *vice* John Atkinson Pickworth (517) (dec.). Of the 3rd (East Kent) Regiment (the Buffs). Occupied No 5 L F. He was with the Cape Mounted Riflemen in the Kaffir War of 1847, and served in the Kaffir War of 1850-52 (medal). At his death, 5 April 1920, no appointment was made to the Lower Foundation.

547. Colonel Dunbar Douglas Muter   1899–1909
Admitted 9 March 1899 L.F. *vice* Francis Cornwallis Maude (540) (dec.). Admitted 31 July 1901 R.F. *vice* John Augustus Tighe (544) (dec.). Of the 60th (The King's Royal Rifle Corps) Regiment, later, The 51st (2nd Yorkshire North Riding)The King's Own Light Infantry. Occupied No 4 L F. He served in the Punjab Campaign in 1848-49, including the siege and capture of Mooltan and the battle of Goojerat, the pursuit and surrender of Shere Singh, the occupation of Attock and Peshawar (medal and two clasps). Also in the campaign of 1857-58 against the mutineers in India. He commanded a wing of the 60th Rifles at Meerut and was present at the siege of Delhi and the assault and capture of the city and the final attack on the Palace 20 September. He succeeded to the command of the attacking column on Kishingunge on the fall of Major Reid(Brevet Major). He served as D.A. Adjutant-General to the Roorkee Field Force during the campaign in Rohilcund, including the actions of Bugawalla and Nugena, the relief of Moradabad, the action on the Dojura, the assault and capture of Bareilly, the attack and bombardment of Shahjehanpore, the capture of the Fort off Bunnai, pursuit of the enemy on the bank of the Goomtee, and the destruction of the Fort of Mahomdee (medal with clasp). He was on board the troopship *Eastern Monarch* when she blew up and was burnt, 3 June 1859. At his death, 7 October 1909 Lieutenant Colonel Arthur Campbell Money (565) was appointed L.F.

548. Major Clement Headington Dale   1900–28 July 1915
Admitted 4 June 1900 L.F. *vice* Richard Molesworth (543) (dec.). Admitted 28 September 1901 R. F. *vice* Maurice George Beaufoy FitzGerald (536) (dec.). Of the Madras Fusiliers (later to become The Royal Dublin Fusiliers). Occupied No 2 Salisbury Tower. He served in the campaign to suppress the India mutineers 1857-58, and was present at the engagements at Bithoor, Mungawar and Alam Bagh, and at the capture of Lucknow. He served also in the campaign in Oude, including the actions at Fyzabad, the passage of the Futehpore (medal with two clasps and a year's service for Lucknow). Serving in 1869 with the Canadian Militia to suppress the rising in the North-West Territories of Canada, as brigade major and senior staff officer in the Alberta Field Force, he was present at the relief of Edmonton and the affair of Fort Pitt and the engagement at Frenchman's Butte (medal with clasp). At his death, 28 July 1915, Lieutenant Colonel Richard Stanley Hawke Moody (575) was appointed L.F.

549.   Captain Edward le Breton Butler   1901–1901

Admitted 21 February 1901 L.F. *vice* Montagu McPherson Battye (545).(prom.). Of the 76th (the West Riding) Regiment of Foot. Died 27 November 1901. [Mon. Insc. South choir aisle (wall)]. At his death Captain Edward Robert Ward Bayley (554) was appointed L.F.

550.   Major Charles George Clarke   1901–1909

Admitted 11 April 1901 L.F *vice* John Augustus Tighe (544) (prom.). Admitted 25 January 1902 R.F. *vice* William Atkinson (541) (dec.). Of the 57th (West Middlesex) Regiment of Foot. He served in the Crimean War 1854-55, and was present at the siege and fall of Sebastopol, and the bombardment and capture of Kinbourn (medal and clasp). He served also in the New Zealand War 1864-65. At his death, 11 December 1909, Lieutenant Colonel George Frend (566) was appointed L.F.

551.   Major Charles Grantley Campbell Norton   1901–1921

Admitted 11 April 1901 L.F. *vice* Henry George Edward Somerset (546) (prom.). Admitted 25 February 1904 R.F. *vice* John Thomas Maguire (542) (dec.). Of the The Royal Welsh Fusiliers. Afterwards Colonel in the Turkish Army. He served in the Indian Campaign of 1857-58, including the relief of Lucknow, the defeat of the Gwalior Contingent at Cawnpore, the siege and capture of Lucknow, and operations across the Goomtee under Outram (medal and two clasps). At his death, 10 April 1921, no appointment was made. See note at (538).

552.   Colonel Thomas George O'Donaghue Hervey   1901–1915

Admitted 31 August 1901 L.F. *vice* Dunbar Douglas Muter (547) (prom.). Admitted 6 October 1904 R.F. *vice* Robert Vaughan Dickens (525) (dec.). Of the Ceylon Rifle Regiment. At his death, 8 February 1915, Major John Morton-Marshall (572) was appointed L.F.

553.   Major Charles Henry Strutt   1901–1908

Admitted 10 October 1901 L.F. *vice* Clement Headington Dale (548) (prom.). Admitted 9 November 1907 R.F. *vice* Henry Dyke Marsh (531) (dec.). Of the Royal (late Bombay) Regiment of Artillery. He served in the Indian Mutiny Campaign 1857-58 with the Centra Field Force, including the siege and capture of Dhar, the action of Mundessore, the battle of Gooraria, the sige and capture of Kalghur, the action of Barodia, the siege and bombardment of Garrakstah, the capture of Fort Barodia, the action of Muddehpore, the siege and storming of Jhansi, the battle of Kooneh, actions before Calpee, the battle of Gallowtee, the capture of Calpee, actions at Moran and Kotah ke Serai, the capture of Gwalior and Powree (Brevet of Major, medal and clasp). At his death, 27 November 1908, Lieutenant Colonel John Grant Anderson (564) was appointed L.F.

554.   Captain Edward Robert Ward Bayley   1902–1912

Admitted 25 February 1902 L.F. *vice* Edward Le Breton Butler (549) (dec.). Admitted 7 December 1904 R.F. *vice* Sir Edward Henry John Meredyth (528) (dec.). He served with the 19th (1st York North Riding, Princess of Wales's Own) Regiment in the Crimean War 1854-55, including the battle of Alma , the siege of Sebastopol (wounded), and the storming of the Redan (wounded) (medal and two clasps, Sardinian and Turkish medals, and the 5th Class of the Medjidie). At his death, 7 may 1912, Lieutenant Colonel Thomas Langhorne Coxhead (569) was appointed L.F.

555.   Major Charles John Burgess   1902–1905

Admitted 12 July 1902 L.F. *vice* Edward le Breton Butler (549) (dec.). Of the 46th (South Devonshire) Regiment. He served in the Crimean War 1854-55, and was present at the siege of Sebastopol (medal and clasp, and Turkish medal). At his death, 15 July 1905, aged 69, Major Arthur Edward Poole (561) was appointed L.F.

556.   Captain John Ball   1902

His Patent was dated 17 January 1902 (Died 7 February 1902, but he died at Brighton 7 February 1902 before he could be admitted. Of the 10th (North Lincolnshire) Regiment. He served in the Indian Campaign against the mutineers 1857-58, including the the advance to Lucknow, and actions of Chanda, Umeerpore, Sultanpoer and Douraha, the siege and capture of Lucknow, the relief of Azimghur, and operations near Judgespore (medal).

557. Lieutenant Colonel William Henry Moffatt   1904–1915

Admitted 17 March 1904 L.F. *vice* Charles Grantley Campbell Norton (551) (prom.). Admitted 15 January 1909 R.F. *vice* Charles Henry Strutt (553) (dec.). Of the 19th (1st York North Riding, Princess of Wales's Own) Regiment. He served in the latter part of the Crimean War from September 1855 (medal with clasp and Turkish medal). Also against the hill tribes of Sikkim during the close of 1860; and later in the Hazara Campaign of 1868, including the expedition against the tribes of the Black Mountain. At his death, 20 June 1915, Lieutenant Colonel Albert William Waite (574) was appointed L.F.

558. Captain Richard Edward Brookes   1904–1906 (Resigned)

Admitted 27 December 1904 L.F *vice* Edward Robert Ward Bayley (554) (prom). Of the 46th (South Devonshire) Regiment. He served in the Crimean War 1854-55, and was present at the fall of Sebastopol (medal and clasp and Turkish medal). He resigned in 1906, when Lieutenant Colonel Montagu Cecil Broun (562) was appointed L.F

559. Major Ernest Gordon Bedingfield   1904–1914

Admitted 11 October 1904 L.F. *vice* Thomas George O'Donaghue Hervey (552) (prom.). Admitted 17 December 1909 R.F. *vice* Dunbar Douglas Muter (547) (dec.). Of the South Staffordshire Regiment, formerly of the 8th Hussars. He served as a special officer for mounted infantry in the South African War 1901 (wounded; Queen's medal with three clasps). At his death, 17 December 1914, Lieutenant colonel Edward Bowater McInnis (571) Was appointed L.F.

560. Major General Edward Henry Courtney CVO   1906–1913

Governor, The Military Knights of Windsor 19 January 1906–1913

Admitted 19 January 1906 R.F. and Governor of the Military Knights in succession to William Maloney (509). Of the Corps of Royal Engineers. He served in the Expeditionary Force in China 1858-60, and was present at the action of Sheksing against the Kwantung rebels 8 January 1859. He accompanied the naval forces under Sir Michael Seymour to the Peilo river, May 1858, and was engaged in the demolition of the forts at its mouth. He served throughout the campaign of 1860 in North China as acting adjutant to the combined force of Royal Engineers and Madras Sappers, and was present at the actions of Sinho Tangku, the siege and capture of the Taku Forts and the surrender of Pekin (medal with two clasps). At his death, 20 June 1913, Major General Carteret Walter Carey 568) was appointed R.F and Governor of the Military Knights.

561. Quarter–Master (Hon. Major) Arthur Edward Poole   1906–1930

Admitted 19 January 1906 L.F. *vice* Charles John Burgess (555) (dec.). Admitted 26 February 1910 R.F. *vice* Charles George Clarke (550) (dec.). Of the 10th (The Prince of Wales's Own Royal) Hussars. He served in the Soudan Excpedition in 1884 (medal and Khedive's star). Also in the South African War 1899-1900. Was present at the Relief of Kimbereley; operations in the Orange Free State 1900, including operations at Paardeburg; actions at poplar grove, Dreifontein, Houtnek (Thoba Mountain), Vet River and Zand River; operations in the Transvaal 1900, including operations near Johannesburg; operations in Cape Colony (Queen's medal with four clasps). At his death, 28 June 1930, John Henry Willis Southey (584) was appointed R. F.

562. Hon. Lieutenant Colonel Montague Cecil Broun   1906–1929

Admitted 10 November 1906 L.F. *vice* Richard Edward Brookes (558) (resigned). Admitted 22 April 1911 R.F. *vice* Stephen Watson (539) (dec.). Of the 15th (The King's) Regiment of Light Dragoons (Hussars) and latterly of the Hants Imperial Yeomanry. At his death in 1929 Brigadier General Cranley Charlton Onslow (582) was appointed R.F.

563. Captain Edward Gould Hasted   1908–1919

Admitted 9 January 1908 L.F. *vice* Charles Henry Strutt (553) (prom.). Admitted 27 July 1912 R.F. *vice* Edward Robert Bayley (554) (dec.). Of the 57th (West Middlesex) Regiment of Foot. He served in the Crimean War from 1855, and was present at the bombardment and capture of Kinbourn (medal and Turkish medal). Also in the New Zealand war 1864-66 and was present at the affairs of Taranki, Wanganui, Kakaramea, Otapowa, Keterimeri and Meremera (medal). At his death, 18 July 1919, Captain Harold Wilberforce Bell (576) was appointed L.F.

564. Lieutenant Colonel John Grant Anderson   1909–1926

admitted 10 March 1909 L.F. *vice* William Henry Moffat (557) (prom.). Admitted 22 September 1914 R.F. *vice* Frederick Hay Swinfen (537) (dec.). Of the 17th (the Leicestershire) Regiment. He served in the Afghan Campaign 1878-79 with the 1st Division of the Peshawar Valley Field Force, and was present at the capture of Ali Musjid, and the action at the Kabul river (medal with clasp). He took part in the Burmese Expedition 1888-89 (medal with clasp). At his death, 5 September 1926, Lieutenant Colonel Henry Hugh Rogers (579) was appointed L.F.

565. Lieutenant Colonel Arthur Campbell Money   1909–1933

Admitted 31 December 1909 L.F. *vice* Ernest Gordon Bedingfield (559) (prom.). Admitted 11 February 1915 R.F. *vice* Ernest George Bedingfield (559) (dec.). Of The Oxfordshire Light Infantry. He served in the New Zealand 1864-66, and was present at the actions of Maketu and Te Tanga (medal). At his death, 26 January 1933, Colonel Walter Willis Chitty (589) was appointed R.F

566, Lieutenant Colonel George Frend CB   1910–1923

Admitted 26 February 1910 L.F. *vice* Arthur Edward Poole (561) (prom.). Admitted 8 April 1915 R.F. *vice* Thomas George O'Donaghue Hervey (552) (dec.). Of the 5th (the Northumberland Fusiliers). He served in the Afghan War 1878-79. He commanded at the defence of the signal post at Sarkai Hill, and acted as Provost Marshal of the 2nd Brigade '2nd Division, Peshawar Valley Field Force, in the first campaign, and as transport officer to the 5th Foot in the second campaign (medal). He served in the Egyptian Campaign of 1882 (medal and bronze star), and in the Soudan Expedition 1885, Suakin (medal and clasp). Also in the South African War in command of the 2nd Battalion until February 1900, including operations in Cape Colony, south of the Orange River 1899-1900 (Queen's medal and clasp). At his death, 22 September 1923, Lieutenant Colonel Walter Edward Webb (578) was appointed R.F.

567. Quarter–Master (Hon. Major) Edward Hampton   1911–1928

Admitted 22 April 1911 L.F. *vice* Montague Cecil Broun (562) (prom.). Admitted 12 February 1916 R.F. *vice* William Henry Moffatt (557) (dec.). Of The The Hampshire Regiment. He served in the Afghan War 1879-80, including actions of Charasiah and Doaba, operations around Kabul and Sherpur (medal and two clasps). Also in the Burmese Expedition of 1885-87 (medal with clasp). Resigned in October 1921, when no appointment was made in his place. Died at Frome 22 September 1928.

568. Major–General Carteret Walter Carey CBE, MVO   1913–1932
Governor, The Military Knights of Windsor 30 September 1913

Admitted 30 September 1913 R.F. and appointed Governor of the Military Knights in succession to Edward Henry Courtney (560) (dec.). Of The Highland Light Infantry. He served as adjutant with the 2nd Battalion of the Highland Light Infantry in the Egyptian Campaign 1882, and was present at the battle of Tel-el-Kebir (medal with clasp, 4th class of the Medjidie, and Khedive's star). He was also in operations on the North-West Frontier of India, 1897-98, with the Malakand and Buner Field Force, and was present at the attack and capture of the Tanga Pass (medal with clasp). he commanded the 2nd Battalion, Highland Light Infantry from December 1900 to December 1904. He commanded No 9 Regimental District (Eastern Counties) from 1905 until his retirement in 1910. During World War 1 he was Acting Governor and Constable of Windsor Castle. At his death, 25 May 1932, Sir Charles Toler McMurrough Kavanagh (586) was appointed R.F and Governor of the Military Knights.

569. Lieutenant Colonel Thomas Langhorne Coxhead DSO, OBE 1914–1939

Admitted 22 September 1914 L.F. *vice* Edward Gould Hasted (563) (prom.). Admitted 12 February 1916 R.F. *vice* Clement Headington Dale (548) (dec.). Of the Royal Regiment of Artillery. He took part in the Burmese Expedition in 1886 and was severely wounded in an engagement at Ningyan (DSO, and medal with clasp). He served on the staff in China 1900 (medal). At his death, 15 November 1939, Edward Herbert Simpson (595) was appointed R.F.

570. Captain John Coley Coley–Bromfield 1914–1922

Admitted 22 September 1914 L.F. *vice* John Grant Anderson (564) (prom.). Admitted 11 November 1919 R.F. *vice* Edward Gould Hasted (563) (dec.). Of the Royal Regiment of Artillery. He served as adjutant with the rank of Captain in the 2nd Sussex Volunteer Artillery. At his death, 6 December 1922, Brigadier-General Cecil Burrington Norton (577) was appointed R.F

571. Lieutenant Colonel Edward Bowater McInnis 1915–Resigned

Admitted 11 February 1915 L.F. Arthur Campbell Money (565) (prom.). Of the 9th (Queen's Royal) Lancers. He served in the Afghan War 1878-80, and was present at the action of killa Kazi Sung, operations around Kabul, and the march from Kabul to Kandahar (medal with two clasps and bronze star). He served later as Inspector General of Police in British Guiana. His father, Captain Peter Mcinnis (505), was a Military Knight 1873-80. At his resignation in 1915 Lieutenant Colonel Arthur Charles Jackson (573) was appointed R.F

572. Riding Master (Hon. Major) John Morton–Marshall 1915–1920

Admitted 8 April 1915 L.F. *vice* George Frend (566) (prom.). Of the 3rd Dragoon Guards. He served in the Afghan Campaign 1878-80, including the action at Sidh Sung and the operations around Kabul (medal with clasp). At his death, 14 April 1920, no appointment was made to the Lower Foundation.

573. Lieutenant Colonel Arthur Charles Jackson 1915–1936

Admitted 25 May 1915 L.F. *vice* Edward Bowater McInnis (571) (resigned). Admitted 21 September 1920 R.F. *vice* Henry George Edward Somerset (546) (dec). Of the East Kent Regiment (the Buffs). He served in the Zulu War 1879, including the action of Inyezane and the occupation of Etshowe (medal with clasp). At his death, 2 June 1936, Colonel Austin Herbert Wightwick Hayward (593) was appointed.

574. Riding Master (Hon. Major) Albert William Waite 1916–1942

Admitted 2 June 1916 L.F. *vice* Edward Hampton (567) (prom.). Admitted 20 June 1921 R.F. *vice* Henry Francis Somerset Bolton (593) (dec.). Of the 10th (Princess of Wales's Own Royal)Hussars. He served in the South African War1899-1900 on the staff (Queen's medal with three clasps). Served in the Great War 1914-18 (promoted Lieutenant Colonel). At his death, 26 January 1942, Brigadier General Raymond Theodore Pelly (598) was appointed.

575. Lieutenant Colonel Richard Stanley Hawke Moody, CB 1919–1930

Admitted 31 October 1919 L.F. *vice* Thomas Langhorne Coxhead (569) (prom.). Admitted 20 june 1921 R.F. *vice* Charles Grantley Campbell Norton (551) (dec.). Of the East Kent Regiment (the Buffs); later of the King's Own (Royal Lancaster Regiment). He served in Griqualand East 1876, and in the Zulu War 1879 (medal and clasp), and in the Boer War 1881. Also in Chitral 1895 with the relief force, including the action of Mamagai (medal and clasp). Served on the North-West Frontier of India 1897-98 at Malakand and operations in Bajaur and in the Mahmund Country (wounded). Served in the South African War 1900-01 in command of the 2nd Royal Irish Fusiliers, as a special service officer, including operations in Orange River Colony 1900 and 1901, and on the Zululand Frantier of Natal 1901 (Queen's medal with three clasps, King's medal with two clasps, and C.B.). Served in the Great War 1914-15 in France and Belgium (British War medal and Victory medal). At his death, 11 March 1930, Lieutenant Colonel John Frederick Plunkett (583) was appointed R.F.

The Garter Ceremony 1937
By Fred Elwell

MKW in St George's Chapel: 2003
En route to the Nave via the Quire

576.   Quarter–Master (Hon. Captain) Harold Wilberforce Bell   1919–1927

Admitted 11 November 1919 *vice* John Coley Coley-Bromfield (570) (prom.). This was the last appointment to be made on the Lower Foundation. Admitted 21 March 1922 R.F *vice* Edward Hampton (567) (resigned). Of the 15th Hussars. He served in the Afghan War 1878-80, acting as Sir Donald Stewart's personal escort at Khandahar (medal). Also in the South African War 1881-82 (medal). At his death, 21 August 1927, Lieutenant Colonel James Hall Martin (580) was appointed R.F.

All appointments after this were made to the Royal Foundation, the Lower Foundation having been absorbed into it

SOLDIERS OF THE GREAT WAR

The war of 1914-18 was waged upon such an unprecedented scale that it would be unsuitable, and even misleading in relation to the services of earlier Military Knights as recorded here, to attempt to give lists of Individual battle honours. It will be sufficient to say that all appointments made since 1923 have been in recognition of distinguished services in the war, whether in France, Flanders, Italy or the Middle EaSt

577.   Lieutenant Colonel (Hon. Brigadier General) Cecil Burrington Norton   1923–1953
CMG, DSO

Admitted 2 March 1923 *vice* John Coley Coley-Bromfield (570) (dec.). Of The Duke of Cornwall's Light Infantry, and formerly of the 12th Lancers. He took part in the operations on the North-West Frontier of India 1897-99, and served with the Tirah Expeditionary Force 1897-98 (medal and two clasps). In the Great War 1914-18 he served in France Belgium and Italy, and was in command of the 95th Infantry Brigade, 5th Division, 1918 (Brevet of Lieutenant Colonel; Chevalier of the Legion of Honour, 1915 Star, British War medal, Victory medal, CMG and DSO). Died in 1953 and was succeeded by Laurence Holbech (603).

578.   Quarter–Master (Hon. Lieutenant Colonel) Walter Edward Webb DSO   1923–1934

Admitted 28 December 1923 *vice* (566) (dec.). Of The King's Own Scottish Borderers. He served in the Afghan War 1878-79, including actions at Kam Daka, Jellalabad, Kabul Pass and Lughman Valley (medal). Also in the Burmese War 1889-90, and the Chin Lushai Expedition (medal and clasp). He served in the South African War 1899-1902, including the actions at Vaal River, Modder River and the relief of Mafeking; operations west of Pretoria, Orange River Colony, the relief of Koffyfontein and the occupation of Jacobsdaal, Boshoff and V ryburg (Queen's medal with three clasps, King's medal with two clasps). He served in the Great War 1914-18 in France and Belgium (1914 Star and clasp, British War medal, Victory medal, DSO). At his death, 24 June 1934, Lieutenant Colonel Bryan Turner Tom Lawrence (591) was appointed.

579.   Lieutenant Colonel Henry Hugh Rogers DSO   1927–1932

Admitted 15 January 1927 *vice* John Grant Anderson (564) (dec.). Of the Royal Field Artillery. He served in the Afghan War 1879-80 (medal), and in the expedition against the Mahsud Waziris in 1881 (medal). Also in the Egyptian Campaign in 1882 in command of the 7th Division Ammunition Column (medal and bronze star). He served in the Great War 1914-18 in France and Belgium (1914-15 Star, British War medal, Victory medal, DSO). At his death, 17 December 1932, Lieutenant Colonel Christopher Lefroy Hodgson (588) was appointed.

580.   Lieutenant Colonel James Hall Martin DSO, MC   1927–1932

Admitted 3 November 1927 *vice* Harold Wilberforce Bell (576). Of the King's Own (Royal Lancaster Regiment) and formerly of the Royal Scots. He served in the South African War 1899-1902, including operations in the Transvaal, East of Pretoria and the action at Belfast; operations in Cape Colony and the Orange River Colony (Queen's medal with three clasps). Also in the Great War 1914-1918 in France and Belgium in the command of the T.F. (Territorial Force) of the Durham Light Infantry from 1917 (wounded; 1914 Star and clasp, British War medal, Victory medal, Medaille Militaire, DSO, MC). Occupied No 8 Lower Ward. Died 30 July 1932 and is buried in Windsor Cemetery. He was succeeded by Lieutenant Colonel Richard Pennell (587)

581.   Major Arthur Frederick Rowan Colquhoun   **1929–1944**

Admitted 30 July 1929 *vice* Montagu McPherson Battye (545) (dec.). Of the The Oxfordshire Light Infantry. he served with the Leicestershire Regiment in the South African War 1899-1902, operations in the Otange River Free State 1900, operations at Paardeburg (wounded). Afterwards temporarily attached to the Army Service Corps, he was present at operations in the Transvaal 1901-02; operations in Orange River Colony 1902 (Queen's medal with four clasps, King's medal with two clasps). He served in the Great War 1915-17 (wounded) (British War medal, Victory medal). He served in Ireland as second in command of his battalion during the Rebellion 1920-22. Died 4 April 1944

582.   Colonel (Hon. Brigadier–General) Cranley Charlton Onslow CB CMG CBE DSO 1930–1940

Admitted 30 January 1930 vice Montague Cecil Broun (562) (dec). Formerly of The Bedfordshire Regiment. He took part in the Isazai Expedition 1892, and served with the Chitral Relief Force under Sir Robert Low 1895 (medal with clasp). He served in the great War 1914-18 in France and Belgium in command of a battalion of the Bedfordshire Regiment (wounded). Afterwards on the Staff as brigade commander from 1916. 1914-15 Star, British War Medal, Victory Medal, CMG., CBE., DSO., Croix de Guerre with palm. Died 16 December 1940 and succeeded by John Alexander Fraser (597).

583.   Lieutenant Colonel James Frederick Plunkett DSO, MC, DCM   **1930–1953**

Admitted 8 May 1930 *vice* Richard Stanley Hawk Moody (575) (dec.). Born 7 March 1877. Enlisted in the Royal Inniskilling Fusiliers in 1896. Rose to the rank of Warrant Officer Class 1. Commissioned from the ranks 23 May 1915. Transferred to the Royal Dublin Fusiliers 23 December 1917. Served in France and Belgium in the Great War 1914-1918. Commanded (1) 19th (5th) Battalion of the Royal Welsh Fusiliers and (2) 13th (5th) Battalion the Royal Inniskilling Fusiliers. Transferred to the East Lancashire Regiment 12-10-1920. He lived in No 9 Lower Ward until 31st March 1947 when, with the permission of the King, he was allowed to leave the Castle for health reasons and live in a house he had purchased in Southwick, Sussex. He remained on the establishment of the Military Knights until his death on 16 September 1953. While living in Southwick, he was allowed to let No 9 Lower Ward to a Miss Hanbury Williams for £100 per annum. Medals, 1914-15 Star, British War Medal, Victory Medal, DSO with 2 bars, MC, DCM, French Croix de Guerre, Mentioned in Despatches 5 times. No record where he is buried. Succeeded by Francis Clere Hitchcock (604).

584.   Lieutenant Colonel John Henry Willis Southey OBE   **1930–1931**

Admitted 21 November 1930 *vice* Arthur Edward Poole (561) (dec.). Of The Princess Charlotte of Wales's (Royal Berkshire Regiment), He served in the Soudan Expedition 1885 at Suakin; also at the reconnaissance to Hasheen; actions at Hasheen and Tofrek; operations and destruction of Tamai (medal with two clasps, Bronze Star). Also in the Soudan 1885-86, with the Frontier Field Force, and present at the action of Giniss. He served in the South African War 1899-1902, performing duties of railway staff officer, Belfast; afterwards acting as district and station commandant. He took part in the operations in the Transvaal, East of Pretoria to November 1900; in the Transvaal West of Pretoria 1900, including the action of Zilikrats Nek; in the Orange River 1900; in the Transvaal 1900-01; Cape Co;ony 1901-02 (Queen's medal with three clasps, King's medal with two clasps). At his death 11 July 1931, Brigadier-General Edward Heneage Finch-Hatton (585) was appointed.

585.   Brigadier General Edward Heneage Finch–Hatton CMG, DSO   **1931–1940**

Admitted 1 October 1931 *vice* John Henry Willis Southey (584) (dec.). Of the East Kent Regiment (the Buffs). He served in the South African War 1899-1902, and was present at the Relief of Kimberley, operations in the Orange River State, including operations at Paarddeburg, operations at Poplar Grove and Dreifontein. Operations East of Pretoria 1900; operations in Orange River Colony (Queen's medal with four clasps, King's medal with two clasps, DSO). Also in the Great War 1914-17, France and Belgium, (wounded). On the Staff as Brigade Commander 1916-17 (1914 Star, British War medal, Victory medal, CMG). At his death, 22 May 1941, Lieutenant Colonel Louis William la Trobe Cockraft (596) was appointed.

586.   Lieutenant General Sir Charles Toler McMurrough Kavanagh   **1932–1950**
KCB, KCMG, CVO, DSO
Governor, The Military Knights of Windsor 29 July 1932

Admitted 29 July 1932 and appointed Governor of the Military Knights *vice* Carteret Walter Carey (568) (dec.). Formerly of the 10th (Princess of Wales's Own Royal) Hussars. He served in the South African War 1899-1902, and took part in operations in the Orange Free State 1900, including actions at Poplar Grove, Dreifontein, Houtnek (Thoba Mountain), Vet River and Zand River, operations in the Transvaal, West of Pretoria 1900, including the action at Wittebergen; operations in the Transvaal 1901 and in Cape Colony 1901-02 (in command of the mobile column). In command of the 10th Royal Hussars from 19 October 1901 (Queen's medal with five clasps, King's medal with two clasps, DSO). He commanded the 1st Cavalry Brigade 1909-13. He served in the Great War 1914-18 (wounded; promoted Major General); 7th Cavalry Brigade, 2nd Cavalry Division, 5th Division, 1st Army Corps, Cavalry Corps. (CB 1909, KCB 1917, KCMG 1919, MVO 1906, CVO 1909, Legion of Honour 3rd Class, Croix de Guerre, Order of St Maurice and St Lazarus of Italy; 1914 Star and clasp, British War medal, Victory medal). Died 20 October 1950.

587.   Lieutenant Colonel Richard Pennell DSO   **1933–1963**
Admitted 11 January 1933 *vice* James Hall Martin (580). (dec.). He served in the Great War in command of the 18th Battalion of The King's Royal Rifle Corps in France (wounded). From 1917 he was engaged in Italy with the same Battalion and returned to France in 1918 (again wounded). After hostilities ceased he was promoted into the Oxford and Buckinghamshire Light Infantry shortly before being invalided out (DSO and bar, 1914 Star, British War medal, Victory medal). Died 13 July 1963. Succeeded by Arthur Ainslie Crook (611)

588.   Lieutenant Colonel Christopher Lefroy Hodgson   **1933–1965**
Admitted 27 February 1933 *vice* Henry Hugh Rogers (579) (dec.). He served with The King's Own (Royal Lancaster Regiment) in the Great War 1914-18, in France and Belgium (wounded) (1914 Star and clasp, British War medal, Victory medal). Died 28 November 1965. Succeeded by Robert Walsh Dobbin (615). Occupied No 14 Lower Ward.

589.   Colonel Walter Willis Chitty CMG, CIE, CVO   **1933**
Admitted 9 May 1933 *vice* Arthur Campbell Money (565) (dec.). Of the Indian Army. He served in British East Africa 1898, including operations against the Ogaden Somalis, and in Uganda 1898-99 in operations against Kaborega (medal and two clasps). He served in the Great War 1914-18, in Iraq 1914-16; taken prisoner at the fall of Kut (Brevet of Colonel, CMG, CIE, Croix de Guerre, 1914 Star, British War medal, Victory medal). At his death, 11 July 1933, Colonel Henry Townsend Corbett Singleton (590) was appointed.

590.   Colonel Henry Townsend Corbett Singleton CMG, DSO   **1933–1934**
Admitted 24 October 1933 *vice* Walter Willis Chitty (589) (dec.). Of the Highland Light Infantry. He served in the South African War 1899-1901 (slightly wounded) as a Special Service Officer , including service as adjutant of the Bechuanaland Protectorate Regiment 1900 (This Regiment fought in the siege of Mafeking). Afterwards on the staff. (Queen's medal with three clasps, King's medal with two clasps, DSO). Served in the great War 1914-18 in France and Belgium. On the staff as (1) DAA & QMG, 1915-16; and (2) AA & QMG from 1916 (wounded; Brevet of Lieutenant Colonel, Legion of Honour 5th class, 1914 Star and clasp, British War medal, Victory medal, CMG). At his death, 9 November 1934, Major Henry Kenny Clough (592) was appointed.

591.   Lieutenant Colonel Bryan Turner Tom Lawrence VC   **1934–38 (Resigned)**
Admitted 12 October 1934 *vice* Edward Webb(578) (dec.). Of the 18th Royal Hussars (Queen Mary's Own). He served in the South African War, 1899-1902. He was awarded the Victoria Cross for an act of great bravery on the 7 August 1900 at Essenbosch Farm, South Africa. As a Sergeant serving with the 17th Lancers, when his comrade, Private Hayman, he was riding with was wounded and his horse shot under him while attacked by a party of twelve to fourteen Boers, He put the man on his own horse and sent him back to safety, whilst he held off the enemy. He then retired on foot for two miles, keeping the enemy at bay until assistance arrived. Queen's Medal with five clasps. Served in the Great war 1914-18 in France and Belgium on the Staff Captain

and as Brigade Major; 1914 Star and Clasp, British War medal and the Victory medal. He served on the General Staff, Eastern Expeditionary Force 1919, and on the General Staff, Iraq Levies 1923-24. He commanded a mobile Column in operations in East Kurdistan 1925-26. At his resignation in 1938 Reginald Heaton Locke Cutbill (594) was appointed. He died on 7 June 1949 at Nakuru, Kenya. He was cremated and there is no memorial or tablet

592.   Major Henry Kenny Clough OBE   **1935–1970**
Admitted 29 January 1935 *vice* Henry Townsend Corbett Singleton (590) (dec.). He occupied No 7 Lower Ward. Of the King's Own (Royal Lancaster Regiment) and formerly of The Highland Light Infantry. He served in the South African War 1899-1902, including operations in the Transvaal in 1900; operations in Natal 1900, including Laing's Nek; operations in the Transvaal 1900-1902 (Queen's medal with two clasps, King's medal with two clasps). He served in the Great war 1914-18; France and Belgium 1915 (wounded). (1914 Star, British War Medal, Victory Medal, O.B.E.). Major Clough features in a book, 'The Kiss' by Hugo Vickers which gives a description of his death and funeral. It is reported that the Governor MKW forgot to order a bugler for the funeral, so there was no 'Last Post ' or 'Reveille'. He also features in a painting, hanging in the Vicar's Hall showing the West steps of St George's Chapel at the end of the Garter Service. He died 10 September 1970. He was succeeded by Charles Arthur Harvey (618)

593.   Colonel Austin Hubert Wightwick Haywood CMG, CBE, DSO   **1936–1965**
Admitted 29 October 1936 *vice* Arthur Charles Jackson (573) (dec.). Of the Royal Regiment of Artillery. He served in West Africa (Southern Nigeria) 1905-06, including operations in the Kwale-Ishan district. He commanded a Field Column in Kamarun 1914-16. He served in the Great War in France 1917-18 (Brevet Lieutenant Colonel; 1914-15 Star, British War medal, Victory medal, CMG, DSO, Croix de Guerre, Legion of Hon our). Died 28 March 1965. Occupied No 10 Lower Ward. Succeeded by Lieutenant Colonel Harry Graham Duncombe (614)

594.   Colonel Reginald Heaton Locke Cutbill CMG, DSO, Legion of Honour   **1938**
Admitted 2 October 1938 *vice* Bryan Turner Tom Lawrence (591) (Res.). Of the Royal Army Service Corps. He served in the Matabel campaign in 1896 (medal) and in the South African War 1899 - 1902 including operations in the Transvaal and in the Transvaal West of Pretoria 1900; operations in Cape Colony, north and south of the Orange River (Queen's Medal with three clasps, King's Medal with two clasps). He served in the Great War 1914-18 in France and Belgium. (1914 Star, British War medal, Victory medal, CMG, DSO, Legion of Honour).

595 .   Major Edward Herbert Simpson OBE, MC   **1940–1955**
Admitted 27 June 1940 *vice* Thomas Langhorne Coxhead (569) (dec.). He served in the South African War 1899-1902 with the South African Light Horse, including operations in Cape Colony, south of the Orange River 1899. He was present at the Relief of Ladysmith, including the action at Liang's Nek; operations in Orange River Colony 1902 (Queen's medal with six clasps, King's Medal with clasp). He served in the Great War 1914-18 in France and Flanders with the King's Regiment (wounded). He was awarded the OBE. and the MC. He had the 1914 Star, British War Medal and the Victory Medal.

596.   Lieutenant Colonel Louis William la Trobe Cockcraft DSO   **1940–1963**
Admitted 9 December 1940 *vice* Edward Heneage Finch-Hatton (585) (dec.). Of the Royal Field Artillery. He served in the South African War 1900-02 including operations in the Orange Free State 1900; operations in the Transvaal, East of Pretoria 1900; operations in the Orange River, 1900. Served in the Intelligence Department 1902 (Queen's medal with three clasps, King's medal with two clasps). Also in operations in West Africa 1906-08, and in the Great War 1914-18, at the Suez Canal 1914; Cape Helles, Gallipoli 1915-16 (dso), France 1916-18 (1914 Star, British War medal, Victory medal, Belgian Croix de Guerre, Brevet Lieutenant Colonel). Died 15 April 1963 and succeeded by Lieutenant Colonel George Frederick Goodwin Turner (610). Occupied No 8 Lower Ward

597.   Colonel John Alexander Fraser DSO, DCM   **1941–1962**

Admitted 10 May 1941 *vice* Cranley Charlton Onslow (582) (dec.). Of the 2nd Dragoon Guards (Royal Scots Greys). he served in the South African War 1900-02, and in the Great War 1914-15 with the Queen's Bays and 1917-18 in command of the 5/6 Royal Scots (severely wounded). (British War medal, Victory medal, DCM, DSO and two bars, Croix de Guerre, Brevet Lieutenant Colonel). Died 1962 and was succeeded by William Parr Aldous Robinson (608). Occupied No 19 Lower Ward.

598.   Brigadier General Raymond Theodore Pelly CB, CMG, DSO   **1942–1952**

Admitted 12 June 1942 *vice* William Albert Wait ((574) (dec.). Of the Loyal Regiment (North Lancashire). He served in the South African War 1900-01, including operations in the Transvaal West of Pretoria 1900; operations in the Orange Free State 1900, and actions at Lindley and Rhenoster River; operations in Cape Colony 1901 (Queen's medal with four clasps). He served in the Great War 1914-18. In command successively of the 8th Royal Irish Rifles (Ulster Division), Princess Patricia's Canadian Light Infantry and the 91st Infantry Brigade (7th Division) in France and Belgium and in Italy. (Brevet Major, Brevet Lieutenant Colonel, 1914 Star, British War medal, Victory medal, CB, CMG, DSO and bar, Italian Croce di Guerra, Order of St Maurice and St Lazarus of Italy, Died 28 June 1952. Occupied No 4. During the Second World War, as a Military Knight of Windsor, he acted as adjutant to 8th Battalion The Berkshire Home Guard. He also maintained a diary from 1942 to 1952 some extract from which feature in this history.

Brigadier Pelly was the last to be appointed during the Second World War

599   Major Douglas Philip Jervoise Collas   **1946–1955**

Appointed 3 August 1946 *vice* Colonel R H L Cutbill (594) (resigned). Commissioned in The Loyal Regiment (North Lancashire) 1906. He served in South Africa 1906-09; India 1909-14; East Africa 1914-17; Egypt and Palestine 1917-19. 1914-15 Star, British War and Victory Medals, 1939-45 Defence and War Medals, Order of the Nile 4th Class 1919 and was twice Mentioned in Despatches. Occupied No. 16. He died 29 December 1955 aged 69 and was succeeded by Lieutenant Colonel E P O Boyle (607)

600   Major (Hon. Lieutenant Colonel) John Munro Mackenzie DSO   **1946–1964**

Appointed 16^{t} December 1946 *vice* Major A F R Colquhoun 581 (dec.). Commissioned in The Argyll and Sutherland Highlanders 1900 and transferred to The Royal Scots 1903. He served in South Africa 1900-02; India 1902-10; with King's African Rifles, Somaliland and East Africa 1910-15; with The Royal Scots, France (wounded) and Salonika 1915-18. DSO, South Africa (Queen's Medal) and South Africa (King's Medal), 1914-15 Star, British War and Victory Medals, 1939-45 Defence and War Medals, Queen Elizabeth II Coronation Medal and was Mentioned in Despatches. Occupied No. 3. He died 12 March 1964 aged 81 and was succeeded by Lieutenant Colonel L W Giles (613)

601   Major General Sir Edmund Hakewill Smith KCVO, CB, CBE, MC, JP.   **1951–1980**
Governor of the Military Knights of Windsor

Appointed Governor of the Military Knights of Windsor 1951 *vice* Lieutenant-General Sir Charles T McM. Kavanagh (586) (dec.). He was mobilised with the South African Defence Force, 1914, but given a Colonial Nomination to the Royal Military College, Sandhurst. Commissioned in The Royal Scots Fusiliers in 1915. He served in France and Germany 1915-18 (wounded twice); Constantinople 1920; India 1921-23: Regimental Duties, Staff College and staff 1924-40. He was CO 5th Battalion, The Devonshire Regiment TA (MG), CO 4th/5th Battalion, The Royal Scots Fusiliers and commanded 157th (Highland) Infantry Brigade all in 1941; Director of Organisation, War Office 1942; commanded 155th Infantry Brigade 1943; GOC. 52nd (Lowland) Division, TA throughout operations in Holland and Germany 1943-45; GOC. Lowland District and 52nd Lowland Division TA 1946-49. He was Colonel of The Royal Scots Fusiliers 1946-57 and a JP in Windsor. KCVO, CB, CBE, MC, 1914-15 Star, British War and Victory Medals, 1939-45 North West Europe Star, Defence and War Medals, Queen Elizabeth II Coronation Medal, Silver Jubilee Medal, Order of St Olaf second class, Grand Officer of the Order of Orange - Nassau and was three times Mentioned in Despatches. Occupied

Mary Tudor Tower. Retired 1980 and was succeeded by Major General Sir Peter Gillett (626). Died 15 April 1986 aged 90 at Hampton Court

602   Colonel Alexander Smith Turnham OBE 1953–1954

Appointed 6 February 1953 *vice* Brigadier R T Pelly (598) (dec). Enlisted in the 10th Royal Hussars (Prince of Wales's Own) 1905 and commissioned in that Regiment 1915. Attached Machine Gun Corps 1915-21 and served in France and Belgium 1917-18. Officer i/c RAC Records 1938-40. OBE, 1914-18 British War and Victory Medals, 1939-45 Defence and War Medals. Occupied No. 4. He died 4 January 1954 aged 68 and was succeeded by Lieutenant Colonel R F Squibb 605

603   Lieutenant Colonel Laurence Holbech CVO, DSO, OBE, MC 1953–1963

Born 6 March 1888, 2nd son of Canon Hugh Holbech. Married Francis Betty Eleanor Clayton 29 June 1943. Son Timothy Charles born 30th January 1950. Appointed 1953 *vice* Brigadier General C B Norton (577) (dec). Commissioned in the Grenadier Guards 1916. He served in France and Flanders 1916-18 (gassed). He was ADC. to GOC. London District 1918; ADC. to Governor of Ceylon 1921-31; Private Secretary and ADC. High Commissioner for the U.K. 1931-35; ADC to the Governor of Southern Rhodesia 1937-47. CVO, DSO. OBE., MC, 1914-18 British War and Victory Medals and Mentioned in Despatches. Occupied No. 18. He died 12 October 1963 aged 75 and was succeeded by Lieutenant-Colonel R.J.L. Penfold (612)

604   Captain (Hon. Lieutenant Colonel) Francis Clere Hitchcock OBE, MC 1954–1962

Appointed 27 May 1954 *vice* Lieutenant Colonel J F Plunkett (583) (dec). Commissioned in The Prince of Wales's Leinster Regiment (Royal Canadians) 1915 and transferred to The East Surrey Regiment 1922. He served in France and Belgium (gassed); India 1919-29. Retired on medical grounds 1929. OBE, MC, 1914-15 Star, British War and Victory Medals, India General Service Medal (clasp Malabar), 1939-45 Defence and War Medals. Occupied No. 9. He died 6 July 1962 aged 76 in Beaconsfield where he had moved by special permission whilst remaining a Military Knight and was succeeded by Major T W Garnett (609)

605   Captain & Brevet Major (Hon. Lieutenant Colonel) Reginald Frederick Squibb MC 1954–1977

Appointed 26 June 1954 *vice* Colonel A S Turnham (602) (dec). Enlisted in The Royal Hampshire Regiment 1909 and commissioned in The Loyal Regiment (North Lancashire) 1916. He served in South Africa and Mauritius 1909-14; France and Belgium 1914-16 (wounded); East Africa and Northern Rhodesia 1917-18; staff duties AA Command 1939-46. MC, 1914 Star and Clasp, British War and Victory Medals, General Service Medal, 1939-45 Defence and War Medals and was twice Mentioned in Despatches. Occupied No. 4. but moved to No. 15 on his second marriage in 1955. He died 15 May 1977 aged 86 and was succeeded by Brigadier J F Lindner (623)

606   Colonel (Hon. Brigadier) Edward Keith Byrne Furze DSO, OBE, MC 1955–1971

Appointed 3 March 1955 *vice* Major E H Simpson (595) (dec). Enlisted The Queen's Regiment (Special Reserve) 1908 and commissioned in The Queen's Royal Regiment (West Surrey) 1912. He served in Bermuda and South Africa 1912-14; France and Belgium 1914-18 (wounded three times, the last time severely whilst commanding 1st Battalion, The Wiltshire Regiment and taken prisoner). Transferred to the Royal Army Educational Corps 1920 and served in India 1939-41; Egypt 1941-43. DSO, OBE, MC, 1914 Star and Clasp, British War and Victory Medals, 1939-45 Star, Africa Star, Defence and War Medals and six times Mentioned in Despatches. Occupied No. 4. He died 23 October 1971 aged 81 and was succeeded by Lieutenant-Colonel A J Spratley (620)

607   Lieutenant Colonel Edward Patrick Ogilvie Boyle MVO 1956–1966

Appointed 1 March 1956 *vice* Major D P J Collas (599) (dec). Commissioned in The Royal Scots Fusiliers 1913. He served in Gibraltar 1913; France and Belgium 1914-18; prisoner of war 1918; Repatriation Commission, Holland 1919; Constantinople 1920-21. He was ADC to the Governor of Bengal 1921-26 and Military Secretary to the Governor-General of New Zealand 1926-30. MVO 4th Class, 1914 Star and Clasp, British War and Victory Medals, General Service Medal (clasp Palestine), 1939-45 Star, Burma Star, Defence and War

Medals. Occupied No. 16. He died 7 December 1966 aged 73 and was succeeded by Lieutenant-Colonel P U Campbell (616)

608   Lieutenant–Colonel (Hon. Brigadier) William Parr Aldous Robinson MC   1962–1978

Appointed 5 April 1962 *vice* Colonel J A Fraser (597) (dec). Commissioned in the Royal Artillery 1915. He served in France 1915-16 (wounded) and as a Pilot Officer, Royal Flying Corps 1917-18; Sudan (Egyptian Army, Bimbashi) 1922-26. He commanded the Cheshire Royal Horse Artillery, North Africa 1940-42 and was CRA 19th Indian Division, India and Burma 1942-44. Wounded three times. MC, 1914-1915 Star, British War and Victory Medals, 1939-45 Star, Africa Star, Burma Star, Defence and War Medals, Queen Elizabeth II Silver Jubilee Medal, the Order of the Nile and was three times Mentioned in Despatches. Occupied No. 19. He died 6 April 1978 aged 81 and was succeeded by Brigadier A C Tyler (624)

609   Major Thomas William Garnett MBE   1962–1976

Appointed 2 August 1952 *vice* Lieutenant-Colonel F C Hitchcock 604 (dec). Enlisted in the Grenadier Guards 1911 and commissioned as Quartermaster 1940. He served in France 1914; Turkey 1922-23; Egypt 1936-37; France 1940; France and Germany 1944-45. He served as Camp Commandant, Garrison Adjutant and Staff Captain 1945-50. M.B.E., 1914 Star and Clasp, British War and Victory Medals, 1939-45 Star, France and Germany Star, Defence and War Medals, King George V Silver Jubilee Medal, King George VI Coronation Medal, Long Service and Good Conduct Medal with Bar and Meritorious Service Medal. Occupied No. 9. He died 18 February 1976 and was succeeded by Major A E Woolaston 621

610   Major (Hon. Lieutenant–Colonel) George Frederick Goodwin Turner OBE, DCM. 1963–1968

Appointed 10ᵗ July 1963 *vice* Lieutenant-Colonel L W La T Cockraft (596) (dec). Enlisted in the Grenadier Guards 1915 and commissioned as Quartermaster 1939. He served in France, Flanders and Germany 1916-19; Egpyt 1922-23; France 1939-40; North Africa 1942-43; Germany 1944-45: OBE, DCM, 1914-18 British War and Victory Medals, 1939-45 Star, Africa Star, France and Germany Star, Defence and War Medals, King George V Silver Jubilee Medal, Kind George VI Coronation Medal, Queen Elizabeth II Coronation Medal, Meritorious Service Medal, Long Service and Good Conduct Medal, and Croix de Guerre. Occupied No. 8. He died 12 October 1968 aged 70 and was succeeded by Major H Smith (617)

611   Brigadier Arthur Ainslie Crook DSO   1963–1981

Appointed 11 October 1963 *vice* Lieutenant Colonel R Pennell (587) (dec). Commissioned in the Royal Artillery 1918 and transferred to The Northamptonshire Regiment 1930. He served with the King's African Rifles, Tanganyika 1926-31; India 1933-35; as Brigade Major SSVF (Singapore) 1939-42; CO 5th Battalion, The Northamptonshire Regiment, North Africa 1942-43; commanded 6th (West African) Brigade, Burma 1944-46. He was Colonel G.S. British Military Mission, Greece 1947, commanded Cyprus Brigade District and was Military Attaché, Siam 1950-52. DSO, 1914-18 British War and Victory Medals, 1939-45 Star, Africa Star, Burma Star, Defence and War Medals, Queen Elizabeth II Silver Jubilee Medal, Gold and Silver Greek Military Crosses and was three times Mentioned in Despatches. Occupied No. 17. He died 1 February 1981 aged 81 and was succeeded by Major J C Cowley (628)

612   Lieutenant Colonel Richard John Linzee Penfold   1964–1982

Appointed 15 January 1964 *vice* Lieutenant-Colonel L Holbech (603) (dec). Commissioned in the Royal Artillery 1916. He served in Egypt 1917-18; France and Germany 1919; Gibraltar 1920-27; India 1936-38; Hong Kong 1939 and then as a prisoner of war 1941-45. 1914-18 British War and Victory Medals, 1937 India General Service Medal (clasp North West Frontier), 1939-45 Star, Pacific Star, Defence and War Medals, Queen Elizabeth II Silver Jubilee Medal. Occupied No.18. He died 12 July 1982 aged 83 and was succeeded by Brigadier C J Codner (629)

613   Major (Hon. Lieutenant Colonel) Leslie William Giles OBE, MC   1964–1976

Appointed 1 July 1964 *vice* Lieutenant Colonel J M MacKenzie 600 (dec). Commissioned in The Oxfordshire and Buckinghamshire Light Infantry (43rd and 52nd) 1915. He served in France and Belgium 1916-18; North

Russia 1919; North West Frontier, India 1926-27. He commanded the Airborne Forces Depot and School 1943-44 and was Group Commander, Royal Pioneer Corps in France, Belgium, Holland and Germany 1944-46. OBE, MC and Bar, 1914-18 British War and Victory Medals, 1939-45 Star, France and Germany Star, Defence and War Medals and the Cadet Forces Medal and was twice Mentioned in Despatches. Occupied No 3. He died 21 November 1976 aged 79 and was succeeded by Brigadier A L Atkinson (622)

614   Lieutenant Colonel (Hon. Colonel) Harry Graham Duncombe, DSO   1965–1980
Appointed 9^t June 1965 *vice* Colonel A H W. Haywood (593) (dec). Enlisted in the Scots Guards 1916 and was commissioned in The Queen's Royal Regiment (West Surrey) 1926. Transferred to The East Surrey Regiment. He commanded 2nd Battalion, The Queen's Regiment 1943; 1st Battalion, The Queen's Regiment in Burma 1943-44; 1st/5th Battalion, The Queen's Regiment in Berlin 1945; 1st/6th Battalion, The Queen's Regiment in Lebanon and Palestine 1946; 2nd Battalion, The East Surrey Regiment in Palestine and Egypt 1947-48. Commander West Rhine (Colonel) 1949-52. DSO, General Service Medal (two clasps), 1939-45 Star, Africa Star, Burma Star, Defence and War Medals, Queen Elizabeth II Silver Jubilee Medal and was Mentioned in Despatches. Occupied No 10. He died 29 November 1980 aged 78 and was succeeded by Major L W Dickerson (627)

615   Major (Hon. Lieutenant Colonel) Robert Wakeham Dobbin OBE   1966–1989
Appointed 29 April 1966 *vice* Lieutenant Colonel C L Hodgson 588 (dec). Commissioned in the Royal Artillery 1921. He served in Gibraltar 1921-25; India 1926-31 and 1933-37; France 1940; GHQ Far East, South West Pacific and British Mission, Java 1941-42; prisoner of war, Java and Japan 1942-45. OBE, 1939-45 Star, Pacific Star, Defence and War Medals, Queen Elizabeth II Silver Jubilee Medal and was Mentioned in Despatches. Occupied No 14. He died 7 August 1989 and was succeeded by Major P H Bolton (634)

616   Lieutenant–Colonel Patrick Usmar Campbell DSO   1968–1970
Appointed 7 May 1968 *vice* Lieutenant-Colonel E P O Boyle (607) (dec). Commissioned in The Highland Light Infantry 1925. He served with 3rd Battalion, The King's African Rifles 1928-31; Malta 1931; Egypt 1936; France 1939-40; Dakar Operation 1940; Iceland 1941. He commanded 2nd Glasgow Highlanders, France 1944; the Fieldcraft and Mountain Wing, School of Infantry 1944-45; was GSO1 Singapore District 1945-47 and commanded 5th/6th Battalion, The Highland Light Infantry 1948-52. DSO, 1939-45 Star, North West Europe Star, War and Defence Medals and General Service Medal (clasp Malaya). Occupied No 16. He died 27^t October 1970 and was succeeded by Lieutenant Colonel A R Clark (619)

617   Major Herbert Smith MBE, RVM   1969–1990
Appointed 31 January 1969 *vice* Lieutenant Colonel G F G Turner (610) (dec). Enlisted in the Scots Guards 1920 and commissioned Quartermaster 1946. He was Staff Captain 32nd Guards Brigade, Cyprus and Egypt 1952-54; War Office, Special Duties (Intelligence) 1954. Awarded MBE for services in formation of 5th (Ski) Battalion, Scots Guards. MBE, RVM. (Silver), 1939-45 Defence and War Medals, King George VI Coronation Medal, Queen Elizabeth II Silver Jubilee Medal, Meritorious Service Medal and Long Service and Good Conduct Medal with Bar. Occupied No 8. Died 24 November 1990. Succeeded by Lieutenant-Colonel H F Rogers (635)

618   Major (Hon. Lieutenant Colonel) Charles Arthur Harvey   1971–1986
Appointed 8 February 1971 *vice* Major H K Clough (592) (dec). Commissioned in The Highland Light Infantry 1926. He served in Malta 1929-31; as ADC to the Captain-General and Commander in Chief, Jamaica 1934-36; India 1936-38; Palestine 1938-40; Eritrea 1940-42; North West Europe 1944-46 (wounded); and as GSO1 Physical Training, BAOR. 1949-54. India General Service Medal (clasp Waziristan), General Service Medal (clasp Palestine), 1939-45 Star, Africa Star, North West Europe Star, Defence and War Medals, Queen Elizabeth II Silver Jubilee Medal. Occupied No 11. He retired as a Military Knight of Windsor on medical grounds 1986 and died 4 March 1987. He was succeeded by Major G R Mitchell (631)

619   Major (Hon. Lieutenant Colonel) Alfred Reeves Clark MC   **1971–1987**

Appointed 26 May 1971 *vice* Lieutenant-Colonel P U Campbell (616) (dec). Enlisted in The Life Guards 1925, commissioned in The Royal Leicestershire Regiment 1940 and seconded to The Parachute Regiment 1941-48. He served in North West Europe 1944-45 (wounded); Egypt and Aqaba 1948-52. Various staff appointments with 1st and 6th Airborne Divisions and Airborne Forces HQ MC, 1939-45 Star, France and Germany Star, Defence and War Medals, Queen Elizabeth II Silver Jubilee Medal, Long Service and Good Conduct Medal. He was ordained Deacon (Church of England 1955 and Priest 1957; served as a Missionary in West Pakistan 1956-64; Chaplain H.M. Prisons, Liverpool 1964 and Parkhurst 1965-69. Occupied No 16. He retired on 16th March 1987 and was appointed a Supernumerary Military Knight of Windsor by H M The Queen; the first known case of such an appointment. He was succeeded by Lieutenant Colonel R L C Tamplin (632). He died 9 January 1992

620   Lieutenant Colonel Arthur James Spratley MBE, MM   **1973–1978**

Appointed 8 August *vice* Brigadier E K B Furze (606) (dec). Enlisted in the Grenadier Guards 1926 and commissioned Quartermaster 1949. He served in Egypt 1933-36; France and Belgium 1939-40; Germany 1944-45; Palestine and North Africa 1948-49; North Africa and Egypt 1951-54. MBE, MM, 1939-45 Star, France and Germany Star, Defence, War and Medals, General Service Medal (clasp Palestine), Queen Elizabeth II Silver Jubilee Medal, Meritorious Service Medal and Long Service and Good Conduct Medal. Occupied No 7. He died 4 October 1978 aged 68 and was succeeded by Major W L Thompson (625)

621   Captain (Hon. Major) Arthur Ernest Wollaston MVO   **1976–1991**

Appointed 12 November 1976 *vice* Major T W Garnett (609) (dec). Enlisted in the Royal Engineers 1926 and commissioned 1945. He served in the British Expeditionary Force 1939-40; Middle East 1940-42; Italy 1942; Prisoner of war 1942-45. He was District Works Officer, Windsor Castle from 1968-76. MVO, 1939-45 Star, North Africa Star, Defence and War Medals, Queen Elizabeth II Silver Jubilee Medal. Occupied No 6. He died 26 December 1991 and was succeeded by Major R J Moore (637)

622   Brigadier Arthur Leslie Atkinson OBE   **1977–1999**

Appointed 26 September 1977 *vice* Lieutenant Colonel L W Giles (613) (dec). Commissioned in the Royal Corps of Signals 1935 (Seniority 1932, University Candidate). Seconded to The King's African Rifles 1938-42. He served in East Africa, India and Burma 1939-45; Staff College, Quetta 1943; British Mission Prague 1946-47; Malaya 1947-49; Korea 1951-52; Joint Services Staff College 1953; GSO 1 Joint Planning Staff (Ministry of Defence) 1953-55; Hong Kong 1956-58; Colonel GS.Allied Land Forces Central Europe 1958-59; NATO Military Standing Group (London and Washington DC) 1959-62; CSO Southern Command 1962-64. Honorary Colonel TA. OBE, 1939-45 Star, Africa Star, Burma Star, Defence and War Medals, General Service Medal (clasp Malaya), Korean Medal, United Nations Medal (Korea), Czechoslovakia Military Cross and was Mentioned in Despatches. Occupied No 9. Died 16 August 1999 and was succeeded by Colonel B E Colston (642)

623   Colonel (Hon. Brigadier) John Frederick Lindner OBE, MC   **1977–2004**

Appointed 2 November 1977 *vice* Lieutenant Colonel R F Squibb (605) (dec). Commissioned in the Royal Artillery 1932. He served in Malta 1935-36; Gold Coast 1936-40; East Africa 1940-42; Gold Coast and Gambia 1942-43; North West Europe 1944-45; Staff College 1946-47; Malaya 1948-51; AMS Anti Aircraft Command 1953-54; commanded the Singapore Regiment RA 1954-57; GSO1 Whistler Committee 1958; CRLS Southern Command 1958-59; commanded 8 Anti-Aircraft Brigade 1959-61; Jamaica Defence Force 1961-64. OBE, MC, 1939-45 Star, Africa Star, France and Germany Star, Defence and War Medals, General Service Medal (clasp Malaya), Independence Medal (Jamaica), Queen Elizabeth II Golden Jubilee Medal and was Mentioned in Despatches. Occupied No 15. Died 11 November 2004, and was succeeded by Lieutenant Colonel S A Watts (647)

624 Brigadier Arthur Catchmay Tyler CBE, MC, DL

1978–91

Appointed 12 June 1978 *vice* Brigadier W P A Robinson (608) (dec). Commissioned in The Welch Regiment 1933. He served in India 1934-37; East Africa 1941-42; India and Burma 1942-45; USA 1952-54; Canada 1960-63. During his service he was instructor, Senior Officers' School, India 1943-44; commanded AHFS. and Mountain Warfare School 1945-46; Staff College 1946-47; War Office 1947-50; Joint Services Staff College 1951; Secretary (Lieutenant Colonel) BJSM., Washington 1952-54; CO 4th Battalion, The Welch Regiment 1954-57; AAG War Office (Colonel) 1957-60; SLO and Military Adviser to the High Commissioner, Canada 1960-63; Assistant Chief of Staff (Operations and Plans) Allied Forces Central Europe 1963-65. Retired at own request 1965 to become Secretary of the Territorial Army Council until 1972. He was appointed Brevet Lieutenant-Colonel 1953; Deputy Lieutenant, Surrey 1968; Hon. Colonel 7th Battalion, The Queen's Regiment 1971-74. CBE, MC, 1939-45 Star, Africa Star, Burma Star, Defence and War Medals and was Mentioned in Despatches. Occupied No 19. Appointed a Supernumerary Military Knight by HM The Queen 9th November 1991 and was succeeded by Brigadier T W Hackworth OBE (636). Died 6 October 1998

625 Major Walter Louvain Thompson MVO, MBE, DCM

1978–2003

Appointed 19th December 1978 *vice* Lieutenant-Colonel A J Spratley (620) (dec). Enlisted in The Life Guards 1933 and commissioned Riding Master 1952. He served at the School of Equitation 1937; Royal Military College, Sandhurst 1938-39; with the Guards' Armoured Division, Europe 1940-46; Chief Instructor, Army School of Equitation, 1966-68. After retiring he was called to Windsor to instruct HRH The Duke of Edinburgh, in coach driving and to oversee the schooling of the carriage horses. MVO, MBE, DCM, 1939-45 Star, France and Germany Star, Defence and War Medals, George V Silver Jubilee Medal, Queen Elizabeth II Silver Jubilee Medal, Queen Elizabeth II Golden Jubilee Medal, Long Service and Good Conduct Medal. Occupied No 7. Appointed a Supernumerary Military Knight of Windsor by HM The Queen 1st November 2003 and was succeeded by Lieutenant-Colonel C I P Webb (646)

626 Major General Sir Peter Bernard Gillett, KCVO, CB, OBE

1980–89

Governor of the Military Knights of Windsor

Appointed 3 June 1980 *vice* Major-General Sir Edmund Hakewill Smith (601) (retired). Commissioned in the Royal Artillery 1934. He served in Waziristan 1938-39; Burma 1944; Germany 1945 and East Africa 1953-55. During his service he was Instructor, School of Artillery, India 1940; Staff College, Quetta 1942; Instructor AFV School, India 1943; course at Command and General Staff School, USA 1946; Instructor, Staff College, Camberley 1947-49; Battery Commander, The Chestnut Troop, RHA, Egypt 1949; GSO1 AA Command 1951; MA to GOC-in-C. East Africa 1953; commanded 5th Regiment RHA, BAOR. and UK 1955; CRA., 3rd Division 1959; Imperial Defence College 1962; Chief of Staff Eastern Command 1962; GOC. 48th Division TA 1965; He retired in 1968 and was Colonel Commandant, Royal Artillery 1968-78 and Secretary to the Central Chancery of the Orders of Knighthood 1968-79. KCVO, CB, OBE, India General Service Medal (clasp Waziristan), 1939-45 Star, Burma Star, France and Germany Star, Defence and War Medals, Africa General Service Medal (clasp Kenya), Queen Elizabeth II Silver Jubilee Medal. Occupied Mary Tudor Tower. He retired 13th February 1989 and was succeeded by Major-General P A Downward (633). He died on 4 July 1989

627 Major Leslie William Dickerson

1981–97

Appointed 2 February 1981 *vice* Colonel H G Duncombe (614) (dec). Commissioned in The Manchester Regiment 1939 after peacetime service in the Honourable Artillery Company. He served with the Royal West African Frontier Force in Nigeria and Burma 1939-45; in Europe 1946-47 and as Permanent President, Courts Martial in U.K., Germany, Middle East and Far East 1957-72. 1939-45 Star, Burma Star, Defence and War Medals, General Service Medal (clasp Cyprus), Queen Elizabeth II Silver Jubilee Medal, Territorial Efficiency Medal. Occupied No 10. Died 12 June 1997 and was succeeded by Major A H Clarkson (640)

628 Major James Charles Cowley OBE, DCM

1981–2009

Appointed 28 October 1981 *vice* Brigadier A A Crook (611) (dec). Enlisted in the Coldstream Guards 1937 and commissioned Quartermaster 1953. He served at the Guards Depot 1938-40; RSM Glider Pilot Regiment 1942-43; 5th Battalion, Coldstream Guards, Guards Armoured Division, Europe 1944-46 (wounded); Guards

Parachute Battalion, Palestine 1947; School of Infantry 1948-52; Guards Training Battalion 1953-53; 1st Battalion, Coldstream Guards, Egypt 1953; QM 2nd Battalion, Coldstream Guards 1953-56; Camp Commandant H.Q. 1st Guards Brigade and HQ 51st Brigade, Cyprus 1957-62; QM Honourable Artillery Company 1963-65; Malta 1966-68. Retired at own request 1968. OBE (Civil), DCM, 1939-45 Star, France and Germany Star, Defence and War Medals, General Service Medal (clasps Palestine and Cyprus), Queen Elizabeth II Coronation Medal, Queen Elizabeth II Golden Jubilee Medal, Long Service and Good Conduct Medal. Occupied No 17. Granted Supernumerary 2006. Died 21 December 2009. Succeeded by Colonel R B Watson (648)

629   Brigadier Christopher John Codner CBE, MC   1983–86

Appointed 3 June 1983 *vice* Lieutenant-Colonel J L Penfold (612) (dec). Commissioned in the Royal Artillery 1939. He served in North West Europe 1944-45; 6th Regiment RHA., India 1945-47; Singapore 1947; Airborne Regiments, Palestine 1947-49; Staff College 1950; GSO, 2 RA, HQ BAOR. 1951-53; GSO. 2 Far East Defence Secretariat, Singapore 1956-58; 5th Field Regiment RA, Hong Kong 1958-59. He commanded 14th Field Regiment RA 1959-61; was AA & QMG, 4th Division, BAOR 1962-63; AAG, AG6, MoD. 1963-65; CRA. 48th Division 1966-67; DDPS. (Army) MoD. 1967-70; Brigadier AQ 1st British Corps, BAOR 1970-74. After retiring he was Secretary (Retired Officer Grade 2) of the Royal Artillery Institution. CBE, MC, 1939-45 Star, France and Germany Star, Defence and War Medals, General Service Medal (clasps Palestine and Malaya) and was Mentioned in Despatches. Occupied No 18. He died 25th May 1986 aged 67 and was succeeded by Lieutenant Colonel N L West (630)

630   Major (Hon. Lieutenant Colonel) Norman Laurence West   1987–96

Appointed 24 March 1987 *vice* Brigadier C J Codner (629) (dec). Enlisted in the Royal Artillery 1939, commissioned in that Regiment 1941 and transferred to The King's Own Scottish Borderers 1944. He served in Gibraltar 1943-44 and with 1st Battalion, The King's Own Scottish Borderers in North West Europe 1944-45 and Palestine 1945-47. He was an Instructor 164 OCTU 1948-50; at London University 1950-52; Interrogation Centre, Salonika 1952-53; with 1st Battalion, The King's Own Scottish Borderers, Northern Ireland 1953-54; Training Major 5th Battalion, The King's Own Scottish Borderers 1954-56; 1st Battalion, The King's Own Scottish Borderers Malaya 1956; Instructor (Pentathlon) ASPT. 1957-59; AMA, Athens 1959-61; second-in-command Royal Sierra Leone Regiment 1961-61; Military Attaché, Sofia 1963-65; DOAE 1965-67; GCHQ 1967-68. After retiring he served in Intelligence Duties, MOD 1968-85. 1939-45 Star, France and Germany Star, Defence and War Medals, General Service Medal (clasps Palestine and Malaya), Territorial Efficiency Medal. Occupied No 18. He died 22 May 1996 and was succeeded by Major R J de M Gainher (639)

631   Major Gordon Ross Mitchell MBE, BEM   1988–2002

Appointed 10 December 1987 *vice* Lieutenant Colonel C A Harvey (618) (dec). Enlisted in The Argyll and Sutherland Highlanders 1941, commissioned in General List for SAS. 1962 and transferred to Scots Guards 1967. He served with the 70th (Young Soldiers) Battalion, The Argyll and Sutherland Highlanders 1941-42 and with 5th (Scottish) and 1st Battalion, The Parachute Regiment in Africa, Sicily and Italy 1942-43. He was with 1st SAS. Regiment in North West Europe and Norway (wounded) 1944-45; 1st Parachute Battalion in Palestine 1946-48; 1 (Guards) Independent Company, The Parachute Regiment in BAOR 1948-51; 1st Battalion, Scots Guards in Egypt and the UK 1951-56; at Royal Military Academy, Sandhurst 1956; with 1st Battalion, Scots Guards 1957-59 and R.H.Q. Scots Guards 1959-62. On being commissioned in 1962 he served with 22nd SAS Regiment in the UK and Borneo until 1965; with 1 (Guards) Independent Company, The Parachute Regiment 1965-67; 1st Battalion, Scots Guards 1967-70; Guards Depot 1970-73 and Camp Commandant, Headquarters London District 1973-77 during which period he took part in the Zaire River Expedition 1974-75. On retiring he became Warden of the Leonard Cheshire Home in Godalming 1977-88. MBE, BEM, 1939-45 Star, Africa Star, Italy Star, Defence and War Medals, General Service Medal (clasp Palestine 1945-48), General Service Medal (clasp Borneo 1962-65), Long Service and Good Conduct Medal and was Mentioned in Despatches. Occupied No 16. Died 20 September 2001 and was succeeded by Colonel D R Axson (644)

632   Lieutenant–Colonel Richard Lyndon Cedric Tamplin   **1988–2000**

Appointed 8 February 1988 *vice* Lieutenant Colonel A R Clark (619) (retired). Enlisted in the 17th/21st Lancers 1941 and commissioned in that Regiment 1943. He served with his Regiment in Italy, Austria and Greece 1944-49. He was at the War Office 1950-51; Regimental Duty, West Germany 1952-57; on the Staff, Headquarters East Africa, Kenya 1957-59; Belgian Staff College 1960; on Staff, Headquarters NATO 1960-62 and on Regimental Duty Aden and Germany 1962-64. He commanded the Sherwood Rangers Yeomanry 1964-67; was Defence Attaché, Khartoum 1968-70; NATO Defence College, Rome 1971 and on the Staff, Allied Forces Central Europe in Holland 1971-73. After retiring he was Regimental Secretary 17th/21st Lancers 1973-88. 1939-45 Star, Italy Star, Defence and War Medals, General Services Medal (clasp Palestine) and was Mentioned in Despatches. Occupied No 11. Died 6 May 2000 and was succeeded by Lieutenant Colonel T B F Hiney (643)

633   Major–General Sir Peter Aldcroft Downward KCVO, CB, DSO, DFC   **1989–2000**
Governor of the Military Knights of Windsor

Appointed 13 February 1989 *vice* Major-General Sir Peter Gillett (626) (retired). Enlisted in The Rifle Brigade 1942 and was commissioned in The South Lancashire Regiment (Prince of Wales's Volunteers) in 1943. He served with 13th Battalion (Lancs.), The Parachute Regiment in North West Europe 1944 to mid 1945; in India, Singapore, Java and Malaya 1945-46. He was GSO3, 10th Infantry Brigade, in Salonika and Palestine 1947. In late 1947 he was seconded to the Glider Pilot Regiment and was training in the United Kingdom 1948; second pilot in the Berlin Airlift (attached 206 Squadron, Royal Air Force) 1949; Airborne Forces Depot 1950 and commanding 1913 Flight (Reconnaissance) Korea 1951-53. He served with his regiment in the United Kingdom, Berlin and the Canal Zone 1953-57; attended the Royal Air Force Staff College 1958; was GSO2 Land/Air Warfare, War Office 1959-60; Brigade Major 127th Infantry Brigade 1961-63; CO 1st Battalion, The Lancashire Regiment 1964-65 in UK and in Aden 1966-68; GSO1 Headquarters Allied Forces Northern Europe, Oslo 1968-69; Chief Instructor, School of Infantry 1970-71; Commander Berlin Infantry Brigade 1972-74, Commandant School of Infantry, 1974-76; and GOC West Midland District 1976-79. He was appointed Lieutenant Governor, The Royal Hospital, Chelsea, 1979-84; Colonel, The Queen's Lancashire Regiment 1978-83; Colonel Commandant, The King's Division 1979-83 and Honorary Colonel Liverpool University Officers' Training Corps. KCVO, CB, DSO, DFC, 1939-45 Star, France and Germany Star, Defence and War Medals, General Service Medal (clasps SE Asia, Palestine), Korea Medal, United Nations Medal (Korea), General Service Medal (clasp South Arabia), Queen Elizabeth II Silver Jubilee Medal. Awarded KCVO in 1999. Occupied The Mary Tudor Tower. He retired in 2000 and was succeeded by Major General Sir Michael Hobbs (641)

634.   Captain (Hon. Major) Peter Henry Bolton MBE   **1990–**

Appointed in 15 March 1990 *vice* Lieutenant Colonel R W Dobbin (615) (dec). He joined The Argyll & Sutherland Highlanders in April 1941, and was commissioned into The Seaforth Highlanders in October 1943, serving in the war with No.9 Commando in Yugoslavia, Greece and the final battles in Italy. Served in 5th Battalion, The Parachute Regiment 1947, Palestine 1948, Tripoli & Malta 1949-51, 1st Battalion, The Nigeria Regiment 1951-52, BAOR 1952-55, Malaya, on secondment to the Malaysian Forces during the emergency there. From 1955 to 1959 he was with the All Arms Training Centre in Sennelager BAOR He was with the Aden Intelligence Staff from 1961 to 1963 and from 1963 to 1965 he served with Malaysian Rangers in Malaysia and Borneo. He transferred to the Royal Corps of Signals in 1965 and served at RAF. Laarbruch. His final posting was to Hong Kong, where he retired from the Army, starting work the next day with the Royal Hong Kong Police as Superintendent. After thirteen years, and having been honoured with an MBE, he retired to Spain, before coming to Windsor. MBE (Civil), 1939-45 Star, Italy Star Defence and War Medals, General Service Medal (clasps Palestine, Malaya), General Service Medal (clasp Malay Peninsular) and the Queen Elizabeth II Golden Jubilee Medal. He also holds the Pingaat Khidmat Berbakti and Pingaat Kerana Perkhidmatan'Am (Malaysia). He has been awarded two medals that are not worn, The Greek War Medal and the Royal Hong Kong Police Disbandment Medal. He occupies No 14

635. Lieutenant Colonel Hugh Francis Rogers MBE   1991–1995

Appointed 29 May 1991 *vice* Major H Smith (617) (dec). Enlisted into The Lancashire Fusiliers 17th June 1954. Commissioned into The Border Regiment 15 December 1955 from RMA Sandhurst. Served with 1st Battalion, The Border Regiment in Germany and Berlin 1956-57. 1st Battalion, The Loyal Regiment (North Lancashire) in Malay, Germany and UK. Adjutant 5th Battalion, The Loyal Regiment (North Lancashire) (TA). Company instructor RMA Sandhurst 1965-67. 1st Battalion, The Loyal Regiment (North Lancashire) 1967-68 in Malta and Libya. GSO2, HQ 1st (British) Corps. 1st Battalion, The Queen's Lancashire Regiment Osnabruck and Northern Ireland 1974-75. DAA & QMG H.Q. 39th Infantry Brigade 1975-76, National Defence College (Latimer) 1976-78, GSO1 Defence Policy Staff MOD 1978-1980. Commanded 4th Battalion, The Queen's Lancashire Regiment; 1980-83 SO1 SD, HQ Director of Infantry; 1982-83, SO1 Tactics DOAE 1983-87. Retired April 1987. M.B.E., General Service Medal (clasp Malaya) and General Service Medal (clasp Northern Ireland). Occupied No 19. Died 1 October 1995. Succeeded by Lieutenant Colonel R R Giles (638)

636. Colonel (Hon. Brigadier) Timothy William Hackworth OBE   1992–

Appointed 19 May 1992 *vice* Brigadier A C Tyler 624 (Supernumerary). Served from 20th September 1951 as a National Serviceman, followed by a National Service Commission. Regular Commission in the Royal Corps of Signals on 17th January 1954. Served in Catterick, Shrivenham, Aden (twice), Germany (three times), London (twice), Aldermaston and Canada. Active service in Aden and Kuwait (1961). He attended the National Defence College at Latimer before taking Command of 16 Signal Regiment in Germany 1973 to 1976. The Regiment had a squadron in Northern Ireland in an infantry role. After a period in London heading an Operational Requirements branch, he spent six years seconded to the Foreign Office, being appointed Defence and Naval Attaché Jordan, closely followed by Defence Attaché Korea where his principal task was Commonwealth Member of the UN Military Armistice Commission at Panmunjom. Retired from the Army in 1988. In retirement he worked as a Director of the British Computer Society. He achieved the degree of a Doctor of Philosophy in the mathematics of computation from the University of London (2004). Treasurer of the Military Knights 1995 to 2002. OBE 1976, General Service Medal (clasps Aden and Radfan), Queen Elizabeth II Golden Jubilee Medal. Occupies No.6

637. Major Richard John Moore   1992–

Appointed on 20 September 1992 *vice* Major A E Wollaston (621) (dec). He joined the army for National Service on 20 September 1951 and completed basic training in the Royal Artillery. After attending Eaton Hall Officer Cadet School, Chester, he was commissioned into The Royal Inniskilling Fusiliers and served in the 2nd Battalion in UK. He transferred to the 1st Battalion, The Royal Inniskilling Fusiliers, extended to a Short Service Commission and served with them in Kenya where he was Mentioned in Despatches. On returning to the UK he was the Battalion Machine Gun Officer at the School of Infantry, Warminster. He transferred to the RASC on obtaining a Regular Commission and served with the Gurkha Army Service Corps in Kluang, Malaya. There followed tours of duty in the Royal Corps of Transport in Germany. He attended the Advanced Transportation Course 1968. Commanded C Squadron, 12 Training Regiment RCT 1969-70. He served in Aden in 1967 with 17 Port Regiment RCT and Cyprus 1970-73 Commanding 10 Port Squadron RCT and as Port Commandant Famagusta. He retired in 1979. In 1982 became an Intelligence Officer (HIO) with the Ministry of Defence Intelligence Staff. He took over the duties of Staff Officer to the Military Knights in 1996, handing it over to Colonel Colston in 2001. He holds the Africa General Service Medal (clasp Kenya), General Service Medal (clasp Malaya), General Service Medal (clasp South Arabia), Queen Elizabeth II Golden Jubilee Medal and was Mentioned in Despatches. He is a Member of the Chartered Institute of Transport. Occupies No 8

Note: On the 20 of November 1992 fire broke out in the Queen's private Chapel in the State Apartments. As a result St George's Hall, the Grand Reception Room, The Red Drawing Room., the State Dining Room and the Small Dining Room were all completely burned out. All the Military Knights and their wives assisted in the removal of furniture, pictures and artefacts. It was six years before the Castle was fully restored.

The picture showing the Military Knights on the 20th of November was taken by the BBC and published in the Radio Times to advertise the Christmas Songs of Praise.

638. Lieutenant Colonel Raymond Roland Giles 1996–

Appointed 21 May 1996 *vice* Lieutenant Colonel H F Rogers (635) (dec). Enlisted in the Royal Horse Guards (The Blues) in 1949 rising through the ranks to become Regimental Corporal Major in 1969. From 1949 to 1959 he was carrying out military and trade training in Windsor and Ceremonial duties in London. From 1959 to 1970 he carried out further Regimental duties in Windsor and Cyprus including 4th Armoured Division exercises in BAOR in Denmark and a tour of the Eastern United States in 1968. Awarded a Special Regular Commission to Captain in 1971. Served with the Household Cavalry Mounted Regiment (HCMR) and The Blues and Royals (RHG/D) Armoured Regiment holding appointments of second-in-command of a Sabre Squadron on a United Nations tour of Cyprus and OC H.Q. Squadron in both HCMR and RHG/D in Windsor and an exchange tour in Jamaica in 1974. Transferred to a Quartermaster (QM) Commission in late 1974 and was QM RHG/D 1974-81, which included two tours in Northern Ireland in the Infantry role and Battle Group live firing exercises in Alberta Canada.. As QM of The Royal Yeomanry 1981-85 he was based in Westminster and was responsible for supporting detached Light Armoured Squadrons in England and Belfast. As a Light Armoured Recce Regiment The Royal Yeomanry visited BAOR on exercise in support of 1st (British) Corps. In 1985 he was posted to H.Q. London District as SO2 G.4. Projects. On retirement from Regular Service in 1986 after which he remained in the same post as a Retired Officer Grade 2 until retirement in 1996. He holds the United Nations (Cyprus) Medal, General Service Medal (clasp Northern Ireland), Queen Elizabeth II Silver Jubilee Medal, Queen Elizabeth II Golden Jubilee Medal and the Long Service and Good Conduct Medal. He occupies No 19

639. Major Robin James de Majendie Gainher 1997–2009

Appointed 23 April 1997 *vice* Lieutenant Colonel N L West (630) (dec). Attended RMA Sandhurst 1957-58. Commissioned into The Loyal Regiment (North Lancashire), served in 1st Battalion in Malaya 1959, BAOR 1960-61, served in 1st Battalion, The King's Own Border Regiment in British Cameroons, with 1st Battalion, The Loyal Regiment (North Lancashire) in BAOR and UK Seconded to Malaysian Army, 2nd Battalion, Malaysian Rangers, Malaya and Borneo 1963-66. Served with the Junior Tradesmen's Regiment, Troon 1966-68, Adjutant 1st Battalion, The Loyal Regiment (North Lancashire) and 1st Battalion, The Queen's Lancashire Regiment 1968-70. Staff Captain Q Quartering HQ FARELF and HQ ANZUK 1970-72. Company Commander 1st Battalion, The Queen's Lancashire Regiment in BAOR and Northern Ireland 1972-74. GSO 2 Tactics, Army School of Transport 1975-77. Retired 1977. Served as a contract officer in Sultanate of Oman 1979-84. He holds the General Service Medal (clasp Malaya), General Service Medal (clasps Borneo, Malay Peninsular, Northern Ireland), Sultan of Oman's General Service Medal (Jebel War), Sultan of Oman's 10th Anniversary Medal. Occupied No 18. Died 16 February 2010

640. Major Alan Hill Clarkson 1998–

Appointed 1998 *vice* Major L W Dickerson (627) (dec). Enlisted into the Army as a Boy Apprentice in 1950 aged 14 and mustered into the Royal Artillery 1953. He was trained as a Surveyor RA and as such served practically all his non-commissioned service in the survey and locating world of the RA rising to the rank of Warrant Officer Class 1 in late 1969. In this capacity he remained as a Troop Commander at the Junior Leaders Regiment Royal Artillery, Bramcote until commissioning in early 1970. As an officer he served in 24th and 50th Missile Regiments in a number of capacities including Troop Commander, Battery Captain and Adjutant until being promoted to Major in late 1974. Up until 1980, when he was appointed to a Quartermaster commission, he commanded a Missile Battery and he also commanded Headquarter Battery on two occasions. As a Quartermaster he held the post in 50th Missile Regiment and 4th Field Regiment and his last military appointment prior to his retirement was that of SO3 Arty Log HQRA 4th Armoured Division in 1988. On retirement he was appointed to the post of Station Staff Officer (Retired Officer Grade 2) until his retirement in 1998 when he was appointed to a Military Knight of Windsor. He holds the Long Service and Good Conduct Medal. Occupies No 10

Parade at Buckingham Palace for HM's Golden Jubilee 5th July 2002
Her Majesty's Body Guards and Royal Companies

© G3 Media Ops London Digital

J F Lindner   BE Colston   TW Hackworth   AH Clarkson   R J Moore   TBF Hiney   Sir M F Hobbs
              W L Thompson   J C Cowley   R R Giles   G R Mitchell

© Photographer Julian Calder

119

641.   Major General Sir Michael Frederick Hobbs KCVO, CBE   **2000–**
Governor of The Military Knights of Windsor

Appointed 2000 *vice* Major General Sir Peter Downward (633) (retired). Commissioned into the Grenadier Guards as National Service Officer 14 April 1956. Regular Commission 28 February 1958. DAA & QMG HQ 4 Guards Armoured Brigade 1970 -72. Instructor Staff College 1974-77. Commanded 1st Battalion, Grenadier Guards in England and Northern Ireland 1978-80. Colonel GS ASD 3 DASD. 1980-82. Commanded 39th Infantry Brigade Northern Ireland 1982-83. Director Public Relations (Army) MOD 1984-85. General Officer Commanding 4th Armoured Division 1985-87. On Retirement became Director, Duke of Edinburgh's Award 1988-98, Director, Outward Bound Trust 1995. Governor Military Knights of Windsor 2000. KCVO 1998, MBE 1975, OBE 1979, CBE 1982, General Service Medal (clasp Northern Ireland) and was Mentioned in Despatches. Occupies Mary Tudor Tower

642.   Colonel Brian Edward Colston   **2000–2009**

Appointed 29 September 2000 *vice* Brigadier A L Atkinson (622) (dec). Commissioned into the Royal Army Service Corps from Mons Officer Cadet School on a Short Service Commission 11th September 1959. Following a series of junior officer appointments in Singapore, Malaya, Cyprus and the United Kingdom he returned to the Far East to be Adjutant of 32 Regiment RCT, he then undertook a further tour as Adjutant, this time with 155 Regiment RCT TAVR following a serious rugby injury to his spine. His subsequent appointment as OC 7 Squadron RCT (3rd Division) was curtailed pending surgery to his neck. He regained fitness behind a desk as SO3 Q Movements Plans/Coord and returned to active soldiering to command 21 Squadron RCT (4th Armoured Division). This was followed by a return to staff work as DAA & QMG. HQ Training Group RCT. Promotion to Lieutenant Colonel followed with three appointment: Commander Transport HQ London District 1980-82, S.O.1 Q Movements 2 1982-85 and SO1 Transport HQ 1st (British) Corps 1985-87. Following promotion to Colonel in 1987, he was Director Logistics (Movements) 1987-89 and Deputy Commander Transport and Movements HQ BAOR 1989-91. Prior to early retirement in October 1991 he enjoyed Pay of Higher rank when he was Commander Transport and Movements for 6 months during the Gulf War recovery period. He holds the General Service Medal (clasp Northern Ireland) and the Queen Elizabeth II Silver Jubilee Medal. On retirement he was SO1 (Retired Officer Grade 1) Project Sponsor H.Q British Forces Cyprus. Staff Officer to the Military Knights from 2001. Occupied No 9. Died 2 May 2009. Succeeded by Lieutenant Colonel W J Willans (649)

643.   Lieutenant Colonel Thomas Bernard Felix Hiney MC   **2001–2003**

Appointed 23 April 2001 *vice* Lieutenant Colonel R L C Tamplin (632) (dec). Enlisted in the West Yorkshire Regiment in March 1954. Attended The Royal Military Academy, Sandhurst and was commissioned into the Royal Leicestershire Regiment in July 1956. Served with 1st Battalion The Royal Leicester Regiment in Cyprus 1957-58. He served with the Ghana Army in the Congo 1960-61 where he was awarded the MC.

He was with the 1st Battalion, The Royal Leicestershire Regiment in BAOR in 1962, Sultan's Armed Forces in the Oman in 1963-64 and with the 4th Battalion, The Royal Anglian Regiment in Malta 1966-67. In 1971 he transferred to the Royal Army Chaplains Department and served as a chaplain in BAOR, Northern Ireland, Cyprus and Supreme Headquarters Allied Powers Europe between 1971-89. He was chaplain to the Royal Hospital Chelsea for nine years. He holds the MC, Order of St John, General Service Medal (clasps Cyprus, Northern Ireland) and the United Nations Medal (Congo). He occupied No 11 until relinquishing his appointment as a Military Knight in 1st September 2003

644.   Colonel David Robin Axson   **2002–**

Appointed 16 May 2002 *vice* Major G R Mitchell (631) (dec). Attended The Royal Military Academy, Sandhurst and was commissioned in the Corps of Royal Electrical and Mechanical Engineers in 1957. He served in Aden and Bahrain, the British Army of the Rhine and the United Kingdom. He commanded 65 Station Workshop REME 1963-64; 13th/18th Royal Hussars (QMO) LAD REME. 1964-66; 5 Field Workshop REME 1976-76; 5 Armoured Workshop REME 1980-83; Vehicles and Weapons Branch REME 1984-88 and the School of Electronic Engineering 1988-92. He held staff appointments as Staff Captain Ministry of Defence AG21 1966-69; DAA & QMG Headquarters REME Training Centre 1972-74; DAAG Ministry of Defence Manning 6

(Army) 1976-77 and GSO1 DGEME Secretariat 1977-80. He served as the Corps Secretary REME (Retired Officer Grade 1) from 1995 to 2002. Treasurer of the Military Knights from 2002 and Honorary Secretary, Guild of Stewards of the College of St George from 2003 to 2007. From 2007 he has been Clerk to the Friends and Companions. He is a graduate of London University, a Chartered Engineer and Fellow of the Institution of Mechanical Engineers. Occupies 16 Lower Ward

645. Lieutenant Colonel John Gilmour Humphreys–Evans.   2003–

Appointed 8 December 2003 *vice* Lieutenant Colonel T B F Hiney (643) (retired). On leaving The Royal Military Academy Sandhurst in December 1958 he was commissioned into The Royal Welch Fusiliers. He joined the 1st Battalion, The Royal Welch Fusiliers in Cyprus 1959. Instructor at the Infantry Junior Leaders Battalion in Oswestry 1961-1963. From 1963 to 1967 he served with 1st Battalion, The Royal Welch Fusiliers in BAOR. Adjutant of the Welsh Volunteers in Cardiff 1968-69. 1970 Adjutant of 1st Battalion, The Royal Welch Fusiliers in Hong Kong. GSO3 (Operations) in H.Q. 39th Infantry Brigade in Belfast 1971-73. Company Commander with 1st Battalion, The Royal Welch Fusiliers in UK, Belize and Northern Ireland. 1974-75. DAQMG (Ops) in HQ UK Land Forces 1976-77. Senior Major of 1st Battalion, The Royal Welch Fusiliers in BAOR and Northern Ireland 1978-79. DAAG/DAMS in HQ Berlin, British Sector 1980-81. Chief Instructor at Anti-Tank Division, School of Infantry 1982. Commanded the 3rd Battalion, The Royal Welch Fusiliers 1983-85. He was Senior British Officer (Colonel) in the Multi-National Force SINAI from 1985-86. Finally he was SO1 G1 HQ UK Land Forces 1987-89. He holds the General Service Medal (clasp Northern Ireland) with Mentioned in Despatches, United Nations Medal (Cyprus) and the Multi-National Force, Sinai Medal (1986). After retiring he worked for the Foreign Office (Organisation for Security and Co-operation in Europe). Occupies No 11

646. Lieutenant Colonel Charles Ian Patrick Webb   2004–

Appointed 5 June 2004 *vice* Major W. L. Thompson (625) (retired). Attended The Royal Military Academy, Sandhurst 1960-61. Commissioned into the 3rd Carabiniers (Prince of Wales's Dragoon Guards), Regimental Duty 1962. Merton College Oxford 1962-65 (MA (Oxon)). Regimental duty in BAOR and Libya 1965-68. Attended Long Armour Course at Bovington 1969-70. Attached to The Royal Scots Greys (2nd Dragoons), Edinburgh, 1970-71. Royal Scots Dragoon Guards (Carabiniers and Greys) from 1971, Regimental Duties Edinburgh, Northern Ireland, BAOR 1971-72. GSO2(W) Armoured Trials and Development Unit, Bovington 1972-75. H.Q. Squadron Leader Royal Scots Dragoon Guards BAOR/Northern Ireland 1975-77. GSO2(W) Ministry of Defence (Procurement Executive) St Christopher House 1977-79. Training Major Bristol University OTC 1979-81. SO2 G3 (Policy and Operational Requirements) HQ BAOR, 1981-83. GSO2 (CD/OR) H.Q. Royal Brunei Armed Forces 1983-87. SO1(W) RARDE (Vehicle Division) Chertsey 1987-91. SO1 G3 (O.R) JHQ High Wycombe January to April 1991. SO2(W) Light Armoured Vehicles Ministry of Defence (Procurement Executive) 1991-94. Retired in January 1994, has worked for Christie's/Spinks since then as head of Militaria Auctions and Medal Services. Also serves as Assistant Historical Adviser to Army Dress Committee. General Service Medal (clasp Northern Ireland), Brunei General Service Medal, Brunei Armed Forces 25th Anniversary Medal. Occupies No 7

647. Lieutenant Colonel Stuart Alastair Watts OBE   2005

Appointed 6 June 2005 *vice* Brigadier J F Lindner (623) (dec). Enlisted as a Band Boy 1960 into the Royal Horse Guards aged 15. Junior Leaders Regiment Royal Armoured Corps (Bovington) 1960-61. Pupils' Course Royal Military School of Music, Kneller Hall studying Cornet, (Trumpeter at Princess Alexandra's Wedding) 1961-63. Equitation Course, HCR Knightsbridge 1963. Musician/Lance Corporal Band of The Royal Horse Guards, stationed in London and Windsor 1963-71. Student Bandmasters' course RMSM 1971-73 (lead Trumpeter Princess Anne's wedding). Appointed WO1 (B.M.) 3rd Battalion, The Royal Anglian Regiment serving in BAOR, U.K., Cyprus, NI 1974. BM Queen's Division Junior School of Music, Bassingbourn 1980. Commissioned Captain (Director of Music) The Parachute Regiment, Aldershot 1982. Director of Music Junior Musicians' Wing, Guards Depot, Pirbright 1985 (served in The Blues and Royals) (three month secondment to Swaziland, preparation of bands for the Coronation of King Maswati III 1986). Director of Music Brigade of Gurkhas, badged, 2nd King Edward VII's Own Gurkha Rifles (The Sirmoor Rifles) served in

Hong Kong 1987. Director of Music Grenadier Guards, London 1988-92. Senior Instructor RMSM 1992-94, 1994-96 Director of Music Welsh Guards. Principal Director of Music (Army), RMSM 1997-2000. Since retirement from the Regular Army he has been Director of Music Honourable Artillery Company. He has the Advanced Certificate of the RMSM (psm) and LRAM. He holds the O.B.E., General Service Medal (clasp Northern Ireland), Queen Elizabeth II Golden Jubilee Medal and Long Service and Good Conduct Medal. Occupies No. 15

648.   Colonel Robert Bruce Watson   2006–

Appointed 24 April 2006 *vice* Major J C Cowley (628) (Supernumerary). Enlisted into the Intelligence Corps in 1960 as a Junior Leader aged 16. Attended RMA Sandhurst 1962-64 and was commissioned into the Royal Army Service Corps, re-badging to the Royal Corps of Transport in 1965, and, 28 years later, to the Royal Logistic Corps. Junior appointments in Cyprus, Germany, Northern Ireland, and the Ministry of Defence. Attended the Army Staff College in 1977. Further appointments in Germany included command of an independent transport squadron, Deputy Secretary of the Commanders'-in-Chief Committee British Forces Germany, and Second in Command of an armoured division transport regiment. After a further Ministry of Defence tour with Army Staff Duties, he was posted to Headquarters British Forces Hong Kong as Commander Transport & Movements and then to an exchange post with the US Army in Fort Lee, Virginia. His final post was as Colonel (Training) with the Army School of Mechanical Transport. He attended London Bible College in 1994/95 prior to employment with the Ex-Services Mental Welfare Society, followed by a number of charity and care industry posts. General Service Medal (clasp Northern Ireland). Occupies No 17.

649.   Lieutenant Colonel William Jolyon Willans   2009–

Appointed 30 November 2009 vice Colonel B E Colston (642) (dec). Commissioned into the Royal Warwickshire Fusiliers on 14 February 1963 from Mons Officer Cadet School on a Short Service Commission. Served with the 1st Battalion The Royal Warwickshire Fusiliers in Hameln, Minden, Watchet in Somerset, Hong Kong, Singapore, Borneo, at the conclusion of The Emergency, and Gibraltar. 1968-69 at The Fusilier Brigade Depot in Sutton Coldfield, then rejoined the Battalion, now 2nd Battalion The Royal Regiment of Fusiliers, in Berlin. Adjutant of that Battalion in Catterick and Northern Ireland 1972-74. Captain Instructor at RMA Sandhurst 1975-77. GSO3 in ASD 2 DASD 1977-79. Company Commander 3rd Battalion The Royal Regiment of Fusiliers Fallingbostel and Londonderry 1979-81. DAAG 2nd Armoured Division in Lubbecke 1981-83. Student at Joint Services Defence College 1984 before commanding 3rd Battalion The Royal Regiment of Fusiliers in Catterick, South Armagh and Cyprus with the United Nations 1985- 1987. Joint Secretariat HQ NORTHAG/2ATAF Rheindahlen 1987-1990. SO1 G3 Plans HQ AFNORTH Oslo 1990 – 1992. Adviser with British Military Mission to the Saudi Arabian National Guard in Jeddah 1993 – 1996. As an RO1 (MSF C1) he was the Regimental Secretary of The Fusiliers at its RHQ in HM Tower of London 1996-2008. General Service Medal (Northern Ireland) and United Nations Medal (Cyprus). Occupies No 9

650.   Colonel David Kirkwood Paige Steele MBE   2010 –

Appointed 1 June 2010 vice Major R J de M Gainher (639) (dec). Commissioned into The Royal Regiment of Artillery from the Royal Military Academy Sandhurst on 17th December 1963. Served in British Army of the Rhine between 1966 and 1971 with emergency tours in Northern Ireland and as Officer Commanding the Island of St Kilda. 1971 to 1976 served with 95 Commando Forward Observation Unit in the United Kingdom and Malta with an operational tour in Southern Oman. 1976 to 1978 TA Adjutant in Bristol and 1978 to 1980, GSO3 Training at 23rd Artillery Brigade in Chester. Transferred to 1st Battalion, The Argyll and Sutherland Highlanders (Princess Louise's) in 1981 and served as a Company Commander in Northern Ireland and Cyprus. 1982 to 1984 Deputy Chief Operations, Plans and Training at Headquarters Allied Forces Central Region in Holland. 1984 to 1987, SO2 MS (Coord) at MOD Stanmore. After a short tour as Training Major of 1st/51st (Highland Volunteers) in Perth, Second in Command of the Scottish Division Depot in Penicuik, Midlothian from 1987 to 1990. 1990 – 1991 SO2 (Instructor) at the Zimbabwe Military Academy. 1992 to 1995, SO1 Land Operations (Joint Operations, Operational Readiness and Multinational Training) at Supreme Headquarters Allied Powers Europe. 1995 to 1996, SO1 and subsequently Officer in Charge, Combined Manning and Records Officer, Exeter. From 2001, Commander Recruiting Scotland until retiring from the

Army in 2008. During this period was also Commandant of The West Lowland Battalion of the Army Cadet Force. From 2008 to 2010 worked for Combat Stress as Regional Welfare Officer for the West of Scotland. He holds the MBE, GSM (Clasps Northern Ireland and Dhofar), Queen Elizabeth 11 Golden Jubilee Medal and The Army Cadet Force Medal.

Banner Ceremony and Memorial Service

The Banner of Sir Edmund Hillary KG ONZ KBE carried through St George's Chapel at his Memorial Service. 3 April 2008

© Getty Images

The Military Knights of Windsor
2009

The Military Knights assembled before Sunday Matins

R R G   R J de M G   Sir M F H   D R A

J G H-E   S A W

T W H

P H B   R B W   A H C   C I P W

(Absent R J M)

Regulations for the Governance of the Military Knights of Windsor

Queen's Regulations for the Army, 1975

Chapter 9 Manning, Part 1 Officers, Annex B, Special Appointments, Part 2 Conditions for Appointment….. Paragraph 4. Military Knights of Windsor.

The Regulations for the Governance of the Military Knights of Windsor are issued by the Keeper of the Privy Purse on the authority of Her Majesty The Queen. These are issued from time to time the latest being in 1988. One copy is issued to each Military Knight. There have been no more recent versions as there have been no material changes.

The Governor of the Military Knights is responsible to the Constable and Governor of Windsor Castle for the discipline of the Military Knights and for every aspect of command, conduct, administration and their duties in Windsor Castle.

The Keeper of the Privy Purse is the Household Authority responsible to the Sovereign for administrative matters relating to the Military Knights. He is the channel of communication with the Ministry of Defence and the Household Property department. He is the ultimate authority for the selection of a new Military Knight and for the submission of his name to the Sovereign.

The Dean of Windsor is responsible for the general welfare of all Military Knights. The Governor of the Military Knights is responsible to the Dean for the attendance of the Military Knights and for their participation at services. The Staff Officer of the Military Knights attends the weekly planning meeting and briefs the Governor on any special requirements.

In amplification of the Keeper of the Privy Purse's Regulations the Governor of the Military Knights has issued a folder entitled " Notes for the Guidance of the Military Knights of Windsor". In addition to expanding on the Regulations they give details of the drills required at special occasions such as Royal Funerals, Banner Ceremonies, Garter Day, State Visits and Installations. A copy is handed to each Military Knight at installation.

The Uniform of a Military Knight is laid down in "Dress Regulations for Officers of the Army" (1969 Edition Pamphlet 7).

The Garter Star surmounted by the Crown is the badge on the Brass plate on the sword belt.

The Constable and Governor of Windsor Castle, Surgeon Vice Admiral I L Jenkins CB, CVO, QHS, FRCS (died 2009) leading the Military Knights of Windsor, the Heralds and the Knights of the Garter on Garter Day 2008

© Photographer Eva Zielinska-Millar

Garter Day 2010

On their way up to the State Entrance to assemble for the Garter Procession.

Colonel DKP Steele
(650)

Lieutenant Colonel CIP Webb
(646)

Lieutenant Colonel CIP Webb Colonel RB Watson
(648)

Lieutenant Colonel WJ Willans
(649)

The Funeral of HRH Princess Margaret, February 2002. Coffin guards Lt. Col R R Giles and Brig T W Hackworth OBE.

© Press Association

129

ABBREVIATIONS

AA	Anti Aircraft
AAG	Assistant Adjutant General
AA&QMG	Assistant Adjutant & Quarter Master General
ADC	aide-de-camp
AFV	Armoured Fighting Vehicle
AG	Adjutant General
AMA	Assistant Military Attache
AMS	Assistant Military Secretary
ANZUK	Australia, New Zealand, United Kingdom
Arty Log	Artillery Logistics
ASPT	Army School of Physical Training
BAOR	British Army of the Rhine
Bart	Baronet
BEM	British Empire Medal
BM	Band Master
CB	Companion of the Order of the Bath
CBE	Commander of the Order of the British Empire
CH	Companion of Honour
CIE	Companion of the Order of the Indian Empire
CMG	Companion of the Order of St Michael and St George
CO	Commanding Officer
CRA	Commander Royal Artillery
CRLS	Command Recruiting and Liaison Staff
CSO	Chief Signals Officer
CVO	Commander of the Royal Victorian Order
DAMS	Deputy Assistant Military Secretary
DCM	Distinguished Conduct Medal
DDPS	Deputy Director Photographic Services
DFC	Distinguished Flying Cross
DGEME	Director General Electrical & Mechanical Engineers
DL	Deputy Lieutenant
DOAE	Department of Army Education
Dr	Doctor
DSO	Companion of the Distinguished Service Order
FARELF	Far East Land Forces
GCHQ	Government Communications Headquarters
GHQ	General Headquarters
GOC	General Officer Commanding
GS	General Staff
GSO	General Staff Officer
HCMR	Household Cavalry Mounted Regiment
Hon.	Honorary
HQ	Headquarters
HQRA	Headquarters Royal Artillery
HRH	His/Her Royal Highness
Insc.	Inscribed
JHQ	Joint Headquarters
JP	Justice of the Peace
KCB	Knight Commander of the Bath
KCIE	Knight Commander of the Indian Empire
KCMG	Knight Commander of St Michael and St George
KCVO	Knight Commander of the Royal Victorian Order
KG	Knight of the Garter
KH	Knight of Hanover (Guelphic Order)
Kt	Knight
LAD	Light Aid Detachment
L.F.	Lower Foundation
LRAM	Licentiate Royal Academy of Music
MA	Master of Arts
MA to ….	Military Assistant to
MBE	Member of the Order of the British Empire
MC	Military Cross
MG	Machine Gun
MM	Military Medal
MOD	Ministry of Defence
Mon.	Monument
Mus Doc	Doctor of Music
MVO	Member of the Royal Victorian Order
NATO	North Atlantic Treaty Organisation
OBE	Officer of the Order of the British Empire
OCTU	Officer Cadet Training Unit
QM	Quarter Master
OTC	Officer Training Corps
RA	Royal Regiment of Artillery
RAC	Royal Armoured Corps
RAF	Royal Air Force
RARDE	Royal Army Research & Development Establishment
RASC	Royal Army Service Corps
RCT	Royal Corps of Transport
REME	Corps of Royal Electrical and Mechanical Engineers
RF	Royal Foundation
RHA	Royal Horse Artillery
RHG/D	Royal Horse Guards/Dragoons
RHQ	Regimental Headquarters
RMSM	Royal Military School of Music
RSM	Regimental Sergeant Major
Rt Hon	Right Honourable
RVM	Royal Victorian Medal
SAS	Special Air Service
SD	Staff Duties
SLO	Senior Liaison Officer
SO	Staff Officer
SSVF	Singapore Special Volunteer Force
TA	Territorial Army
TAVR	Territorial Army Volunteer Reserve
UN	United Nations
VC	Victoria Cross

REGIMENTS

Regiment No	Name	MKW Nos
	HOUSEHOLD CAVALRY	
	Life Guards	625, 436, 434, 396, 270, 214,
	Royal Horse Guards Blues	638, 428, 238 (Oxford's), 236 (Oxford's),
	Blues and Royals RHG/D	638
	LINE CAVALRY	
2nd	Dragoon Guards (Queen's Bays)	597
3rd	Dragoon Guards	572,
5th	Dragoon Guards	537, 447,
6th	Dragoon Guards (Carabineers)	516, 646, 265
1st	Royal Dragoons,	426, 421
2nd	Dragoons (Royal Scots Greys)	646, 597
4th	Light Dragoons	522
8th	Light Dragoons (Hussars),	517
9th	(Queen's Royal) Lancers	504, 571
10th	Light Dragoons	422, 393,
10th	Royal Hussars	602, 586, 574, 561
11th	Light Dragoons	471, 438,
13th	Light Dragoons	541, 474, 435, 425,
15th	Light Dragoons (Hussars),	576, 453, 562, 392,
16th	Lancers	536
17/21st	Lancers,	632
18th	Hussars	591 VC,
21st	Light Dragoons	439
	Staff Corps of Cavalry	439,
	Thomas Fairfax Troop	269
	CORPS	
	Royal Horse Artillery	626 (5th, Chestnut Troop)
	Royal Regiment of Artillery	540 VC, 452, 570, 569, 553 (Bombay), 579,
	Royal Regiment of Artillery	640, 629, 626, 624, 623, 615, 612, 608, 596,
	Corps of Royal Engineers	621, 560,
	Royal Corps of Signals	636, 622,
	Army Air Corps	633
	FOOT GUARDS	
1st	Grenadiers	641, 620, 610, 609, 603, 268, 267,
2nd	Coldstream	628,
3rd	Scots	633, 617, 482
4th	Irish	
5th	Welsh	

Regiment No	Name	MKW Nos
	LINE INFANTRY	
1	Royal Scots (The Royal Regiment)	600, 481, 263,
2	Queens (West Surrey) Regiment	614, 606,
3	Buffs (Royal East Kent) Regiment	585, 575, 573, 546,
4	King's Own (Lancaster)	592, 588, 580,
5	Royal Northumberland Fusiliers	566, 469, 397, 331,
6	Royal Warwickshire Fusiliers	527, 649
7	Royal Fusiliers (City of London)	261, 449, 465, 451, 649
8	King's Regiment (Liverpool)	475 (Half Pay), 459, 390,
9	Royal Norfolk Regiment	460,
10	Royal Lincolnshire Regiment	556, 545, 524, 440,
11	Devonshire Regiment	
12	Suffolk Regiment	
13	Somerset Light Infantry	494,
14	West Yorkshire Regiment	468 (Buckinghamshire), 441 (Bedfords), 417,
15	East Yorkshire Regiment	431,
16	Bedfordshire & Hertfordshire	582,
17	Royal Leicestershire Regiment	643, 619, 581, 564,
18	Royal Irish Regiment	538,
19	Green Howards	557, 554, 543,
20	Lancashire Fusiliers	514 (East Devon), 461 (East Devon), 410, 400,
21	Royal Scots Fusiliers	607, 601,
22	Cheshire Regiment	
23	Royal Welch Fusiliers	645, 551, 529, 475, 354,
24	South Wales Borderers	
25	King's Own Scottish Borderers	630, 578, 526,
26	Cameronian Scot Rifles	474, 454,
27	Royal Inniskilling Fusiliers	637, 583, 521, 490, 445,
28	Gloucestershire Regiment	
29	Worcestershire Regiment	539, 409, 407, 396, 389, 326,
30	East Lancashire Regiment	474 (Cambridge), 464 (Cambridge),
31	East Surrey Regiment	
32	Duke of Cornwall's Light Infantry	577,
33	Duke of Wellington's Regiment	
34	Border Regiment	635,
35	Royal Sussex Regiment	486, 398,
36	Worcestershire 2nd Bn	
37	Royal Hampshire Regiment	567, 262 (Merediths Regt),
38	South Staffordshire Regiment	559,
39	Dorsetshire Regiment	513, 470,
40	South Lancashire	437 (2nd Somerset),
41	Welch Regiment	624, 515,
42	Black Watch (Royal Highland R)	489,
43	Oxfordshire & Buckinghamshire L I	613, 565, 479 (Mon), 467, 456, 427, 423, 399,

Regiment No	Name	MKW Nos
44	Essex Regiment	505,
45	Sherwood Foresters	475, 466,
46	Duke of Cornwall's L I 2nd Bn	558 (S Devon), 555 (S Devon), 518, 500, 478,
47	Loyal (North Lancashire) Regiment	639, 605, 599, 598, 535, 476, 455,
48	Northamptonshire Regiment	611, 443,
49	Royal Berkshire (Marines)	584, 511 (Herts),506(Herts),499(Herts),457 (H)
50	Queen's Own Royal West Kent	462, 424,
51	King's Own Yorkshire Light Infantry	472, 402,
52	Oxford & Bucks Light I 2nd Bn	480 (Oxfordshire), 414,
53	King's Shropshire Light Infantry	530,
54	Dorsetshire Regiment 2nd Bn	
55	Border Regiment 2nd Bn	542(Westmoreland), 493(Westmoreland), 485,
56	Essex 2nd Bn	461, 395,
57	Middlesex Regiment	563, 550, 507, 446,
58	Northamptonshire 2nd Bn	386,
59	East Lancashire 2nd Bn	
60	King's Royal Rifle Corps	587, 547, 458, 542,
61	Gloucestershire 2nd Bn	533,
62	Wiltshire Regiment	503,
63	Manchester Regiment	627, 475 (West Suffolk), 474 (West Suffolk)
64	North Staffordshire	525,
65	York & Lancaster Regiment	448,
66	Royal Berkshire Regiment 2nd Bn	450, 391,
67	Royal Hampshire 2nd Bn	532,
68	Durham Light Infantry	
69	Welch Regiment 2nd Bn	
70	East Surrey 2nd Bn	544, 512,
71	Highland Light Infantry	618, 616, 590, 568,
72	Seaforth Highlanders	634,
73	Black Watch 2nd Bn	488 (Died before admit)
74	Highland Light Infantry 2nd Bn	483,
75	Gordon Highlanders	
76	Duke of Wellington's 2nd Bn	549 (West Riding),
77	Middlesex 2nd Bn	498, 477, 433,
78	Seaforth Highlanders 2nd Bn	502,
79	Queen's Own Cameron Highlanders	
80	South Staffordshire 2nd Bn	509,496,
81	Loyals 2nd Bn	491 (Loyal Lincoln Volunteers),
82	South Lancashire 2nd Bn	633, 531,
83	Royal Ulster Rifles	
84	York & Lancaster 2nd Bn	432,
85	King's Shropshire L I 2nd Bn	495 (Bucks Volunteers King's L I)
86	Royal Ulster Rifles 2nd Bn	
87	Royal Irish Fusiliers	528, 526, 463,

Regiment No	Name	MKW Nos
88	Connaught Rangers	
89	Royal Irish Fusiliers 2nd Bn	487, 484,
90	Cameronians 2nd Bn	404,
91	Argyll & Sutherland Highlanders	631, 600, 650
92	Gordon Highlanders 2nd Bn	501
93	Argyll & Sutherland 2nd Bn	
94	Connaught Rangers 2nd Bn	
95	Rifle Brigade	442,
96	Manchester 2nd Bn	510,
97	Queen's Own R West Kent 2nd Bn	
98	North Staffordshire 2nd Bn	
99	Wiltshire Regiment 2nd Bn	
100	Leinster Regiment	604,518(Prince of Wales Royal Canadian Regt)
101	Royal Munster Fusiliers	
102	Royal Dublin Fusiliers	548,
103	Royal Dublin Fusiliers 2nd Bn	492 Royal Bombay Fusiliers,
104	Royal Munster Fusiliers 2nd Bn	
105	King's Own Yorkshire L I 2nd Bn	
106	Durham Light Infantry 2nd Bn	
107	Royal Sussex 2nd Bn	463,
108	Royal Inniskilling Fusiliers 2nd Bn	463,
109	Leinsters 2nd Bn	
	Royal Marines	466,
	Parachute Regiment	633, 631, 634,
	Special Air Service	631
	Glider Pilot Regt	633, 628,
	Army Commandos	634,
	Brigade of Gurkhas	637, 647,
	SERVICES	
	Royal Army Chaplains Department	643
	Royal Army Service Corps	642, 637, 594,
	Royal Corps of Transport	648, 642, 637, 513 (Land Tpt Corps), 544,
	Royal Army Ordnance Corps	395 (Barrack Master), 269 (Commissary)
	Royal Logistical Corps	648,
	Royal Army Medical Corps	392 (Surgeon)
	Corps of Royal Electrical & Mechanical Engineers	644,
	Adjutant General's Corps	
	Royal Army Veterinary Corps	
	Small Arms School Corps	
	Royal Army Dental Corps	
	Intelligence Corps	643,
	Royal Pioneer Corps	613,

Regiment No	Name	MKW Nos
	Royal Army Educational Corps	606,
	Royal Army Pay Corps	431 (Paymaster).
	Army Physical Training Corps	
	Corps of Army Music	647,
	Royal Gibraltar Regiment	
	COLONIAL FORCES	
	South African Light Horse	595,
	Bechuanaland Protectorate Regt	590.
	Ceylon Rifle Regt	552,
	Indian Army	589, 520,
	4th West Indian Regt	523,
	3rd West Indian Regt	519, 462,
	5th West Indian Regt	508
	2nd West Indian Regt	497
	8th West Indian Regt	462, 429,
	Colonial Forces	403,
	Singapore Regiment	623,
	Malay Regt/Malaysian Rangers	633, 639
	King's African Rifles	616, 622, 611, 600,
	Royal West Africa Frontier Force	634, 627,
	Sultan of Oman Forces	639, 643,
	Royal Sierra Leone Regiment	630
	Canadian Militia	548,
	Princess Patricia's Canadian L I	598,
	Ghana Army	643
	Jamaica Defence Force	623.
	YEOMANRY/ TA	
	2 Yorkshire Militia	461,
	Royal Veteran Corps	444, 420, 418, 415, 413, 412, 405, 401, 396,
	7th Royal Veteran Bn	439,
	East Kent Yeomanry Cavalry	436,
	South Yorkshire Fencibles	411,
	Ind Coy of Invalides	408, 406, 397,
	Banffshire Fencibles	401,
	South Staffs Militia	394,
	Sherwood Rangers Yeomanry	632,
	Honourable Artillery Company	647, 628, 627
	Royal Yeomanry	639
	2nd Glasgow Highlanders	616

THE BATTLE OF WATERLOO

The Military Knights of Windsor who fought in the battle.

No	Name	Regiment
424	Lt. W. Jones	50th , or West Kent Regiment
428	Q.M. T. Varley	Royal Horse Guards, Blues
436	Lt. A. Heartley	Royal Horse Guards, Blues
438	Lt. G. Sicker	11th ,Light Dragoons. Carried Regimental Standard
442	Maj. R. Cochrane	95th, The Rifle Brigade
445	Capt. T. Cradock	27th, Enniskilling Regiment of Foot. Wounded.
452	Q.M. J. Whiteman	Royal Artillery. Wounded.
453	Lt. H. Griffiths	15th , (King's) Light Dragoons (Hussars))
468	Q.M. S. Goddard	14th , or Buckinghamshire Regiment
472	Capt. F. Minchin	51st , Light Infantry (Second Yorkshire West Riding)
473	Q.M. A. Hendry	Unknown
474	Lt. Col. P.P. Neville	30th , or 1st Cambridge Regiment
475	Lt. Col. A.G. Sedley	63rd, West Suffolk Regiment of Foot. Wounded.
480	Maj. G.F.Berkley	52nd, (Oxfordshire) Regiment of Foot, Light Infantry
481	Col. R. Blacklin	3rd Bn. 1st , or Royal Scots. Carried King's Colour
482	Q.M. G. Copeland	Scots Fusilier Guards
485	Capt. L. White	55th , Westmoreland Regiment
486	Lt. Col. W. Rainforth	35th , or Sussex Regiment
489	Lt. A. Innes	42nd , (The Royal Highland) Regiment of Foot

Burials

Military Knights buried in the Catacombs

In 1849 a vault was constructed to the North West of St George's Chapel. It was enlarged in 1863 and a stone cross erected over it in 1879. It became known as the Catacombs. The following Military Knights are buried there:-

432	Allen, Captain John
481	Blacklin, Colonel Richard
454	Campbell, Lieutenant Colonel Adam Gordon
442	Cochrane, Major Robert
466	Douglas, Captain Joseph
458	Ellison, Captain Andrew
437	Fernyhaugh, Captain Thomas
457	Fitzgibbon, Colonel James
461	Hollinsworth, Captain, Henry
467	Hopkins, Major Sir John Paul K.H.
459	King, Captain John Duncan
439	McDermott, Lieutenant, Thomas
472	Minchin, Captain Francis
447	Moore, Major Charles
474	Lieutenant Colonel, Park Percy Neville,
441	Wathen, Major, George.

Cross marking the Catacombs

Tombs now non- existent

184, 206, 218, 220, 227, 244, 246, 252, 253, 255, 256, 257, 266, 268, 290, 299, 362, 374.

Monuments/Tombs

Dean's Cloister

West wall:	287, 397, 432, 447, 451.	**St Albans**	055
West Pavement:	235	**Reigate**	320
East Side low wall:	441, 454.	**Kensal Green Cemetery**	532
East Pavement:	195, 351, 366.	**Windsor**	536
North East Corner:	389	**Windsor Town Cemetery St Leonards Rd**	540, 580
North Wall:	221, 236, 250, 382, 385, 387, 388, 395, 481.		
South Inner wall:	421		
South Pavement:	356, 399. 587, 601, 605, 606, 607, 608, 609, 610, 611, 613, 615, 616, 618, 620, 622, 626, 628		

Choir Aisles

South Aisle Wall;	507, 526, 531, 539, 540, 547. 549
South Aisle Pavement:	286.
North Choir Aisle:	333, 586

Nave

North Aisle Wall:	203
South side:	377
Rutland Chapel Wall:	467, 477
Bray Chapel Pavement:	301

Outside in the Green

411, 429, 463.

Outside South Side Pavement

619, 621, 623, 624, 627, 630, 631, 632, 635, 639, 642, 637(Wife),

Sir Francis Crane's Foundation/Lower Foundation

During the Commonwealth the number of the Poor Knights was increased from thirteen to eighteen. The five additional Poor Knights were those first appointed to Sir Francis Crane's new Foundation, described later as the Lower Foundation. Eighteen Poor Knights attended Oliver Cromwell's funeral in 1658.

The operation of Crane's bequest had been long delayed by a protracted series of law-suits. Sir Francis Crane had at one time been the Chancellor of the Order of the Garter. A legacy had been left to him by Sir Peter le Maire, his brother-in-law, to be employed by him for such charitable purposes as he should think fit. Before carrying out any plan Sir Francis died, and by his will , dated 27 August 1635, he greatly increased le Maire's benefit that was designed to add five more Poor Knights to the existing thirteen and to provide accommodation for them in the Castle.

There were several law-suits involving Sir Richard Crane, brother of Sir Francis and executor of his will and William Crane, heir to Sir Richard mainly concerning the provision of finance for the construction of the houses and the maintenance of the Poor Knights.

Five houses were constructed on the site currently occupied by the Guard Room. They are clearly visible in the watercolours by Thomas and Paul Sandby, ca. 1760. The houses were demolished in 1863. After their demolition the Military Knights of the Lower Foundation, as they then had become, occupied various lodgings around Salisbury Tower and Henry VIII's Gate.

From 1833 it became the regular custom for the senior Military Knights on Crane's Foundation to be promoted to the Royal Foundation when a vacancy occurred. Fresh Letters Patent were issued and the promoted Knight would move to the vacant house. Promotion also meant an increase in stipend.

In 1919 Crane's Foundation was absorbed into the Royal Foundation and in due course the number of Military Knights reverted to thirteen.

Sir Francis Crane

The Naval Knights of Windsor

The Naval Knights of Windsor were established in 1795 from a bequest by Samuel Travers who left money to care for seven elderly naval officers at Windsor.

Travers' College was built below Windsor Castle to house the seven Naval officers in what is now St George's School. Each was provided with a sitting room, bedroom and kitchen. They were expected to lead 'devout lives and attend services in St George's Chapel'. They were not 'to haunt the town or taverns'. Having to attend Mattins and Evensong daily required climbing over one hundred steps from the college to the chapel. Having arrived at the castle/town level in the morning they tended to stay there.

There were stories of the elderly naval men getting very drunk and behaving outrageously. When drunk they used to unstrap and beat one another with their wooden legs.

They were disbanded in 1892. The money for their upkeep was diverted to a special ' Travers Pension' fund, which was payable to elderly and infirm naval officers. It was reported that the last Naval Knight refused to leave and was prepared to defend himself with a blunderbuss from being ejected by bailiffs.

Memorials to some of the knights may be found in the Dean's Cloister.

A full history and list of the Naval Knights, 62 in all, may be found in 'Mariners Mirror' volume 60, page 41.

NAVAL KNIGHTS OF WINDSOR BILL.
House of Lords Debate 16 June 1892 vol. 5 cc 1221-8

SECOND READING.

Order of the Day for the Second Reading, read.

★*LORD ELPHINSTONE*

My Lords, this is a very short Bill which I think I can explain in a very few words. It appears that in 1724 a Mr. Travers left a sum of money in aid of superannuated or disabled lieutenants of English men-of-war; he left a property of 1,140 acres in Essex, but coupled with certain conditions. The Knights were to be single, they were to have no children, they were to be inclined to lead a virtuous, studious, and a devout life, they were to live in a collegiate manner, they were to keep their mess together in the Common Hall, and were to attend divine service daily in St George's Chapel. This bequest was some time after supplemented by Lieutenant Brathwaite, R.N., who left £18,000 for the same object, but the conditions imposed have been proved by the experience of over three-quarters of a century to be entirely inconsistent with and unsuited to the habits and wants of naval officers at the present day. My Lords, I think that the Memorandum at the beginning of the Bill will explain as simply as possible what the object of the Bill is. Owing to these conditions we have experienced great difficulty in finding officers eligible to fill the vacancies, which is shown by the fact that at present we have only four Knights instead of seven. Under those circumstances, as the Memorandum states, it has been decided to dissolve the Corporation of the Naval Knights of Windsor, and to appropriate the funds in a more useful manner, for the direct benefit of a large class of deserving naval officers in whose interest the Trust was originally founded. The income of the property thus transferred will be granted in the form of pensions to naval officers of the rank of lieutenant of the Navy or who have retired from that rank, and the arrangement so made by the Admiralty will be submitted for approval to Her Majesty in Council. That is really the whole Bill. I will only add that it passed through the House of Commons without comment or amendment; and under those circumstances I trust your Lordships will give it a Second Reading. Moved, 'That the Bill be now read 2ª. '—(The Lord Elphinstone.)

TOWERS OF STRENGTH

Eaden Lilley Photography

Caroline Marden/Rex

Sygma

Windsor Castle's order of Military Knights: just hours later, the fire (left) had taken hold

Two hours after posing for our picture above, on the steps of St George's Chapel, Windsor Castle, members of the castle's ancient order of Military Knights were among the human chain helping salvage works of art from the fire.

The 13 knights – all distinguished retired army officers – form part of the 300-strong community that lives in the castle.

One, Major Jim Cowley DCM, talks about his life and his faith in this week's *Songs of Praise*, which was recorded at Windsor Castle a few days after the fire, and includes a reading by the Duchess of Kent.

The programme-makers themselves saw action on the day of the fire, 20 November. The outer gates of the castle had been secured as soon as fire broke out and the advance guard of the *Songs of Praise* team were locked in for the day. "All we could see was billowing smoke, because we were about 300 yards from the Upper Ward, where the fire broke out," says researcher Julia Powell.

"What impressed me most was the way the community pulled together and the way life returned to normal afterwards. No one was going to let the fire interfere with Christmas preparations."

Songs of Praise
Sunday 20 Dec BBC1

Maj R J Moore
Lt Col R L C Tamplin   Lt Col H F Rogers   Brig T W Hackworth   Maj P H Bolton
Maj J C Cowley   Maj G R Mitchell   Lt Col N L West
Maj W L Thompson   Brig A L Atkinson   Maj Gen P A Downward   Brig J F Lindner   Maj L W Dickerson

The Constable and Govenor of Windsor Castle, Air Chief Marshal Sir Richard Johns GCB, KCVO, CBE, FRAeS leading the Military Knights of Windsor, the Heralds and Knights of the Garter on Garter Day 2007.

John Norton (99) c. 1596 - 1617

Warning! Poor Knight No 99 uses strong language!

First mentioned in 1596 in the Chapter Acts as being admonished for speaking contemptuously about the statutes for the government of the Poor Knights[1]. In August 1602 he was charged with 'divers contempts and misdemeanors, including striking Mr Hook (107) and was suspended from attending chapel. He 'contumaciously' attended both Morning and Evening prayer and was subsequently excommunicated and had his stipend and pay stopped. In September he expressed sorrow and after making a public confession during Sunday service received absolution. In June 1606 John Norton, being the senior Poor Knight was required to attend with one other to bring John Massingberd (109) to the Governor's place. He refused declaring Massingberd to be a 'Pycard, no gentleman and no soldyer'. Norton's wages were stopped again until such time as he acknowledged his offences. In September 1606, he and John Salisbury (112) were fined Five pounds and four shillings for continued tumultuous and disobedient behaviour. In October they both acknowledged themselves to be 'sorye'. On 4 April 1617 he was succeeded by Read Wildgos (138).

The following extract is taken from the 'The Chapter Acts of the Dean and Canons of Windsor 1430, 1523-1672 ' Edited by Shelagh Bond 1966.

'1595. Januarii. 19. beinge Mundaye betwene three and foure of the Clocke in the afternoone John Norton gent one of her Majestes poore Knightes of Windesor in the house of Mr William Wilson one of the Canons of her Majestes Frechappell of Windesor in the presence of him the said Mr Wilson and Mr William Glover Citizen and founder of London spake contemptuouslye of her Majestes orders and statutes geven to this house under the greate seale of England for the government of the poore Knightes of the said Chappell. viz That if there were a thousand statutes he would break them all to trye whether he could be expelled or no. And that his patent of his place was better then that the statutes could touch him. Also that he made no more reaconynge of the said statutes then of a coale in the fier which he then pointed unto. of the Canons he also spake as followeth

Turde in all your teethe, a fart for you all. you are a sorte of peysantlye priests.

And beinge tolde howe Contemptuously he sent answere to Mr Frenche beinge Chaunter and the deanes Lieuetenant, When the said Mr Frenche heeringe him lowde in the Churche sent unto him to desier him to be silente

He rapte out and oathe Blood and Woundes he Cared not a button for Frenche nor any that tooke his parte let them all doe their woorst a sort of Curmuggens

Theis thinges are testified by the said Mr Glover in a Writinge Under his hande, remaynynge in the Custodie of the said Mr William Wilson'.

377. Sir John Dineley [or Dineley-Goodere] Bart.   1798-1809

Admitted 16 April 1798 in succession to John Morrison (342) © National Portrait Gallery

Extract from the 'Oxford Dictionary of National Biography'.

Dineley [*formerly* Dineley-Goodere], Sir John, fifth baronet (*c.*1729–1809), eccentric, was born at Burhope, Herefordshire, the second of three sons of Samuel Goodere (1687–1741), landowner and naval officer, of Burhope, and his second wife, a widow, Elizabeth, *née* Watts (*d.* 1742). The claim that Dineley-Goodere once practised physic is unsubstantiated and probably derived from his regular purchases of medical books. Dineley-Goodere's father, Samuel, lived on bad terms with his elder brother, Sir John Goodere, third baronet, who adopted the name Dineley-Goodere as heir to his maternal ancestors. He married Mary Lawford but their only son died young and unmarried. Because of this bad feeling Sir John threatened to disinherit Samuel in favour of his niece's husband, John Foote of Truro. To prevent this threat being carried out Samuel, then in command of the naval vessel *Ruby*, caused his brother to be kidnapped at Bristol, and then to be strangled by two sailors on board his vessel. The murder took place on the night of Sunday 18 January 1741, and on 15 April following the fratricide Samuel was hanged with his two accomplices at Bristol. The precise status of the baronetcy thereafter is unclear. It is possible that Samuel's eldest son, Edward, succeeded as baronet, or was merely granted a courtesy title. On Edward's death in March 1761, aged thirty-two, the title of fifth baronet passed to his brother John, assuming that his father never inherited the title. What little remained of the family estates he soon wasted. About 1770 he was obliged to part with Burhope to Sir James Peachey and he lived for a time in a state bordering on destitution. At length his friendship with the Pelhams, coupled with the interest of Lord North, procured for him the pension and free residence of a poor knight of Windsor. From then on he seems to have only used the surname of Dineley.

By the oddity of his dress, demeanour, and mode of life Dineley became one of the chief sights of Windsor. Each morning he locked up his house in the castle, which no one entered but himself, and went forth to purchase provisions. According to the Penny Magazine:

> He then wore a large cloak called a roquelaure, beneath which appeared a pair of thin legs encased in dirty silk stockings. He had a formidable umbrella, and he stalked along upon pattens. All luxuries, whether of meat, or tea, or sugar, or butter, were renounced … Wherever crowds were assembled—wherever royalty was to be looked upon—there was Sir John Dineley. He then wore a costume of the days of George II—the embroidered coat, the silk-flowered waistcoat, the nether garments of faded velvet carefully meeting the dirty silk stocking, which terminated in the half-polished shoe surmounted by the dingy silver buckle. The old wig, on great occasions, was newly powdered, and the best cocked hat was brought forth, with a tarnished lace edging. He had dreams of ancient genealogies, and of alliances still subsisting between himself and the first

Dineley's second preoccupation was his search for a wife whose wealth he hoped would allow him to establish his lineage:

> To secure for himself a wife was the business of his existence; to display himself properly where women most do congregate was the object of his savings. The man had not a particle of levity in these proceedings; his deportment was staid and dignified. He had a wonderful discrimination in avoiding the tittering girls, with whose faces he was familiar. But perchance some buxom matron or timid maiden who had seen him for the first time gazed upon the apparition with surprise and curiosity. He approached. With the air of one bred in courts he made his most profound bow; and taking a printed paper from his pocket, reverently presented it and withdrew. (Penny Magazine).

More than once he paid court to some lad dressed up as a fine lady. His marriage proposals were crudely printed by himself. Occasionally he advertised in the newspapers. He also printed some extraordinary rhymes under the title of 'Methods to get husbands … with the advertised marriage offer of Sir John Dineley, bart., of Charleton, near Worcester, extending to 375,000*l*., to the reader of this epistle, if a single lady, and has above one hundred guineas fortune'.

Although obsessed by his search for a wife and for his lost inheritance, in other matters Dineley was both sane and shrewd. Twice or thrice a year he visited Vauxhall Gardens and the London theatres, taking care to apprise the public of his intention through the medium of the most fashionable daily papers. Wherever he went the place was invariably well attended, especially by women. Dineley persevered in his addresses to the ladies until the very close of his life, but without success. When he failed to appear at chapel one morning his door was broken open. His passage was filled with coals, his sitting room with his printing materials; there was little furniture. Dineley was found in bed. He died a few days later, in November(?) 1809, aged about eighty. On his death the baronetcy became extinct.

Died 18 October 1809 and buried at St George's Chapel on 21 October [Mon. Insc. outside the Chapel South side]. Succeeded by Edmund Taylor (392).

Major Charles Henry Strutt

553. Major Charles Henry Strutt   1901- 1908

Admitted 10 October 1901 L.F. *vice* Clement Headington Dale (548) (prom.). Admitted 9 November 1907 R.F. *vice* Henry Dyke Marsh (531) (dec.). Of the Royal (late Bombay) Regiment of Artillery. He served in the Indian Mutiny Campaign 1857-58 with the Centra Field Force, including the siege and capture of Dhar, the action of Mundessore, the battle of Gooraria, the sige and capture of Kalghur, the action of Barodia, the siege and bombardment of Garrakstah, the capture of Fort Barodia, the action of Muddehpore, the siege and storming of Jhansi, the battle of Kooneh, actions before Calpee, the battle of Gallowtee, the capture of Calpee, actions at Moran and Kotah ke Serai, the capture of Gwalior and Powree (Brevet of Major, medal and clasp).

The Great Planchette Case

In 1903 a case came up for trial that caused a major sensation. It was known as the 'Great Planchette Case.' A young man of fortune named Henry Sheppard Hart Cavendish, aged twenty-six, brought an action against a Major Charles Henry Strutt, his wife Madeline, and a solicitor named Alfred Washington Guest Ranger, to set aside a voluntary settlement whereby he gave Major Strutt and his wife almost absolute control of his estate. Cavendish pleaded 'undue influence,' as Mrs. Strutt, who dabbled in the occult, had persuaded him by spirit messages purporting to come from his deceased mother and the archangels Gabriel, Michael, and Uriel. These 'messages' arrived *via* table-tipping, Mrs. Strutt's automatic writing, and especially the planchette. Mrs. Strutt herself interpreted these messages. After several days' hearing   Mr. Justice Byrne said he would reserve judgment. This was delivered two months later (May 13, 1903), and he ordered the settlement to be set aside - with costs.

During the hearing in the Chancery Division, Mr Justice Byrne severely criticised the conduct of one of the parties, a Military Knight, Major Charles Strutt (553). The criticism was considered so serious that Council's opinion was sought as to whether Strutt could be dismissed. The advice was that nothing could be done since despite the judge's strictures upon Strutt's conduct he had not offended against the Elizabethan Statutes. This result led to the issue in 1905 of Letters Patent declaring that Military Knights hold office and may be dismissed at the Sovereign's pleasure.

The Stater of Eucratides

One of the British officers who brought back gold from India was Major Charles H. Strutt. In the middle of the 19th century, Major Strutt amassed a fair collection of Bactrian and Indian coins.   What was obtained from on the hand of an Afghan officer as a ring, that the learned major immediately recognized as a coin of great rarity. No other a Stater of Eucratides.

When it passed into Strutt's possession, he decided that it should become a coin again. In a determined operation to remove the ring, the reverse was caught up with the 2000 years of scarring that the obverse had already suffered. The stubborn weld would not come free of the prancing horses. Like a wad of chewing gum, it sits there still. Worst of all, in a desperate attempt to cut the blemish away, the new owner chiselled deep into it and inadvertently sawed clear across the design. His effort to pry loose the offending lump peeled up the edges of the wound, and let his long blade bite into the soft metal. Tiny striations on the edge, just in front of the king's face, betray the grip of the pliers which held it hard during the terrible ordeal.

The numismatic rarity more than compensated for the battered condition. Major Strutt conveyed it to 13 Wellington Street in London, the distinguished home of Sotheby's, the art auctioneers. Major Strutt's entire collection ('featuring a unique Stater of Eucratides ') was exhibited for sale. On the afternoon of January 26, it was purchased from the collection of Major Strutt by a Colonel Strutt with a bid of £25

Many years later, Colonel Strutt sold the coin to a collector, Hyman Montagu.

At his death, 27 November 1908, Lieutenant Colonel John Grant Anderson (564) was appointed L.F.

ACKNOWLEDGEMENTS AND THANKS

Her Majesty The Queen for granting permission to use the following pictures from the Royal Collection:-
Group photograph of Her Majesty with the Military Knights
Interior of St George's Chapel by Wenceslaus Holler
Three prints by Thomas and Paul Sandby
Coloured print of Mattins in St George's Chapel 1837 by Joseph Nash
Coloured print of Garter Ceremony 1840
Garter service 1937 by Fred Elwell

The British Museum:-	Two Poor Knights in the Garter Procession 1663. by Sir Peter Lely.
The Ashmolean Museum Oxford:-	Captain Nicholas Burgh by Cornelis de Neve.
The Dean and Canons of Windsor:-	Photograph by Charlotte Manley, 2009. Marching through the Choir
Getty Images	Banner Ceremony, Sir Edmund Hillary, KG, ONZ, KBE
BBC:-	BBC Radio Times Magazine December 1992 showing the Castle fire .
Press Association	HRH Princess Margaret's Funeral
National Portrait Gallery	Sir John Dineley, Bart
The College of Arms:-	For researching the shields of the Poor Knights.
The Military Knights of Windsor:	Group photograph with Her Majesty The Queen, Mrs Eva Zielinska-Millar
	Painting Lieutenant George Sicker 11th Light Dragoons
	Group on Chapel steps 1899
	Group on Lower Ward path 1930.
	The Garter Procession in Lower Ward.
	Group outside MTT by Julian Calder

People

The Revd Michael Boag	For his help and advice.
Lieutenant Colonel Charles Webb (646)	For his military research
Colonel David Axson (644)	For his help and advice and production of a PDF version.
Mr Hugo Vickers	For help with illustrations
Miss Bridget Wright	For proof reading
Mrs Ann Willis	For her help and advice
Mr Philip Moore	For his help and advice
Robert Noel Esq. Lancaster Herald	For researching Poor Knights' shields

Publications/ Sources

The Military Knights of Windsor , 1352 – 1944. The Revd Edmund H Fellowes, CH, MVO, MA, Mus Doc
Antiquities of Windsor. Joseph Pote   The Oxford Dictionary of National Biographies.
The Chapter Acts of the Dean and Canons of Windsor
The Military Knights of Windsor. Peter Begent   Regiments of Foot. HL Wickes
A History of the British Army. Hon J W Fortesque   The Journal of the House of Lords
The Gentleman's Magazine   The Windsor and Eton Express
The Diary of Brigadier Pelly   Wikipedia Encyclopaedia

Alphabetical Index

60	Johns H.	439	McDermott T.	248	Ormsby J.
443	Johnson S.	571	McInnis E.B.	19	Ottelinger, Sir
251	Jones P.	505	McInnisP.	152	Ousley R.
424	Jones W.	412	McIntosh W.	352	Padmore J.
281	Jordan T.	396	Mclean J.	319	Palairet P.
586	Kavanagh C.T. McM★	52	Meautis J.	202	Palmer E.
66	Kemp T.	386	Meggs P.	135	Palmer J.
301	Kemys R.	510	Menzies J.	80	Palmer T.
15	Kiderowe J.	528	Meredyth, Sir E.	81	Palmer W.★
459	King J.D.	97	Metcalf S.	337	Papon P.
155	King W.	156	Meysey W.	164	Parker C.
12	Koker, Sir A.	472	Minchin F.	111	Parker R.
427	Lalor T.	631	Mitchell G.R.	110	Parkhurst A.
444	Lamb J.	557	Moffatt W.H.	383	Parsons T.Z.
345	Lamb J.	84	Molesworth J.	70	Pasfield J.
183	Lambe B.	543	Molesworth R.	277	Peart H.
350	Lane J.	565	Money A.C.	598	Pelly R.T.
426	Langford C.	347	Monnet S.	612	Penfold R.J.L.
137	Langley R.	389	Monsell W.	587	Pennell R.
357	Lauzun D.	226	Montgomery E.	469	Pennington J
591	Lawrence B.	575	Moody R.S.H.	522	Percy W.
435	Lawrence G.	447	Moore C.★	113	Pesemede F.
360	le Cointe J.M.	637	Moore R. J.	24	Pesmerch J.
305	le Grand P.	395	Moore S.	187	Peters T.
269	Llewellyn M.	72	More J.	259	Phillips H.
351	Loddiges L.	93	Morgan J.	121	Phillips W.
324	Lodge S.	141	Morris R.	517	Pickworth J.A.
465	Loggan G.	342	Morrison J.	122	Pierson J.
421	Lorimer C.H.	572	Morton-Marshall	311	Pineda P.
241	Loudon R.	71	Mounteney H.	527	Platt C.R.
150	Lowe W.	285	Mozen G.	583	Plunkett J.F.
18	Lowyk, Sir R.	114	Muffett J.	194	Pochin R.
13	Lyle, Sir W.	9	Muschet G.	355	Pollock W.
180	Mabb R.	120	Muse T.	561	Poole A.E.
359	MacCulloch D.	547	Muter D.D.	212	Poole B.
398	Mackay J.	449	Nantes R.	238	Pope D.
245	Mackenzie J.	393	Neale I.	364	Porny M.A.
600	Mackenzie J.M.	182	Nest S.	368	Potter H.
446	Maclachlan D.	474	Neville P.P.	513	Powell J.
396	Mclean J.	329	Neville R.	433	Powell J.
479	Maclean J.L.	207	Newans T.	161	Pratt R.
483	Macqueen D.J,	306	Newton J.	91	Price D.★
542	Maguire J.T.	265	Nicholson W.	192	Price W.
224	Mainwaring R.	577	Norton C.B.	276	Prince J.
509	Maloney W.★	551	Norton C.G.C,	302	Prince S.
391	Mansell W.	99	Norton J.	293	Pritchard W.
531	Marsh H.D.	184	Norwood T.	534	Purcell J.
95	Martin G.	415	O'Meara R.	420	Ragg S.
580	MartinJ.H.	199	Odingsell	477	Raines J.R.
109	Massingberd.★	370	Ogg R.	486	Rainforth W.
540	Maude F.C.	227	Ogilvy D.	456	Rand S.
221	Mauleverer J.★	287	Olivier J.★	205	Ranger F.
335	Maxted J.	166	Olner	229	Rashleigh N.
167	Mayes	582	Onslow C.C.	240	Rayer W.
422	McDermott J.	496	Ormsby A.	371	Redman J.

330	Reeve T.	123	Stafferton R.	88	Tyndesley R.
333	Richardson J.	4	Stanle R.	186	Tyrwhitt W.
340	Richardson T.	650	Steele D.K.P.	428	Varley T.
407	Riches I.	404	Steel T.	203	Vaughan R.
270	Rivers C.	346	Steidel G.	521	Versturme L.
367	Robertson A.	165	Stephens	535	Villiers C.C.
608	Robinson W..	511	Stevens W.	85	Waferer N.
171	Roe	408	Stewart W.	574	Waite A.W.
635	Rogers H.F.	516	Stilman J.	73	Walkley T.
579	Rogers H.H.	252	Storey A.	168	Wallinger J.
288	Rogers H.★	45	Stoughton W.	309	Walton J.
338	Rome R.	431	Strange A.	441	Wathen G.
189	Rowlandson W.	553	Strutt C.H.	349	Watson J.
312	Rush J.	7	Sturmy, Sir H.	648	Watson R. B.
126	Russell W.	537	Swinfen F.H.	539	Watson S.
343	Sadleir J.	632	Tamplin R.L C.	495	Watts J.J.
112	Salisbury J.	147	Tanfield, Sir F.	647	Watts S. A.
455	Sall W.	266	Tattersall B.	646	Webb C. I. P.
17	Salusbury J.	2	Taune T.	578	Webb W.E.
103	Sampson R.	392	Taylor E.	502	Webster J.
145	Sanders H.	318	Taylor H.	291	Webster R.
503	Sanderson J.	385	Taylor J.	82	Wentworth R.
28	Sanderson W.	106	Teshe R.	630	West N.L.
519	Saunders H.F.	64	Thackwell G.	54	Westby B.
8	Say, Sir N.	44	Thame R.	157	Westcote S.
223	Sayer G.	96	Thistlethwaite	258	Whalley J.
478	Scoltock S.	32	Thomas D.	260	Wharton A.
460	Scott J.	283	Thompson J.	263	White A.
475	Sedley A.G.★	119	Thompson N.	485	White L.
39	Sewall H.	253	Thompson R.	196	White R.
492	Shaw R.L.	625	Thompson W L	11	Whithors, Sir
403	Shaw W.	399	Thorne W.	58	Whiting M.★
101	Sheffield G.	242	Thornton R.	104	Whittacres N.
274	Short J.	544	Tighe J.A.	452	Wightman J.
438	Sicker G	295	Tildesley R.	138	Wildgos R.★
29	Sigemond J.	262	Timson T.	649	Willans W.J.
53	Sigemond J.	43	Tonge R.	423	Williams D.
595	Simpson E.H.	219	Trappes T.	275	Williams R.
590	Singleton H.	16	Trebell, Sir J.	261	Williams W.
411	Skilton E.	254	Trevanion H.★	255	Williams W.
317	Smart E.	191	Trumball S.	197	Willoughby A.
380	Smart S.	102	Tucker T.	310	Wise C.
617	Smith H.	363	Tucker W.	332	Wittewrong, Sir
374	Smith J.	278	Tuer W.	621	Wollaston A.E.
89	Smyth N.	610	Turner G.F.G.	217	Wood C.
546	Somerset H.	78	Turner W.	90	Worseley R.
584	Southey J.H.W.	602	Turnham A.S.	218	Wright T.
50	Spencer H.	529	Twisleton-Wykeham-	239	Wye G.
620	Spratley A.J.		Fiennes F.N.	499	Young W.
605	Squibb R.F.	624	Tyler A.C.		
480	St John G.F.B.	378	Tyler R.		